Domestic Violence:

The 12 Things You Aren't Supposed to Know

D0096723

FEB 0 8 2005

Domestic Violence:

The 12 Things You Aren't Supposed to Know

by
Thomas B. James, J.D.

cP
Aventine Press LLC

"All I want is the truth. Just give me some truth."
--John Lennon

Contents

Introduction

Telling the truth about domestic violence is a risky business, particularly when the truth challenges the traditional notion that violence is exclusively a male phenomenon. Scientists who have tried to speak the truth have received death threats, threats of harm to their careers and reputations, and even threats to kill or harm their children. Some scientists who have discovered evidence that women and men are equally culpable of domestic violence have even admitted that they sat on their findings for years before revealing them, for fear of what might happen to their careers, reputations and lives if the findings from their research were disclosed..

I am fully aware of these risks. I also know that upon publication of this book, I will be labeled a misogynist[1] and an anti-feminist.[2] There will be those who will accuse me of being a wife-beater myself. That is what always happens whenever anyone dares question the gospel that violence is exclusively a male phenomenon.[3]

This kind of reaction strikes me as somewhat hypocritical, particularly when it comes from the mouths of people who support the expansion of the definition of abuse to include name-calling.

I am not a woman-hater. I am a strong believer in the right of women to equality under the law. Do I beat my wife? I have been married to the same woman for over ten years and have never abused her in any way. She is the love of my life and the mother of our children.

It is probably the risk of being made the target of a smear campaign that accounts for the fact that so far very few men have been brave enough to publicly challenge the "facts" about domestic violence that are routinely recited by government officials, educators and the media. The stigma of being a woman-hater is a difficult one to shake, even when it has absolutely no basis in truth. This is probably why the most outspoken proponents of the notion that some women may also be prone to violence have been *women*: Cathy Young, Erin Pizzey, Suzanne Steinmetz, Katherine Dunn, Kathleen Parker, Paula Pearson. Erin Pizzey was the founder of the first battered women's shelter in England, yet she defends the position that women and men are equally prone to violence more vigorously than any man I know.

Is anyone who dares suggest that some women may be as violent as some men an anti-feminist? The women mentioned in the foregoing paragraph do not consider themselves anti-feminists. Feminist writer Katherine Dunn has remarked that "with the possibility of genuine equality visible in the distance, it is self-destructive lunacy to deny the existence of women's enormous fighting heart."[4]

Am I an anti-feminist? Trying to answer that question is like trying to answer the question, "Have you stopped beating your wife?" The question cannot be answered with a "yes" or "no" because *feminism* is a loaded term. If, by *feminism*, is meant the belief that women are inherently more moral or more valuable than men, or that women should enjoy rights and protections that are denied to men, or that women are naturally superior to men, then I would have to admit that I am opposed to those notions. If, on the other hand, feminism is defined as the belief that women and men derive their dignity and worth entirely from the fact that they are human beings and therefore should have equal rights and responsibilities, then no, I am not an anti-feminist.

Beyond the affixing of labels, the most common objection to revealing the truth about domestic violence is the fear that telling the truth might jeopardize funding for battered women's shelters. I cannot emphasize enough that by telling the truth about domestic violence it is not my intention to eliminate shelters. To the contrary, I am acutely aware of the need for them.

As a family law attorney, I have had first-hand experience with the need for domestic abuse shelters. One of my first clients was a battered woman whose husband had obtained a gun and threatened to kill her with it. The man was arrested and a protection order was issued, but we both knew that if he was really intent on harming her, a piece of paper wasn't going to stop him. I referred her to several area battered women's shelters. She called each of them, but was turned away from every one. She said she was told that there might be room for her but not for her three children. Her parents refused to take her in, as they were more afraid of her ex-husband than she was, and none of her friends were willing to put her up for more than one night at a time. She called upon members of her church for help, as did I, but no help was forthcoming there, either. I helped secure alternative housing for her as long as I could, but eventually she and her children wound up living in their car. Drawing on various community resources, she was eventually able to secure employment, help with child care and a permanent home, but I have every reason to believe that the memory of being on the run, living in daily fear with no idea where they would be from one day to the next, will remain with those children for the rest of their lives. I strongly believe that no one should have to go through that.

Does any of this mean that the truth about domestic violence should be misrepresented or concealed? Certainly not. To the contrary, what the experience teaches is that shelters for victims of domestic abuse are badly needed. It also suggests that shelter intake priorities may need to be re-examined. Frankly, I do not know what each shelter's policies are with respect to the intake of children, but if, as my client claimed, people are being turned away because they are not single women, then shelter intake policies most definitely do need to be re-examined. Children should be the first priority, not the last.

The experience also demonstrates that as a people we need to do some serious thinking about our own selfish attitudes. I don't mean women; I don't mean men; I mean *all of us*. Public service announcements are doing a good job of raising consciousness about the plight of domestic abuse victims, but they all seem to imply that our public responsibility ends by calling the police and having the abuser arrested. It doesn't. People who, out of an unwillingness to give up some of their space for a little while, would force friends, family members, fellow parishioners--and *children*--to live in their cars should be ashamed of themselves.

Make no mistake about it: some women are victims and some men are aggressors. Shelters are needed. I am not an apologist for male violence. None of these things, however, is inconsistent with the statement that some men are victims and some women are aggressors. Nor are they even inconsistent with the statement that as many men as women are victims of violence. If revealing the truth about domestic violence will have the effect of forcing shelters to stop discriminating against abuse victims on the basis of their gender, then so be it. Using gender as the criterion for determining whether or not a person's life is worth saving is not feminism; it's supremacism. As the example of the Ku Klux Klan should have made clear many years ago, supremacism is not a good thing. If this is the practice among publicly funded domestic abuse shelters, then they need to stop it. If that means they will lose government funding, then the funding laws need to be changed.

Moreover, the argument that shelters will lose funding if they provide services to men requires one to believe at least one of the following two propositions: (1) government officials are so prejudiced against men that they would rather let a battered woman continue being battered than allow even one dime to be spent on helping a battered man; or (2) existing appropriation laws require shelters to discriminate against men. Concerning the first proposition, it is doubtful that any legislator in his or her right mind would rather permit a woman to be battered than to let any man receive any kind of assistance at all from the government. Misandry may be at an all-time high right now, but legislators know very well that the majority of the voting population is female and that most of them would be outraged if a battered woman were killed because the government decided to shut down their shelters. Politicians are sharp enough to know that allowing even one woman to be killed by an irate husband simply because of the politician's zeal to destroy men is not the way to win the hearts, minds and votes of most women. It would be political suicide. As for the second proposition, if existing appropriation laws mandate discriminatory practices against minority groups[5] then they should be ruled unconstitutional.

Having said that, it would be regrettable if anything in this book were to be used as a basis for eliminating programs and services for abuse victims. On this point, I concur with Steven Easton, founder of a support group for battered men in Canada, that "the scope and visibility of wife battering is something which should never be diminished in our attempts to assist battered men."[6] Calling attention to the untold half of the story about domestic violence should only serve to increase awareness that the problem is even more widespread than we may have thought before; that when the male victims are added in, there are even *more* victims than we previously thought. If anything, the information in this book should therefore impel *more*, not fewer, programs; *more* services, not fewer; *more* research, not less; and ultimately, it should impel the development of treatment methods that are more grounded in reality and therefore more likely to be effective than the current approaches that are not working.

It is my sincere hope that the information in this book will encourage members of both camps in the gender war to lay down their arms and see what we can achieve as a nation by working together, rather than constantly trying to malign, smear and abuse one another. Once we can get past our collective gender myopia, I think we will see that the problem of violence in our country has much deeper roots and much wider branches than most of us realize; that domestic violence is a symptom of a much deeper problem than misogyny, misandry, matriarchy or patriarchy alone. For a long time, the gender wars have been distracting us from this deeper problem. Unfortunately, according to the latest figures, there will come a time in almost all of our lives when each of us will regret having failed to see it until it was too late.

1. Most victims are male

For 13 years, Mary Smith...broke her husband's ribs, ripped entire patches of his hair out, scratched him, bit him, beat him with a baseball bat and kicked him. He never hit back--and he never filed charges.[7]

We all know that violence is a male phenomenon, that 95% of all domestic abuse is men beating up women,[8] that it's all about male privilege, that it's how the patriarchy maintains power and control, right? After all, this is what government officials, college professors, judges, attorneys, and the media always tell us. If you asked the average person on the street, it's what he would tell you. It's what we've all been taught to believe. Guess what. We've all been taught to believe a lie.

I first became suspicious of the "95%" statistic when I read a report from the U.S. Women's Bureau's stating that women are "6 times more likely than men to experience domestic violence." The Women's Bureau cited the U.S. Department of Justice for this statistic. Yet, if 95% of domestic abuse victims are female, then the Women's Bureau would be reporting that women are 19 times more likely than men to be victims, not merely 6 times more likely. A 13-fold difference is not exactly a standard statistical deviation. Something wasn't right.

The Super Bowl Sunday Hoax

The Super Bowl Sunday hoax also fueled some skepticism. The Super Bowl Sunday hoax stemmed from a press conference called

by Sheila Kuehl of the California Women's Law Center to report
that sociologists at Old Dominion University supposedly had found
that police reports of domestic violence increase 40% on Super
Bowl Sundays. The press conference was called just prior to the
Super Bowl in January, 1993. At the conference, journalists were
told that Super Bowl Sunday is "the biggest day of the year for
violence against women." Not a single journalist checked out the
story before publishing and broadcasting it in every major media
outlet across the country. In fact, many members of the media even
added embellishments of their own--such as the Boston *Globe*'s
assertion in a January 29, 1993 article that area women's shelters
are "flooded" with more calls from victims on Super Bowl Sunday
than any other day of the year. (Not true.) The Minneapolis *Star-
Tribune*, like many other newspapers, printed a huge story about
male violence against women on the front page of the sports section
of the Super Bowl Sunday newspaper. The story, titled "Sunday's
victims: Number of battered women rise," was a reprint of an article
that had been written by Joan Ryan for the San Francisco *Examiner*.

Janet Katz, a professor at Old Dominion University and one of
the authors of the study cited by Ms. Kuehl, denied having ever
made any such finding, and indeed denied any correlation between
football and domestic violence in general. To the contrary, the only
finding the Old Dominion study made about football and violence
was that an increase in emergency room admissions is *not* associated
with the occurrence of football games. Eventually, newspapers
(including the Boston *Globe* and the Minneapolis *Star-Tribune*)
acknowledged that they had let themselves be used to perpetrate a
fraud upon their readers, although they good-humoredly maintained
that it was all "for a good cause."[9]

The Intergenerational Cycle of Abuse

Another thing that made me suspicious of the 95% figure has
to do with what social scientists refer to as the *intergenerational
transmission of abuse*, or the *cycle of abuse*.[10] It is well-known
that people who abuse are very likely to have been victims of
abuse themselves: "garbage in, garbage out."[11] The cycle of abuse
principle is frequently used in defense of women who are violent.

The argument goes something like this: "A woman should be excused when she is violent because her violent behavior is simply a consequence of violence that she herself has experienced at some time in her life; therefore, punishing her would be tantamount to re-victimizing the victim." Okay, maybe this is an argument that only judges and juries would buy. The premise upon which it rests, though, is valid: people who abuse have almost always been victims of abuse themselves at some time in their lives.[12] Now, if 95% of all abusers are male, then the cycle of abuse principle would predict that 95% of the people who abuse are abused males. If, as the National Organization for Women maintains, 4 million women are victims of domestic abuse, and if 95% of the perpetrators are men, then the cycle of abuse principle would predict that at least 3.8 million men have been victims of abuse themselves. That's one heck of a lot of abused men!

Astonishing Research

When I began my search for the truth about the "95%" figure, I started by tracing the sources cited for the figure by governmental agencies in their own publications. Before long, however, I found myself stuck in an endless loop, with authors citing one another but none citing any original empirical data from which the statistic was derived.[13] Basically, what it came down to was "a friend of a friend told me"--the stuff of urban legends.

Still, I found it hard to believe that lofty institutions like the United States Department of Justice, the United States Department of Health and Human Services, the California Attorney General's Policy Council on Domestic Violence, et. al., would knowingly proliferate a completely unfounded urban legend. So I decided to do some digging to find out just exactly what the researchers who have conducted responsible research in this field have learned about it. I was astonished at what I discovered.

Contrary to what I had been led to believe by the media (not to mention more than a few judges, legislators and law professors), I learned that most victims of violence in this country are *male*, not female. In fact, among all demographic groups, young males are far and away the most frequent victims of violence in our country, while elderly females are actually the *least* frequent victims of violence.[14]

Overall, males are about twice as likely to be victims of violence as females are,[15] and young white males (20 to 24 years of age) are 10 times as likely to be victims of violence as older white females are.[16] Males between the ages of 16 and 24 are three times as likely to be assault victims as females are, and men overall are nearly twice as likely to be victims of assault.[17] Men of all ages are three times more likely to be murdered than women are, and by some reports they are *four* times more likely to be murdered.[18]

During a twelve-month period, men are nearly twice as likely as women to be victims of violence, and the lifetime likelihood of being a victim of three or more violent crimes is nearly three times as great for a man as it is for a woman.[19]

And these figures *include* the crime of rape.

Of course, these statistics are all from the mid-1980's. A lot can happen in twenty years. So I decided to see if I could find some more recent figures.

I did. Not much has changed. A 1997 Bureau of Justice Statistics report shows that the majority of all assault victims are still male, and two-thirds of all victims of aggravated assault (assault with a deadly weapon, or causing serious bodily harm) are male.[20] According to a recent study of violence by intimates, the general rate of violent victimizations against males over 12 years old is 5.3%; for women, it is 3.7%.[21] A 1998 Bureau of Justice Statistics study reports that 76.3% of all murder victims between 1976 and 1996 were male.[22]

Another Bureau of Justice Statistics survey report,[23] this one issued in June, 2001, confirms that, despite an overall decrease in violent crime between 1999 and 2000, males are still the one demographic group that is most vulnerable to violent victimizations. Even including rape and sexual assaults, the rate of violent victimizations against males is still about 1.5 times the rate of violent victimizations against females. As of the year 2000, men are still nearly 3 times as likely to be victims of aggravated assault as women are and the rate of simple assaults against men is about 126% the rate of victimizations against women.[24]

These figures are borne out by law enforcement agencies.[25] In 1991, for example, Minnesota police agencies recorded 122 murders. Of the victims, 34 were women and 88 were men.[26] And in 1993, the California attorney general reported that 81.5% of homicide victims in that state were male.[27]

The statistics show not only that men are more often victims of violence than women are, but that the violence directed at men is usually much more severe. The homicide statistics cited above are pretty good evidence of that. In addition, the National Crime Survey found that 35% of the violent crimes against men involved the use of guns or knives, while only 14% of the crimes against women involved weapons. A study of homicides in Philadelphia found that women used knives in their crimes four times as often as men did, and concluded that "Offenses against men are significantly more serious in nature than are offenses against women."[28] Indeed, it can be said that as a rule, and with the exception of rape, the more violent the crime the more likely it is that the victim is male.[29] Forcible rape, incidentally, constitutes less than 5% of all violent crimes; crimes of which males are the primary target constitute the other 95%.[30]

Prisoners and jail inmates comprise an often-overlooked population of crime victims. It is common knowledge that male prisoners are routinely raped, but no reliable statistics are maintained as to the rate at which this occurs. The lack of data in this area is most likely attributable to societal indifference toward male prisoners. Many people consider homosexual rape an acceptable part of the punishment we exact for the crimes that prisoners have committed against society.

This doesn't explain the societal indifference to the *murder* of prisoners, though. Given that most prisoners are serving time for drug offenses,[31] does it really comport with our sense of justice to sentence people to death for experimenting with drugs? I don't think so. Might our indifference have more to do with the fact that nearly all prisoners are male and roughly 100% of all prison murders involve male victims?[32]

In the course of studying violence against women, researchers from the National Institute of Justice and the Centers for Disease Control found that 61,584,672 men had been victims of physical assault at some time during their lives, while women had been victims of 52,261,743 physical assaults during their lifetimes. That's nearly 10 million more assaulted men than assaulted women. The researchers also found that even when rape is included, the lifetime likelihood of being a victim of violence is significantly higher for men than for women (66.8% for men, 55% for women) and that at any given time a male is over 1.5 times more likely to be a victim of a rape or assault than a female is. Men are more likely than women to be pushed, grabbed, shoved, thrown at, slapped, hit, kicked, bit, beat up and hit with an object; about twice as likely to be threatened with a gun; nearly three times as likely to be knifed or threatened with a knife; and twice as likely to actually be shot at with a gun.[33]

The Ms. Magazine College Student Rape Hoax

Not long ago, research funded by *Ms.* magazine[34] reported, in effect, that over a quarter of American women of college age had been raped. Like the Super Bowl Sunday statistic, this "fact" made headlines all over the country. And like the Super Bowl Sunday statistic, it was a hoax.

In this case, what the "researchers" did was a little bit trickier than the flat-out lie that was told in the case of the Super Bowl Sunday Hoax. In this case, what they did was invent a new definition of "rape" that would be sufficiently broad to reach the statistical figure they were looking for. Specifically, they invented a definition of rape according to which any time a woman engages in "unwanted" sexual activity of any kind, it is "rape"--even if the woman said yes and even if no trickery, force or threats, express or implied, were used to obtain the woman's consent. Ms. Koss herself acknowledged that the vast majority (73%) of the women she classified as rape victims were not even aware that they had been "raped." In fact, 43% of the women who had been "raped" were still dating the "rapist"![35]

According to the U.S. Department of Education, the truth is that there is, on average, less than one rape per year on each U.S. college campus.[36]

Most of us probably remember reading or hearing about these startling campus rape "findings." On the other hand, since no media coverage was given to Charlene Muehlenhard and Stephen W. Cook's follow-up study, most people are completely unaware of it.

Cook and Muehlenhard tested the *Ms.* methodology by asking men the same questions that previously had been asked only of women. When the results were tabulated, it was found that by the time they were of college age, 63% of *men* had engaged in sexual intercourse in which they had not wanted to engage (which the *Ms.* researchers had defined as "rape"), as compared to only 46% of the women.[37] In fact, when asked whether they had ever engaged in *any* kind of unwanted sexual activity (not just sexual intercourse), 94% of college-age men said they had. In other words, if the "new and improved" definition of rape propounded by the *Ms.* researchers is accepted, then substantially more men than women are victims of rape!

The media also kind of forgot to mention the study that was conducted by M. Aizeman and G. Kelley. That study found no significant difference between the sexes with respect to the perpetration of physical abuse among actively dating college men and women.[38] Also overlooked by the media was the study that found that 38% of men, as compared to 30% of women, reported having been a victim of sexual coercion by their partner.[39]

It is not necessary to stretch definitions in order to establish that violence against men is a serious problem in this country, though[40]. All of the existing reliable data clearly show that it is.

Violence by intimates

When people hear that men are significantly more likely than women to be victims of violence, the usual response is that this is just men hurting other men and at most is just further evidence that men are the ones with the power in our society. This logic is difficult to understand. Would we say to a black crime victim that we don't care if she was attacked by another black person, because it's only black-on-black crime? Well, maybe if we belonged to the Ku Klux Klan we would. But if we believed in equality, we wouldn't. If we found that most crimes against blacks are black-on-black crimes, would we say that it only goes to show you that blacks have more power in our society than whites do? Well, maybe if we were insane we would. The truth is that a victim is a victim, regardless of who the perpetrator is. If our true concern is with protecting victims, and not simply the elevation of one gender over another, then it shouldn't matter who the perpetrator is.

Frankly, it is very difficult to understand how anyone today can believe that the male-always-aggressor/female-always-victim model *isn't* a myth. Lorena Bobbitt was not a man. We all know who she is and what she did. The Chicago woman who shot five elementary school boys, poisoned food at two fraternities, burned down the Young Men's Jewish Council, burned two other boys in their basement, shot her own son and killed an eight-year-old boy (claiming he was a rapist), was not a man.[41] As was noted earlier, a review of arrest reports from law enforcement departments in 1999 reveals that the proportion of female arrests for domestic violence, in some cities, is actually *7 times higher* than the "5%" figure that we have all been taught to believe.[42] In Michigan, there were 7,000 reports to police of men being battered by their wives or significant others in 1995 alone,[43] and this is just the archival data! Nevertheless, the myth persists.

To determine how frequently men are victims of the "domestic" variety of violence, and specifically, of female perpetrators of violence, specialized statistics detailing not only the nature of the crime, but also the nature of the relationship between the perpetrator and the victim, are needed. Studies of this kind are still in their infancy, as compared to studies of crime rates in general, but what studies there are do not support the "95%" figure. They're not even close.

According to the 1996 National Violence Against Women Survey, the ratio of women who had been assaulted or raped, as compared to men who had been raped or assaulted, is about 3 to 2.[44] There are important reasons to believe this ratio was artificially inflated, which I will discuss in more detail later on, but even taking the Survey at face value, it shows that the ratio of female victims to male victims is considerably lower than 19 to 1. It doesn't even support the "6 times higher" figure touted by the Women's Bureau. At best, it shows a ratio of about 1.5 to 1. Even assuming, for the moment, that all of the assaults against women were perpetrated by males (and they weren't), it would still only follow that 62% of all reports of rape or physical assault involved a man attacking a woman. Adjusting for the possibility of female-on-female violence (e.g., in lesbian relationships) would bring the figure even closer to the 50-50 mark.

Bureau of Justice Statistics data show that in the year 2000 alone, 1,585,130 males over the age of 12 were victims of violent crime at the hands of someone they know. The same data also show that substantially more men than women were violently victimized by a friend or acquaintance. Although women are slightly more likely than men to be victims of simple assault at the hands of a nonstranger, men are about 1.5 times more likely to be victims of *aggravated* assault at the hands of someone they know (wife, girlfriend, relative, etc.) than women are.[45]

Prior to the 1990's, women were about equally as likely to be convicted of murdering their husbands and boyfriends as men were to be convicted of murdering their wives and girlfriends.[46] With the advent of female-only defenses to premeditated murder (the "battered women's syndrome" and "raging hormones" defenses, for example), the conviction rate for women has been steadily decreasing relative to that for men. As a result, the archival data now makes it appear that 60% of the people who are convicted of murdering an intimate are male, while 40% of those convicted are female.[47] Even taking this data at face value, however, it would still mean that there were at least 12,686 *unjustifiable, premeditated* murders of husbands by wives who were not suffering from battered women's syndrome or raging hormones at the time and did not hire someone else to do the killing for them (*see* Chapter 11), and 6,879 unjustifiable, premeditated murders of single men by girlfriends who were not suffering from battered girlfriend syndrome or raging hormones at the time of the murder.[48] These figures are not exactly persuasive evidence that domestic violence is strictly a male phenomenon.

Regardless of the number of women who are convicted of murder, it is nevertheless the case that 55% of the victims of family killings are actually male.[49]

Murder by Intimates

Although we often hear startling reports about the high number of women who are killed by men they know, what the research really shows is that men who kill are more likely to kill a stranger or an acquaintance than a wife or girlfriend. Women who kill are actually more likely to target an intimate partner than men are.[50]

In 1993, 70% of California homicide victims were related to or knew their killer. In the same year 81.5% of California homicide victims were male.[51] 8.1% of these men were killed as a result of domestic violence. Putting these numbers together, we see that 6.6% of all California homicides in 1993 involved a male being killed as a result of domestic violence. The same report shows that the figure for women killed as a result of domestic violence is 6.8%. In other words, the rates are almost identical.

Finessing the Statistics

Interestingly, the author of the California study kind of forgot to point this out. Instead, what he reported was that "female homicide victims in California were 15 times more likely than male victims to be killed by their spouse/partner."[52]

How could he construe data that so clearly shows that the rates are nearly identical as if they showed that the ratio is 15-to-1? It requires some ingenuity, but a person who is both intelligent and committed with all his heart and soul to the goal of devaluing men can always find a way. In this case, it was done by comparing apples and oranges: using data about female *victims* as if it was data about the entire female population. As we have seen, the likelihood that a California *female* will be killed by her spouse/partner is about equal to the likelihood that a California male will be killed by his spouse/partner.

To understand this point, an illustration might be helpful. Suppose that in the course of a year 500 black people were killed, while only 2 white people were killed. Suppose, further, that the number of interracial killings was equal--that 1 white person killed 1 black person, and 1 black person killed 1 white person. From this data, we could validly conclude that a white person is equally as likely to be killed by a black person as a black person is to be killed by a white person. On the other hand, since only 1 in 500 of the black victims was killed by a white person, while 1 in 2 of the white victims was killed by a black person, we could *also* say that white victims are 250 times more likely to have been killed by blacks than black victims are to have been killed by whites.[53] Only one of these conclusions would serve the purpose of a person who is committed to the goal of perpetuating fear and prejudice against black people. Can you guess which one?

This is an important distinction to understand because nearly every governmental agency and female supremacist organization in this country manipulates statistics in exactly this way to mask the truth that males are about equally as likely to be victims of domestic violence at the hands of females as females are to be victims of domestic violence at the hands of males.[54]

Take the statistic that appears on page 69 of the California Department of Justice's publication, *Homicide in California, 1993*, for example. According to this agency, many more female *victims* (51.4%) than male *victims* (20.6%) are killed in their homes. If, as the California Attorney General acknowledges, 81.5% of all homicide victims in 1993 were male, and if, as the California Department of Justice reports, 20.6% of this 81.5% occurred in the home, then it follows that 16.8% of all homicides involved a male being killed in his home, while only 10% of all homicides involved a female being killed in her home. Applying the California Department of Justice's and the California Attorney General's assumption that a homicide that occurs in the home is likely to have been the result of domestic violence, then their own data would support the inference that men are substantially more likely to be victims of fatal domestic violence than women are.

Non-lethal Violence

Since the key witness is dead, the truth about lethal violence is difficult to ascertain. As will be seen, however, the statistics on non-lethal forms of domestic violence are clear that domestic violence is approximately a 50-50 proposition. For example, it has been found that the rate of non-lethal domestic violence against males in households with incomes of less than $7,500 is about the same as the rate of non-lethal intimate violence against females in households with incomes of $75,000 or more. This tends to corroborate the anecdotal evidence that our culture permits and encourages women to beat up on men when and if they fail to be good providers for them.[55]

Survey Results

One of the earliest and most controversial studies on the subject of domestic violence was the National Family Violence Survey. The National Family Violence Survey was a longitudinal study that found that *wives are at least as likely to behave violently toward their spouses as husbands are.*[56]

When I first came across this study a few years back, I was so certain it must have suffered from methodological or design flaws that I didn't even bother to read it. But then I ran across a recent figure from the U.S. Department of Justice's National Violence Against Women Survey that made me question my assumptions. Specifically, the National Violence Against Women Survey, although designed to call attention to the need to devote more resources to the problem of violence against women, actually reported that every year *834,700 men are physically abused by an intimate* (wife, ex-wife or current living-together relationship.)[57] That's nearly a million men a year! And this doesn't even count the huge number of male victims of domestic violence who are under the age of 18, or the victims who are abused by an ex-girlfriend, or those men who simply didn't feel comfortable admitting that they had been beaten up or that they are afraid of a woman.

This reminded me of a survey I had read about in a newspaper a few years ago. The survey was conducted jointly by the Minneapolis *Star Tribune* and WCCO Television. It found that men and women use basically the same tactics to deal with conflict, including violence. To my astonishment, the *Star-Tribune*--the same newspaper that had asserted that over-reporting the incidence of violence against women is a good thing--reported that 13% of the men had been abused by their partners, while only 7% of the women had been. 6% of the men had actually been physically attacked by their partners, while only 2% of the women had been. What impressed me the most about this survey was that female reports of perpetration and victimization mirrored almost exactly the male reports of perpetration and victimization, suggesting that neither gender was likely to have been either under-reporting or over-reporting victimizations.[58]

Since then, I have uncovered numerous studies conducted by independent researchers that say basically the same thing. These studies are among the least-publicized and least-known in the history of western civilization, but they have all been conducted in accordance with sound principles of scientific research.[59]

In a 20-year longitudinal study conducted in Dunedin, New Zealand, 12.7% of women and 21.2% of men reported being the victims of severe physical violence by a partner. These figures mirrored the corresponding reports concerning the perpetration of severe physical violence against a partner of the opposite sex.[60] About 50% of women reported perpetrating physical abuse (whether severe or mild) and about 50% of men reported being victims of physical abuse (whether severe or mild); about 42% of men reported perpetrating physical abuse (whether severe or mild) and about 39% of women reported being victims of physical abuse (whether severe or mild.) Male victim reports corroborated what female perpetrators reported: women perpetrate partner violence more frequently than men do.[61]

Recent findings from the British Home Office also confirm that men are just as likely to be victims of domestic violence as women are. The findings reveal that 4.2% of British men and 4.2% of British women were victims of domestic assault in 1996. The findings also reveal that males are most vulnerable to abuse when they are bad providers (under-employed, earning low income, low or negative net worth, or suffering from a long-term illness or disability) and that over 3 million British men are physically assaulted by their wives or girlfriends every year.[62]

A national criminal justice census conducted in Brazil in 1988 showed that 60% of that nation's victims of physical abuse were male and 40% were female.[63]

In 1986, *Marriage and Divorce Today*, a newsletter for family therapy practitioners, reported that 52% of the victims of elder abuse are men.[64]

Between 1976 and 1989 more black men were killed by their wives than black women were killed by their husbands.[65] In fact, it has been pointed out that "black males are twice as likely to be killed by their female intimates than to kill them."[66]

Additional scholarly research[67] supporting the conclusion that women are at least as likely to abuse men as men are to abuse women include: Archer (women more likely than men to "use one or more acts of physical aggression and to use such acts more frequently");[68] Archer and Ray (women significantly more likely than their male partners to commit acts of physical violence);[69] Arias, Samios and O'Leary (30% of men and 49% of women found to have used some form of aggression in their dating histories);[70] Arias and Johnson (more women than men are physically aggressive while dating);[71] Bernard and Bernard (15% of male college students physically abusive to partners while dating; 21% of female college students physically abusive to partners while dating);[72] Billingham and Sack (young women more likely than young men to initiate violence in dating relationships);[73] Bland and Orne (study of Canadian women finding that women engage in domestic violence at higher rates than men do);[74] Bohannon, Dosser and Lindley (among military couples, 11% of wives and 7% of husbands were physically aggressive);[75] Bookwala, et. al. (women and men about equally violent toward each other, but women tend to initiate violence more frequently);[76] Breen (female college students more likely than male college students to be violent in dating relationships);[77] Brinkerhoff and Lupri (Canadian study of 562 couples found twice as much wife-to-husband as husband-to-wife severe violence--10.7% v. 4.8%, respectively; overall violence rates for men were 10.3%, as compared to 13.2% for women);[78] Brush (married men and married women about equally violent toward each other);[79] Brutz and Ingoldsby (study of Quaker families finding a higher ratio of female-to-male violence (15.2%) than male-to-female violence (14.6%));[80] Burke, Stets and Pirog-Good (14% of men and 18% of women reported inflicting physical abuse, the researchers concluding that they observed "no significant difference between men and women in reporting inflicting or sustaining physical abuse");[81] Carlson (men and women equally likely to aggress against their partners);[82] Carrado, et. al. (in a random sample of nearly a thousand British men and a thousand British women, 18% of the men and 13% of the women were victims of physical violence during any of their heterosexual relationships throughout their lives, and more men than women were victims of partner aggression during their current relationship);[83] Cascardi, Langhinrichsen and Vivian (among couples in marriage counseling, husbands and wives equally likely to perpetrate violence);[84] Barling, et al. (same);[85] Caulfield and Riggs (among unmarried college students, women are significantly more likely to commit acts of physical violence against their partners than men are; 13% of women kicked, bit, or hit their partners with a fist, while only 3.1% of men engaged in this activity--a female-to-male ratio of 4 to 1);[86] Claxton-Oldfield and Arsenault (26% of Canadian college women admitted they had initiated physical aggression in order to punish and control their male partners);[87] Coney and Mackey ("epidemiological surveys on the distribution of violent behavior between adult partners suggest gender parity");[88] Deal and Wampler (violence in dating relationships is most often mutual; in cases where it is not reciprocal, women are 3 times more likely to be the perpetrator);[89] Ensminger-Vanfossen (women as violent toward men as men are toward women);[90] Ernst, et. al. (20% of men and 19% of women treated in a New Orleans hospital emergency room are current victims of physical abuse);[91] Fekete ("women in relationships with men commit comparatively as many or more acts of physical violence as men do, at every level of severity");[92] Fiebert and Gonzalez (29% of Southern California college women initiated physical assaults against their male partners, over a 5-year period);[93] Flynn ("men and women in relationships, both marital and premarital, engage in comparable amounts of violence");[94] Follingstad, Wright and Sebastian (college women twice as likely to perpetrate dating violence as college men are);[95] Foshee (among nearly 2,000 adolescents in rural North Carolina, 27.8% of females and 15.0% of males perpetrated dating violence, although only slightly more males than females admitted they had been victimized);[96] Frieze (among college students, women are more likely than men to start physical altercations with a dating partner);[97] Gelles (1974)(comparable rates of physical aggression between husbands and wives);[98] Gelles (1982)(same);[99] Gelles and Straus

(1988)(same);[100] George (14% of men, and 7% of women had been assaulted by a woman at some time in their lives, and the majority of female assaults on men are perpetrated by spouses, partners or former partners);[101] Goodyear-Smith and Laidlaw ("within the general population, women initiate and use violent behaviors against their partners at least as often as men");[102] Harders, et. al. (women significantly more physically aggressive than men, especially with respect to pushing, slapping and punching);[103] Headey, Scott and de Vaus (Australian International Social Science Survey shows that 5.7% of Australian men and 3.7% of Australian women have been victims of domestic assaults);[104] Henton, et. al. (abuse among high school students is usually reciprocal, with both partners initiating violence at similar rates);[105] Jackson, Cram and Seymour (study of New Zealand high school seniors, finding approximately equal rates of injury from domestic violence perpetrated by a partner of the opposite sex);[106] Jouriles and O'Leary (among married couples, rates of violence appear to be about equal);[107] Kalmuss (rate of husband-to-wife severe aggression is 3.8%, while ratio of wife-to-husband severe aggression is 4.6%);[108] Lane and Gwartney-Gibbs (equal rates of violence for males and females involved in dating relationships);[109] Laner and Thompson (similar rates of male and female violence in dating relationships);[110] Langhinrichsen-Rohling and Vivian (64% of wives and 61% of husbands involved in marriage counseling are aggressive);[111] Lo and Sporakowski (women more often perpetrators than victims of abuse);[112] Lottes and Weinberg (31% of American males will be victims of physical abuse perpetrated by a female partner by the time they are in college);[113] Magdol, et. al. (during a 12-month period, physical violence was perpetrated by 37.2% of women and 21.8% of men);[114] Makepeace (roughly equal incidence of violence among men and women);[115] Malone, Tyree and O'Leary (men and women engage in similar amounts of physical aggression both in their families of origin and against their spouses, but women are more aggressive toward their partners than men are);[116] Margolin (about 41% of wives have engaged in physical violence against their husbands, and about 39% of husbands have engaged in physical violence against their wives);[117] Marshall and Rose (more women than men commit acts of domestic violence against a partner of the opposite sex);[118] Mason and Blankenship (women and men about equally violent toward each other);[119] McCarthy (recent study of 1,145 college students revealing that 36% of men and 28% of women have been victims of physical abuse during the previous year);[120] McKinney (38% of women and 47% of college men surveyed had been victims of physical abuse in a dating relationship; 26% of women acknowledge that they have physically assaulted their dating partner);[121] McLeod (women commit more serious forms of violence against men than men do against women);[122] McNeely and Robinson-Simpson (1987)(women are as violent as men in domestic relationships);[123] Mercy and Saltzman (husbands more likely than wives to be stabbed to death by their spouses);[124] Meredith, Abbot and Adams (Nebraska men and women about equally as likely to use severe violence against each other);[125] Milardo (almost all college women are likely to hit their partner, while considerably fewer college men would be likely to hit their partner under any circumstances);[126] Morse (data from the longitudinal National Youth Survey, finding that for each survey year--1983, 1986, 1989 and 1992--the prevalence rates of female-to-male violence were significantly higher than for male-to-female violence);[127] Murphy (men more often victims of heterosexual domestic physical abuse than women are; 20.7% of college men and 12.8% of college women had been kicked, bitten or hit with a fist by their heterosexual partner, and 6% of men and 3.6% of women had been beaten up by their heterosexual partner);[128] Mwamwenda (in a South African survey of mostly female college students regarding domestic abuse witnessed as children, 20% had seen their mother or a female relative beat their husbands, and 26% had witnessed female neighbors beating their husbands);[129] Nisonoff and Bitman (18.6% of men and 12.7% of women have been hit by their spouses);[130] O'Keeffe, Brockopp and Chew (11.9% of high school girls and 7.4% of high school boys have been sole perpetrators of physical violence against a dating partner; 17.8% of girls and 11.6% of boys have been involved in incidents involving mutual violence);[131] O'Leary, et. al. (1989)(wives more physically violent toward husbands than husbands are toward wives--both before and during the marriage);[132] O'Leary, et. al., "Premarital Physical Aggression" (among premarital couples, 34% of males and 40% of females engaged in some form of physical aggression against their mates; 35% of the men and 30% of the women reported being abused);[133] Plass and Gessner (women significantly more likely than men to be aggressors in both courtship and committed relationship violence; in a committed relationship, women are three times more likely than men to slap their partners, and 7 times more likely to kick, bite or hit with the fist);[134] Riggs, O'Leary and Breslin (39% of women and 23% of men had engaged in physical aggression against their current partners);[135] Rollins and Oheneba-Sakyi (a random sampling of 1,471 Utah households revealed that women's rate of severe violence was 5.3%, while the male rate was 3.4%);[136] Rosenfeld (Detroit men more likely to be murdered by their intimate partners than Detroit women are);[137] Rouse, Breen and Howell (men more likely to be physically abused by women than vice versa, in both dating and marital relationships);[138] Russell and Hulson (men and women equally likely to be abusive, but women about twice as likely as men to commit acts of severe physical abuse);[139] Ryan (40% of college men and 34% of college women had been victims of domestic physical abuse);[140] Sack, Keller and Howard (men and women equally likely to engage in acts of physical violence);[141] Schafer, Caetano and Clark (ratio of female-to-male violence higher than ratio of male-to-female violence, among both married and cohabiting heterosexual couples);[142] Shook, et. al. (23.5% of women and 13.0% of men used physical force against a dating partner);[143] Sigelman, Berry and Wiles (college men experience significantly more domestic violence than college women do);[144] Sommer (1994)(Canadian study finding that 39.1% of women have been physically aggressive toward their male partner at some time, while 26.3% of men have been physically aggressive toward their female partner at some time; in addition, 34.8% of men and 40.1% of women reported having observed their mothers hitting their fathers);[145] Smith, S., et. al. (women as abusive as men);[146] Sommer, Barnes and Murray (39% of women physically aggressed against their male partners at some point in their relationship);[147] Sorenson and Telles (women more likely than men to hit, throw objects and initiate violence);[148] Spencer and Bryant (study of 2,094 high school students finding that males are more often victims of dating violence than females are; 30% of rural, and 20% of urban and suburban boys are victims of female violence; 25% of rural girls, 16% of suburban and 13% of urban girls are victims of male violence);[149] Steinmetz (1977-78)(incidence of husband-beating similar to incidence of wife-beating, but wives somewhat more likely than husbands to initiate physical violence);[150] Steinmetz (1981)(cross-cultural study of married couples in Finland, Canada, Puerto Rico, Belize, Israel and the United States, finding that "in each society the percentage of husbands who used violence was similar to the percentage of violent wives");[151] Steinmetz (1980)(women are both perpetrators and victims of domestic violence);[152] Stets and Henderson (22% of single, never married men who are dating, and 40% of single, never married women who are dating, use some form of physical aggression in their dating relationships);[153] Stets and Pirog-Good (1987)(male and female college students similar in their use of intimate violence);[154] Stets and Pirog-Good (1989)(12% of women slapped men they were dating and 8% of men slapped women they were dating; rates at which other violent acts are perpetrated are roughly equal);[155] Stets and Straus (1990)(women as likely as men to initiate physical conflict);[156] Stets and Straus (1989)(among dating, cohabiting and married couples, women perpetrate more physical abuse against men than vice versa);[157] Straus (1980)(study of 325 violent married couples, finding that in 72.2% of the cases, the wife had committed at least one violent act against the husband);[158] Straus (1993) (women initiate physical assaults against their partners as often as men do);[159] Straus (1998)(same);[160] Straus and Gelles (1986)(wives commit slightly more acts of domestic abuse against husbands than husbands do against wives);[161] Straus and Gelles (1990)(same);[162] Straus, Gelles and Steinmetz (Jewish wives 7 times more likely than Jewish husbands to commit abusive violence, defined as "an act which has a high potential for injuring the person being hit," but otherwise men and women are equally violent toward each other; when violence against children is included, women commit more violence than men);[163] Straus, et. al. (1996)(49% of men and 31% of women are victims of physical assault by their partner);[164] Straus and Kantor (wives assault husbands at higher rates than husbands assault wives);[165] Straus and Mouradian (9.9% of college men and 9.4% of college women have been injured by a member of the opposite sex);[166] Sugarman and Hotaling (39.3% of women and 32.9% of men commit acts of domestic violence against the persons they are dating);[167] Szinovacz (wives' rates of physical aggression appear to be somewhat higher than husbands');[168] Tang ("Mothers as likely as fathers to use actual physical force toward their spouses");[169] Thompson (1990)(28.4% of women and 24.6% of men exhibited physical violence toward their dating partners over a two-year period; also, women are twice as likely as men to slap their partners);[170] Vivian and Langhinrichsen-Rohling (no significant differences found to exist between husbands' and wives' reports concerning the frequency and severity of assault victimizations);[171] National Association of Social Workers (adolescent girls are more often violent in dating relationships than adolescent boys are);[172] White and Humphrey (51.5% of 17- and 18-year old females entering college have used physical aggression at least once in their dating relationships and 30.2% admitted physically abusing their male partners at least once in the past year);[173] White, J. W., and R.M. Kowalski ("women equal or exceed men in number of aggressive acts committed within the family");[174] White and Koss (in a representative sample of 2,603 women and 2,105 men, 39% of men and 32% of women had been victims of some form of physical aggression in a dating relationship.)[175]

> *[W]hile repeated studies consistently show that men are victims of domestic violence as often as are women, both the lay public and many professionals regard a finding of no sex difference in rates of physical aggression among intimates as surprising, if not unreliable, the stereotype being that men are aggressive and women are exclusively victims*[176]

The most recent profile published by Statistics Canada (which publishes statistical profiles on an annual basis) confirms that men are still more frequently the targets of domestic violence than women are. According to the statistics, there were 303,000 male victims of domestic violence, as compared to 259,000 female victims. Almost twice as many men were choked, bitten, kicked, battered or hit with an object, as compared to women.[177]

It has been observed that the same study that is cited by women's advocates, politicians, educators and the media for the statistic that "a woman is battered every 15 seconds" *also shows that a man is battered every 14 seconds.*[178] Educators, the media, politicians and other women's advocates always omit the second half of this statistic.

A 1996 survey of college students found that nearly all of them were completely unaware of any of this.[179] Nearly every one, however, had heard about "that research study" according to which "95%" of domestic violence is perpetrated by men against women-- even though no such research study exists.[180]

In his book, *Knights Without Armor: A Practical Guide for Men in Quest of Masculine Soul*, Aaron Kipnis states that "Although we are discouraged from talking about it, nearly all men today have felt victimized, manipulated, scapegoated, dominated or abused by women at various times in our lives."[181] The research is making it increasingly difficult to continue to dismiss this kind of outburst as whiny backlash from an uppity male.

2. Violence against men is just as severe as violence against women

When I tell people about these findings, they always react in exactly the same way: "Well, that may be true," they say, "But when men abuse women, the injury is severe; when women abuse men, it is only mild."[182] The tacit (and sometimes express) assumption, of course, is that men are stronger than women, and consequently more dangerous than women.

Preliminarily, it should be noted that the distinction between "mild" and "severe" abuse is a rather artificial one. The law does not always make this distinction. The crime of battery encompasses *any* unwanted touching, no matter how slight. Men are arrested, charged and convicted of "domestic assault" and "battery" every day for doing things like grabbing car keys from a woman's hand to prevent her from driving drunk, or giving a woman a friendly hug, a slap to the wrist, etc. These men all show up in the archival data as "batterers," right along with the men who beat women so severely that they require medical treatment or protection in a shelter. Those who rely on archival data to support their extraordinary claims about the extent of male violence never seem to have any problem with lumping these offenders together and calling them all "batterers." They don't bother to take the time to distinguish between men who commit "mild" abuse and those who commit "severe" abuse. It is not clear why it is believed that distinctions must be made between "mild" and "severe" violence if the figures show that women commit more violence than men, but not if they don't.

It can also be asked whether it really makes any sense to distinguish between "good" domestic abuse ("mild" abuse

committed by women against men) and "bad" domestic abuse
(*any* kind of abuse committed by men against women, regardless
of severity.) Men bleed when they are cut. Men feel pain when
they are hit. The claim that women suffer emotional harm from
domestic abuse and men don't is ridiculous. Domestic violence,
even of the "mild" variety, significantly increases psychological
distress for male victims, too.[183] In fact, when objective measures
of psychological distress are employed (as distinguished from
subjective self-reports), researchers have actually found that males
sometimes suffer *greater* psychological distress as a result of abuse
than female victims of the same kind of abusive act do.[184] The fact
that male victims have been socialized to hide their emotions, while
female victims have been socialized to express them, does not mean
that men do not experience the pain. Men's tendency to suppress
and/or deny their pain only provides evidence about the societal
response to the experience of pain by persons of the male gender,
not the actual incidence of pain in persons of the male gender.[185]

What, then, does this distinction between "severe" and "mild"
domestic abuse mean? It is usually assumed that sexual abuse is the
most severe form of abuse, while verbal and emotional abuse are
the most mild, and physical abuse runs the spectrum between these
two extremes. Some would argue, however, that emotional abuse
can be worse than physical abuse. For example, should repeatedly
calling a woman "fat and ugly" be regarded a "less serious" form
of abuse than, say, grabbing car keys from her hand to prevent her
from driving drunk? Where along the continuum of abuse is this
imaginary line between "mild" and "severe" to be drawn?

Frankly, I do not know the answer to that question. I suspect it
all depends on the political agenda of the person you ask. For the
sake of argument, however, let's suppose that it does make sense to
distinguish between "mild" and "severe" forms of abuse. While it
may not be possible to state precisely where the line between them
is to be drawn, it may at least be possible to reach a consensus about
the kinds of abuse which most of us would agree are "severe" and
which kinds most of us would agree are not necessarily quite as
"severe."

This is what Murray Straus was after when he designed the
Conflict Tactics Scale. Adopting the methodology applied by

the U.S. Supreme Court to decide obscenity cases ("We may not know how to define it, but we know it when we see it"), certain types of acts were classified as "severe" on the basis that the researchers simply believed them to be more likely to have injurious consequences than other acts that they chose to classify as "mild." Thus, shooting a gun at someone, choking, beating up and stabbing people were all classified as "severe," while name-calling, pushing, shoving and grabbing were classified as "mild."[186] Most forms of emotional abuse were classified as "mild," except that calling a woman fat or ugly was classified as a "severe" form of abuse. All forms of sexual abuse against a female victim were classified as "severe." While these classifications have been assailed by some critics,[187] they come about as close as it is humanly possible to get to an accurate portrayal of the average person's intuitive sense of what constitutes "severe" violence, on one hand, and what constitutes "mild" violence, on the other. The scale developed by Straus may be vulnerable to some criticism (*see* Appendix), but it is still the best instrument available for measuring the severity of abuse, as distinguished from the mere incidence of it. Most of the studies that will be cited in this chapter make use of it in some way.

What the Research Shows

So, then, is it true that female violence against males is milder than male violence against females? To pose the question another way: Is it true that men are more dangerous than women because men are bigger and stronger than women?

It probably is true that men, on average, are taller than women. It is also probably true that some men are physically stronger than some women. On the other hand, some women are actually quite strong, physically. Indeed, if we accept current media portrayals, it would seem that women and girls are all fabulously stronger, both physically and mentally, than any male can ever hope to be. Be that as it may, it is important to keep in mind that even women who are not otherwise as strong as their male partners can be just as dangerous when equipped with a gun, a knife or some other weapon. And studies have shown that women are much more likely to use a weapon against their partners than men are.[188]

Moreover, even a muscle-bound man may be completely incapable of defending himself in his sleep, or when he is hit with an object from behind. The research shows that it is mostly women who assault their partners while they are sleeping, and it is also mostly women who attack their partners from behind.[189]

It is also mostly women who use weapons to assault their partners. According to the National Crime Victimization Survey, males are 20% more likely to be victims of aggravated assault (assault with a weapon or causing serious bodily harm) at the hands of someone they know well than women are, and are twice as likely to be victims of aggravated assault at the hands of an acquaintance as women are.[190]

The Straus and Gelles studies showed that 54.8% of the severe- -not the mild, the *severe*--varieties of domestic spousal abuse are committed by a wife, not a husband.[191] Specifically, Straus and Gelles found that women are at least as likely as men to commit acts of domestic violence at *every* level of severity.[192]

The Straus and Gelles findings have been confirmed by other researchers. Arias, Samios and O'Leary found that a greater percentage of women engaged in severe physical aggression against a dating partner of the opposite sex than men did.[193] A study of 562 married couples in Calgary, Canada uncovered twice as much wife-to-husband as husband-to-wife severe violence (10.7%, as compared to 4.8%.)[194] A U.K. study of people who have been victimized by women found that when a man is the victim, the kind of injury inflicted is more severe than when a woman is the victim.[195] An examination of data from the International Social Science Survey/ Australia reveals that women inflict serious injuries at least as frequently as men do in domestic violence incidents; in fact, 1.8% of men's, as compared to 1.2% of women's injuries, required first aid; and 1.5% of men's injuries required treatment, as compared to 1.2% of women's injuries.[196] Kalmuss found that the rate of wife-to-husband severe aggression is 4.6%, as compared to a 3.8% rate for husband-to-wife severe aggression[197] Langhinrichsen-Rohling and Vivian found that overall, wives involved in marriage counseling are more aggressive than husbands who are involved in marriage counseling. Among those who were aggressive, 25% of the husbands and 11% of the wives engaged only in mild forms of aggression, while 36% of husbands and 53% of wives were classified as severely aggressive.[198] In a longitudinal study, Magdol, et. al. found that 18.6% of women had perpetrated severe violence against their partners over a twelve-month period, as compared to 5.7% of men.[199] A study in Great Britain revealed that although overall husband-to-wife and wife-to-husband rates of violence were equal, 11.3% of the violence committed against husbands was severe, as compared to 5.8% of the violence committed against wives.[200] In a random sample of 1,471 Utah households, it was found that the women's rate of severe violence was 5.3%, as compared to the male rate of 3.4%.[201] A national telephone survey of single, never married men and women currently involved in a relationship revealed that women were "6 times more likely than men to use severe aggression (19.2% vs. 3.4%.)"[202] A cross-cultural study of marital violence in Finland, United States, Canada, Puerto Rico, Belize, and Israel found that "Wives who used violence... tended to use greater amounts."[203] A review article written by social scientists McNeely and Mann in 1990 noted that women are more likely than men to engage in severely violent acts.[204] Vivian and Langhinrichsen-Rohling discovered that among mutually aggressive couples, there is no significant difference between husbands and wives concerning either the frequency or the severity of assault victimizations.[205]

Battering vs. Ordinary Couples Violence

It is sometimes argued that although the aggregate number of severe violent acts may be the same, men are more likely than women to be guilty of a *pattern* of repetitious assaults. Although in law a person does not have to be shown to have engaged in a pattern of violence in order to be convicted of "battery," some social scientists recognize a distinction between "ordinary couples violence" and "battering," with "battering" being defined as the use of repeated acts of violence as a means of maintaining control over one's partner. Survey data such as that obtained by using the Conflict Tactics Scale ("CTS") is often criticized for failing to measure domestic violence according to this special definition of battery. Yet, many research studies have, in fact, included measures of frequency in addition to incidence and severity. The 1975 National Family Violence Survey, which used the CTS, included measures of frequency. It showed that wives who commit acts of violence average 10.1 acts per year, while husbands who are violent average 8.8 acts per year. For severe violence, the mean frequency rate for wives was found to be 8.9 per year, while for men the mean frequency rate was 8.0 per year. Among violent wives, the median frequency for both overall and severe violence was 3.0 per year, as compared to 2.5 per year among those husbands who were violent. The median frequency rate for using or threatening to use a gun or a knife was nearly equal, with women showing a slightly higher frequency than men.[206]   More recently, Straus has found that women who commit acts of domestic abuse carried out an average of 6 minor and 5 severe assaults per year.[207]   Even when the men's interpretation of events was excluded and reliance was placed entirely on the female responses, it was found that women who are violent averaged 7.2 assaults per year, while men who are violent averaged 6.0 assaults per year.[208]

In 1995, Straus observed that the rate of severe violence by women against men has been higher than the rate of severe violence by men against women since at least 1975.[209]   Straus has also observed that since 1975, female violence rates have been growing, while male violence rates have been declining[210] Even in 1975, however, the rates at which husbands and wives perpetrated severe acts of violence against each other were not that far apart; the ratio wasn't even 2-to-1, let alone 19-to-1.[211]

In a study of college students, researchers found that even though men were significantly more likely than women to report that their partners had used only "moderate" physical violence against them, male victims suffered a greater number of injuries requiring medical attention than female victims did.[212] This suggests that men are more inclined to under-report the severity of the harm to which they are subjected than women are.

The National Violence Against Women Survey found that most domestic abuse against women consists of pushing, grabbing, shoving, slapping or pulling hair (not all of which is committed by a male perpetrator.) The percentage of domestic abuse cases involving a female victim in which the woman was actually beaten up was about 8.5%. A gun or knife was used in 1.6% of the cases.[213] This stands in marked contrast to the figures for abused men. When women commit domestic violence, they are substantially more likely to use a weapon than when men do. Studies have shown that overall, 29% of female offenders use a weapon, as compared to 17% of male offenders.[214] And with respect to homicides, a Philadelphia, Pennsylvania study found that knives were used four times as often by women as by men.[215]

McLeod found that, of the male spousal abuse victims in Detroit, 74% of men sustained injury; of these, 84% required medical care.[216] Discovering similar data in other cities, he concluded that "Offenses against men are significantly more serious in nature than are offenses against women."[217] This is borne out by emergency room data which has shown that nationally, 950,000 men, as compared to 600,000 women, are treated in emergency rooms as a result of interpersonal violence every year.[218]

Straus, et. al. found that 16% of male college students, as compared to 14% of female college students, were seriously injured by their partners.[219] Yet, Straus and his colleagues have also found that women are 7.5 times more likely than men to say that they sought or required medical treatment, even though 97% of the women who reported being abused were not injured seriously enough for medical treatment.[220]

Overall, *32%* of the male victims of domestic abuse are seriously injured as a result of the abuse. Only 27% of male victims suffer only "minor" injuries (such as a bruise or a scratch.)[221] Among female victims, 50% did not suffer any physical injury at all.[222]

Data published by the U.S. Department of Justice shows that regardless of the severity of the injury, less than 1% of abused men even sought medical treatment at all, even though substantially more men than women were injured seriously enough to require the services of aparamedic at the scene of the crime.[223]

Among the male victims who receive treatment for physical injuries, a substantially greater percentage had to be transported to the hospital in an ambulance or required the services of a paramedic, and a substantially greater percentage of male victims who received medical treatment required physical therapy as a result of the injury.[224] Substantially more men than women require overnight hospitalization for their injuries.[225]

Taking It Like a Man

One of the things that is becoming increasingly clear from the research is that most men do not tend to seek or receive medical treatment unless and until they have been very severely injured, while women are much more inclined to seek or perceive a need for medical treatment even when the injury is comparatively not as severe. This comports with the societal norm of "taking it like a man." That is to say, it is an American cultural norm that a man is supposed to deny and suppress his pain when he is injured. It also comports with the general societal stigma that attaches to "letting" oneself be beaten up by a woman. This stigma doesn't apply to women because it is assumed in our society that men are physically stronger and therefore can overcome a woman's will. From this frame of mind, the notion that a woman "let" a man beat her isn't even a possibility. This is why it is considered "unmanly" for a man to "let" a woman beat him up, but it is not considered "unwomanly" for a woman to acknowledge that she has been beaten up by a man. This is also why it is that when men do get medical treatment, it is usually provided to them at someone else's request, and it is usually for much more serious injuries than those for which women seek medical treatment.[226]

The fact that more victims of domestic violence requiring intensive medical care are male than female not only confirms that domestic abuse against males is at least as severe as domestic violence against females, but it also suggests that there may be many, many more male victims of abuse than even these statistics can possibly show.[227]

3. Women who abuse are not normally acting in self-defense

One of the biggest frauds perpetrated on the American public in recent times is the myth that women only batter in self-defense. The truth is that women batter for the same basic reasons that men batter, including but not limited to the simple desire to control their partners.

Those who have an interest in perpetuating this myth usually rely on information obtained from law enforcement records and battered women's shelters to support their claims.[228] These kinds of records, however, are inherently unreliable because they are derived from non-representative samples that are not randomly selected. Women's violence is virtually guaranteed not to come to the attention of the operators of a battered women's shelter, since battered women's shelters are designed to house women who have been victims, not women who have been aggressors. For reasons more fully explored in Chapters 9, 10 and 12 (having to do with under-reporting, credibility and gender-bias), female violence is also not very likely to come to the attention of law enforcement officials, and even when it does it is not likely to show up in arrest and conviction records. The most serious problem with the use of such archival data, however, is that it selects only those subjects who have a strong motivation to allege that they were acting in self-defense. A woman who faces the possibility of jail time if she admits she was the aggressor has a strong motivation to tell law enforcement officers (and judges) that she was only acting in self-defense. A woman who is seeking the services of a shelter or a domestic abuse services program of some other kind also has a strong incentive to claim that any violence on her own part was entirely in self-defense. And a woman who is accused of abuse in a family court proceeding has a strong motivation to claim self-defense if custody of children and/or entitlement to alimony is at stake.

The only way to get reliable information about whether or not female violence is "always in self-defense" is to survey randomly selected women from a sample that is representative of the whole population under circumstances in which such motivations to lie are not present. Although women's organizations, politicians and the media never mention them, such studies actually have been done and actually do exist.

What the Research Shows

In the Dunedin study mentioned earlier, it was found that males who committed domestic violence were 19 times more likely to have been victims of females who committed domestic violence than males who did not commit domestic violence were. Women who abused were 10 times more likely than women who do not abuse to have been victims of abuse themselves.[229] This finding means either that females are ultimately responsible for more violence than males are, or that domestic abuse, more often than not, is mutual. I prefer to make the latter conclusion. In either event, the Dunedin study clearly refutes the notion that women who abuse are always doing it in self-defense.

A study of courtship violence among university students revealed that 9% of women had initiated violence at a time when their partner had not, while only 3% of men had done so.[230] A similar study conducted on college students found that 22% of women had initiated violence with a non-violent partner, while the figure for men was 17%.[231] Likewise, DeMaris concluded from a study of college students that "when one partner could be said to be the usual initiator of violence, that partner was most often the woman."[232] A 1997 survey of 225 college women disclosed that 55% admitted that they had initiated physical violence toward their male partners at some time in their lives.[233]

Data from the National Youth Survey reveal that over twice as many women as men had assaulted a partner who had not assaulted them.[234] Among high school students, 7.4% of the female pupils were found to have been sole perpetrators of physical violence against a dating partner.[235]

A study of Canadian men and women also found that women had initiated violence at higher rates than their male partners had.[236] This finding is corroborated by Sommer (1994), who found that among a random sampling of 452 married or cohabiting women and 447 married or cohabiting men in Winnipeg, Canada, 16.2% of the women had perpetrated severe violence against their partners, while 7.6% of the men had done so. Results of this study actually showed that a *man* is more likely to be acting in self-defense when he commits domestic abuse than a woman is (15% of men vs. 10% of women.)[237]

A recent study conducted in Ireland by a team led by Dr. Kieran McKeown found that when violence occurs in a marriage, 41% of the time it is initiated and perpetrated by the wife alone, with neither provocation nor participation by the husband. The husband is the initiator 26% of the time. In the remaining third of the cases, either the wife or the husband initiated the violence, and the other spouse retaliated with abusiveness of his or her own.[238] Dr. McKeown concluded from this that "both men and women are about equally likely to initiate domestic violence and seem to give broadly similar reasons for doing so."[239]

Similar results have been obtained in the United States. For example, Sorenson and Telles found that women are more likely than men to initiate domestic violence; they also found that non-Hispanic American women are more likely than men to strike first more than one time in a relationship.[240] In 1990, Stets and Straus found that in the majority of domestic abuse incidents involving physical violence, women struck the first blow.[241] Even when men's responses were completely disregarded, they found that 52.7% of the women reported that they had been the ones who struck the first blow, while 42.6% reported that the man had struck the first blow.[242] Dr. Irene Frieze, a psychology professor at the University of Pittsburgh recently found that among college students, women are more likely than men to initiate acts of physical violence against their dating partners.[243] A review of the research literature in this area leaves no reasonable doubt that women initiate physical assaults against their partners at least as often at men do.[244]

In sum, the research studies are clear that when women commit domestic violence, they usually are not acting in self-defense. So why do they do it, then? Well, there have been some interesting studies on that subject, too.

Why Women Abuse

While researchers are not in complete agreement about the causes of female violence, some generalizations can be made. Most researchers seem to be in agreement that women who abuse tend to have been abused as children, or to have witnessed abuse as children.[245] That is to say, female violence is a *learned* behavior pattern that will manifest itself regardless of whether or not any need for self-defense exists.[246]

Tyree and Malone have identified a positive correlation between a woman's history of hitting one's siblings when she was a child and hitting her partner when she is an adult.[247] This finding tends to corroborate the theory that domestic violence is a learned control mechanism for some women, just as it is a learned control mechanism for some men.[248]

In fact, research studies show that women's reasons for abusing tend to be nearly identical to men's reasons.[249]

Jealousy is one of the principal factors explaining dating violence among college-age women.[250] Similarly, Straus found that the most frequently cited reason for the perpetration of physical violence by a wife against a husband is sexual unfaithfulness (either real or imagined.)[251]

Stress is another causative factor that researchers have identified.[252]

Mason and Blankenship have identified a strong correlation between "low activity inhibition" and physical abusiveness in women, suggesting that many women may commit violence simply because they do not believe there will be any adverse consequences if they do.[253] In a similar vein, Fiebert and Gonzalez found that many women who aggress essentially believed they could "get away with it" because men are not permitted to retaliate in any way, under any circumstances.[254] In this connection, Straus has observed that while societal approval of a husband slapping his wife declined dramatically between 1968 and 1994 (from 21% to 10%), societal approval of a wife slapping her husband has always been higher than for a husband slapping his wife, and has remained fairly constant since 1964.[255] Straus attributes the overall high approval rate for violence against men, as compared to that for violence against women, to the fact that American public educational policy, while doggedly condemning male violence against females, has refused to recognize and condemn violence by females against males. Indeed, women who physically abuse men often maintain that they earnestly believe either that men do not feel pain or that men's feelings simply do not matter.[256]

In Fiebert and Gonzalez's study of college women who abuse their male partners,[257] selfishness (desire to force partner to focus on her needs and desires rather than his own) was the principal reason cited by most of the women themselves for their acts of violence against their male partners. 46% of the abusive women cited this as a principal reason for their use of violence against a male partner.[258] 44% of the women cited "I wanted to get my partner's attention" as a principal reason for assaulting their partners. 43% said they did it out of anger because their "partner was not listening to me." More than a third of the women rationalized their behavior on the grounds that they did not believe that men get hurt when they are victims of domestic abuse. Self-defense was cited with much less frequency than these reasons.[259]

According to the American Psychological Association, the principal reason women aggress is to express anger.[260]

All of these sources suggest that a great number of women abuse men for power and control reasons, while very few do it in self-defense.

When I've talked about the results, I've heard women say, "Yeah, I hit my boyfriend—it makes me feel powerful"[261] -- Dr. Irene Frieze, Ph.D.

A female researcher studying the "battered wife syndrome" defense (a defense derived from the American need to believe that when a woman is violent it can only have been in self-defense)[262] found that less than 6% of female killers actually had justifiable self-defense as a motive for the killing.[263] Specifically, she found that not a single one of the hundreds of women she interviewed who had been imprisoned for murdering their husbands or lovers had been battered. What she did find is that women tend to kill men when it is realized that the men are worth more dead than they are alive, as where a man is not a great provider but has a handsome life insurance policy.[264] Nevertheless, "battered woman's syndrome" is a viable--and often successful--defense strategy, even in cases involving premeditated murder, in every state in the country and the District of Columbia.[265]

As one researcher has put it: "When battered women are on trial, traditional concepts of criminal law continue to be discarded or oddly twisted, and myths and misconceptions about battered women run rampant."[266] I couldn't have said it better myself.

4. Most child abuse victims are male

The statistics on violence are even more startling when the full range of violence against males is considered.

According to the National Institute of Justice, 3.9 million of the nation's children between the ages of 12 and 17 have been victims of a serious physical assault.[267] It has been estimated that male children between these ages comprise 21.3% of all of the nation's crime victims, while female children in this age group comprise only 13.4% of the nation's victims.[268]

The U.S. Justice Department's Office of Juvenile Justice and Delinquency Prevention has confirmed that most child victims of violence are male.[269]

The Federal Bureau of Investigation reports that over half of the victims of crimes against children under 12 years of age are male[270] and that 83% of juvenile homicide victims are male.[271] As the Office of Juvenile Justice and Delinquency Prevention has put it, "[T]he risk of murder for males in young adulthood far surpasses that for young adult females."[272]

According to a recent Maternal and Child Health Technical Information Bulletin, homicide is now the leading cause of death for young black males.[273]

Of course, not all of these children are killed by their parents. Some are killed by "friends," acquaintances and strangers. Yet, the Children's Bureau of the U.S. Department of Health and Human Services reports that 56% of the children who are killed as a result of domestic child abuse are male.[274] And according to the U.S. Bureau of Justice Statistics, mothers are almost twice as likely to kill their sons as they are to kill their daughters.[275] At least half of the child maltreatment victims reported to child protection agencies nationwide are male,[276] and according to the National Center on Child Abuse and Neglect, among children under 12 years of age, boys are more frequently the victims of domestic physical abuse than girls are.[277]   A Minnesota Department of Human Services report on child abuse has also confirmed that child abuse victims under the age of 12 are more likely to be male than female.[278]

It has been estimated that between 10 and 20% of all American males are molested before they reach the age of 18.[279] The U.S. Office of Juvenile Justice and Delinquency reports that about 27% of all child sexual assault victims are male,[280] a figure in marked contrast to the "less than one-tenth of 1%" figure that is bandied about in the popular literature.

It may surprise you to learn (I know it surprised me!) that the majority of all forcible sodomy (defined as either oral or anal sex) victims of all ages are male, and 59% of the juvenile victims of this crime are male. At least half of all sodomy victims are under 12 years of age, and of these, 64% are male.[281]

According to the National Center on Child Abuse, a disabled male child is about *2.5 times more likely* to be maltreated than a disabled female child is.[282]

Some might attempt to minimize the severity of the problem of violence against children, but it is difficult to imagine any crime that could be considered more severe than sodomizing and killing a disabled child.

Is any of this meant to imply that violence against girls is not severe? Certainly not. Crimes against children of *either* gender should automatically be classified as "severe" for the simple reason that the victim is a child. To those who would suggest that the kinds of abuse to which male children are subjected are less severe than the kinds to which female children are subjected, however, I would point out that studies have shown that boys are more likely to be victims of the most severe forms of abuse--lethal or life-threatening abuse--than girls are.[283]

For those who like to try to minimize the problem of child abuse, talking to some of the inmates of prisons and mental institutions might prove instructive. Ask the prisoner whose mother disciplined him by shooting him in the arms and legs with a pistol, if his injuries were really all that bad. Ask the prisoner whose face and body are covered with grotesque scars from his mother throwing scalding water on him, if his injuries are really all that severe. Or the prisoner whose mother assaulted him in his sleep, attacked him with an ax, threw him out a window and set him on fire.[284]

5. Violence against males is on the rise

Unfortunately, the problem is getting worse, not better. Between 1986 and 1993, maltreatment of male children increased 102%, while the rate of increase of maltreatment of female children was 68%.[285]

With the exception of a slight dip in 1995, violent victimizations by intimates against their male partners steadily increased between the years 1992 and 1996.[286] Between 1997 and 1998 alone, the rate of violent victimizations against men by intimate partners *increased by 50%*.[287]

As long ago as 1986, respected researchers in the field published their observations that domestic violence against men has been steadily increasing since 1975.[288]

The increase in domestic violence against men is not really a new or recently-discovered phenomenon. It's just that for the past twenty years the information has been suppressed.

6. Violence against females is decreasing

The mantra that we always hear from journalists, politicians, educators and feminists alike is that violence against women is getting worse. The truth, however, is that while domestic violence against men has been steadily *increasing* since 1986, violence against women has actually been *decreasing*.

Between 1973 and 1988, rapes decreased by 33%.[289]

Between 1976 and 1996, the percentage of all murders involving a female victim of intimate murder declined from about 35% to less than 30%.[290] During the same time period, the rate of intimate murders of white wives and ex-wives has also steadily decreased.[291] For black victims, *every* category of intimate murders of women (wives, ex-wives, girlfriends, etc.) decreased.[292]

Between 1975 and 1985, domestic violence against women decreased by over 20%.[293] The number of female victims of intimate violence is also known to have declined every year between 1993 and 1996. During those years, the overall rate of decline was 24%.[294] Between 1993 and 1997, the rate of violent victimizations against women by intimate partners decreased by 21%.[295]

National rates of female victimization by intimate partners, rape victimization, and overall violent crime have been declining at levels comparable to the child sexual abuse rate....There has been a 21-percent decline in the rate of female victimization by intimate partners since 1993, a 60-percent decline in the rate of forcible rape since 1991, and a 30-percent decline in the rate of overall violent crime since 1994.[296]

A recent U.S. Bureau of Justice Statistics report[297] discloses that the rate of criminal victimization has been steadily decreasing every year since 1994, and in the year 2000, the number of criminal victimizations was the lowest ever recorded since 1973 when the National Crime Victimization Survey first began. The number of victimizations decreased from 44 million in 1973 to 25.9 million in 2000. The rate of *violent* victimization rates were also the lowest they have ever been since the inception of the Survey in 1973. Between 1994 and 2000, violent crime rates dropped by an average of about 10% every year, and between 1999 and 2000 they dropped by 15%. By 2000, the rate of aggravated assaults was about half what it was in 1994. The rate of simple assaults has also been steadily decreasing since 1994, and in 2000 it reached its lowest level ever.

In other words, the rate of violent victimizations of women by men hasn't been increasing; to the contrary, it has *radically decreased*. The Bureau of Justice Statistics notes that the most significant decrease in violent victimizations is sexual assault (rape, etc.)--the one category of crime in which females are most often the victim and males are most often the perpetrator.[298] Between 1999 and 2000 alone, the rate of sexual assault underwent a *37.5% decrease*.[299] The overall rate of violence against women decreased by 19.4% from 1999 to 2000, a rate of decrease nearly twice the corresponding rate for male victimizations.[300]

7. Violence by males is decreasing

Although the rate of crime in the United States is still higher than other countries, for the past 10 years the crime rate in the United States has actually been going down. This is true of both the homicide rate and the overall rate of crime in general.[301]

Male juvenile crime rates have also been going down.[302] Between 1991 and 1994, the rate of vandalism perpetrated by male juveniles decreased by 20%.[303] Between 1994 and 1995, juvenile male arrest rates for both simple and aggravated assaults also decreased significantly.[304]

Between 1976 and 1996, the number of intimate murders fell from 3,000 to 1,800. In 1976, 13.8% of all homicides involved intimates; by 1996, only 8.8% involved intimates, and by 1997 there were 38% fewer murders of intimates than there were in 1976. Between 1976 and 1996, spouse murders went down 52%.[305]

Between 1975 and 1985, wife-beating underwent a *21% decrease in actual incidence*, even in the face of a tremendous increase in the willingness of female victims to report this kind of crime when it does occur.[306] Among African Americans, the rate of severe violence by husbands against wives *decreased 43%*.[307]

In 1983, the rate of male-to-female domestic violence of any kind was 36.7; by 1992, the rate had dropped to 20.2. The rate of male-to-female serious violence also underwent a dramatic decline between 1983 and 1992, from 9.5 to 5.7.[308]

An article appearing in the *Sacramento Bee* recently reported that area arrests of men for domestic violence went from 3,147 in 1991 to 2,922 in 1996.[309] Thus, even while the definition of domestic violence was being broadened and tougher laws and arrest policies were being enacted to crack down on men, the rate still went down.[310]

Contrary to popular belief, most violent crimes against women are committed by strangers and acquaintances, not their male husbands and boyfriends. Because the development of adequate measures of intimate violence against women is a relatively recent phenomenon, it is difficult to know for certain what the rates have been in the past. Today, however, it is known that violence against women by intimates accounts for only about 10% of all violence against women.[311]

The variety of child abuse most commonly associated with men is sexual abuse. Yet, between 1991 and 1997, there has been a 48% decrease in reports of child sexual abuse. Between 1992 and 1998, substantiated cases of child sexual abuse decreased by 31%, from 149,800 substantiated cases in 1992, to 103,600 in 1998. In 1986, reports of sexual abuse were 16% of all child maltreatment cases; between 1996 and 1998, they accounted for only 8% of all child maltreatment reports.

The popular belief that the incidence of rape is on the rise is also a myth. In truth, there has been a 60% *decline* in the rate of forcible rape against women since 1991.[312]

Taken together, the evidence is pretty clear that men, as a class, have been getting *less* violent, not moreso, over the course of the past twenty years.

8. Violence by females is on the rise

"We are seeing numbers that suggest that young women are getting more aggressive." -- Bonnie J. Campbell, director, United States Violence Against Women Office[313]

While violence by men against women has been going down, violence by women against men has been going up. This is not really as recent a phenomenon as you might think. In fact, a U.S. Bureau of Justice Statistics report issued in 1988--five years before the Violence Against Women Office was created--observed that between 1971 and 1985 the violent crime rate for females rose 38%--a rate nearly 10 times greater than the corresponding male rate.[314] The increase in female violence was also noted in the *Handbook of Family Violence*, which was published in 1988.[315] Both of these reports were available at the time the Violence Against Women Act was under consideration. Both were ignored.

Federal Bureau of Investigation data show that between 1981 and 1990, the rate of violent crimes committed by women increased 61.8%. For the crime of assault, the rate of increase in female offenders was 79.1%, that is, nearly double the rate it was in 1981.[316] Between 1991 and 1995, the rate of female-perpetrated arson increased 27%; the rate of female-perpetrated weapons offenses increased 13%; and the rate of female-perpetrated aggravated assaults (assault with a deadly weapon or causing serious bodily harm) increased 37%.[317] Even the National Institute of Justice recently acknowledged that there has been a "dramatic increase in the number of women offenders."[318]

Just minor women-on-women crimes? Hardly. "Women incarcerated for violent crimes were nearly twice as likely as their male counterparts to have committed homicide, more than twice as likely to have victimized a relative or intimate, and more likely to have victimized men."[319] Among violent offenders in state prisons, women were about 3 times as likely as men to have committed their crime against a spouse, ex-spouse or other intimate partner.[320] 1,900 women commit homicide in the United States every year, and nearly 90% of their victims are male.[321]

Mothers and fathers are about equally as likely to commit the crime of parental kidnapping, but mothers are more likely to illegally abduct children after an adverse custody order has been issued than fathers are, and female custodial parents are more likely than male custodial parents to interfere with the other parent's visitation rights.[322]

A study commissioned by the United States Department of Health and Human Services found that more than 22,000 babies are abandoned in hospitals by their mothers every year. And this statistic only tells how many were left in hospitals; it doesn't include the babies who were discarded in fields, the sides of roads, and garbage dumpsters. Child abandonment is a not a minor crime.

Between 1987 and 1996, the number of juvenile delinquency cases involving female perpetrators increased 76%.[323] Between 1987 and 1994, the overall female juvenile crime rate underwent a 40% increase. During the same time period, the violent crime (murder, rape, robbery and aggravated assault) rate for juvenile females more than doubled, realizing an increase of *120%*. Between 1991 and 1994, the female rate of vandalism also more than doubled. Between 1994 and 1995, the juvenile female rates for both aggravated and simple assault increased, and female arrest rates for weapons law violations nearly tripled. By 1997, the female rate of increase for violent crimes was 4 times greater than the male rate[324]

The increase in domestic violence by women against men is also not a recent phenomenon. As early as 1986, Straus and Gelles observed that the rate of severe violence by women against men had been steadily growing since 1975, and they found that by 1985, 10% of both men and women were perpetrators of domestic violence against members of the opposite sex.[325] At about the same time, a female sociologist studying domestic abuse noted "few differences between husbands and wives in the type and frequency of physical aggression."[326] She also observed that "data from the nationally representative sample...found wives slightly higher in almost all categories (of violence) except pushing and shoving."[327] Furthermore, she found that "not only the percentage of wives having used physical violence exceeds that of the husbands, but that wives also exceed husbands in the frequency with which these acts occur."[328] The 1985 National Family Violence Resurvey found that 11.6% of men and 12.4% of women committed acts of violence against their partners.[329] According to the National Family Violence Survey, wives are more likely to assault their husbands than husbands are to assault their wives.[330] Furthermore, it was found that 54.8% of all violence termed "severe" was actually committed by a wife, not a husband.[331]

Since 1985, the trend documented in the National Violence Surveys and Resurveys has continued.[332] According to the Los Angeles Police Department, the percentage of domestic abuse cases involving a female offender doubled between 1987 and 1995.[333] In Sacramento, California, arrests of women for domestic violence went from 245 in 1991 to 469 in 1996.[334] Data from the California Department of Justice show that arrest rates of women for domestic violence went from 7% to 13% between 1991 and 1994.[335] Nationally, the rate of female-perpetrated domestic violence increased 62% between 1991 and 1995.[336]

Not long ago, the Minneapolis *Star Tribune* reported on a survey taken by Johnston & Murphy, the shoe manufacturers. According to the survey, 40 percent of women have thrown a shoe at a man at some time in their lives. If this is true, just imagine how large the percentage would be if the question posed in the survey had been how many women had thrown *any* kind of object (not just shoes) at a man. Some people may say that throwing things at people is not all that serious; nevertheless, it is a criminal offense in every state, and if directed at or in the presence of an intimate, it constitutes domestic abuse in every state. Men are arrested and jailed for crimes like these every day.

Another poll, conducted jointly by the Minneapolis *Star Tribune* and WCCO Television, found that more women than men used violence to deal with conflicts, and that *more than twice as many women as men hit, pushed, grabbed, slapped or shoved their partners*. This figure corresponded with the number of men who acknowledged being victims of this kind of violence.

The Dunedin Study

The Dunedin study found that 18.6% of young women have perpetrated severe physical violence against their male partners, while only 5.7% of young men had perpetrated severe physical violence against their female partners. Although the ratio of young men acknowledging they had been severely victimized by a woman to young women reporting that they had been severely victimized by a man was not as high as 18.6 to 5.7, nevertheless it was still *almost 2 to 1*. When less severe forms of violence were included--e.g., pushing, grabbing, shoving, slapping, throwing things--the rates were 37% perpetrated by women against men and 22% perpetrated by men against women.[337]

Overall, the Dunedin study found that about 50% of young women had perpetrated some form of physical violence against a male intimate, and that the rates of female violence against men were higher with respect to both severe forms of physical abuse and the milder forms of it. It confirmed that young women today are substantially more likely to commit physical abuse than men are, and they are also substantially more likely to engage in acts of severe violence than men are.[338]

The Dunedin findings were corroborated (again) by the findings of a Marriage and Relationship Counseling Services study issued in June, 2001. The MRCS study found that among married couples where violence occurs, 33% of it is mutual, 41% of it is female-perpetrated and 26% of it is male-perpetrated.[339]

Child Abuse

It has been known for many years that most child abuse is perpetrated by women. Today, even government officials are finding it difficult to cover up the fact that the vast majority of the perpetrators of child maltreatment are female.[340] According to the U.S. Department of Health and Human Services, 95% of maltreatment of an infant (child under one year of age) involved a female perpetrator. Overall, 78% of maltreatment of children of all ages involved a female perpetrator. Although females were involved as perpetrators in only 38% of the sexual abuse cases,[341] females committed a significantly larger proportion of each of the other categories of child maltreatment. For example, 67% of severe physical child abuse cases involved a female perpetrator; 74% of psychological abuse cases involved a female perpetrator; and 95% of medical neglect cases involved a female perpetrator. At all age levels, the vast majority of physical abuse cases in which a female child was the victim involved a female perpetrator, and the vast majority of physical abuse cases reported to child protection agencies in which a male child under the age of fifteen was the victim also involved a female perpetrator.[342] No more than 16% of all child maltreatment is perpetrated by the child's biological father,[343] and more children are killed by their mothers than their fathers.[344]

In general, female perpetrators of child abuse are more likely to seriously abuse younger children (of both genders) than male perpetrators are; when men abuse children, their primary targets appear to be 17-year-old males.[345]

Between 1974 and 1990, annual reports of child abuse rose from 60,000 to over 2,600,000 per year. That's a *43-fold increase in less than twenty years*! Of the 2,600,000 cases reported in 1990, about 1 million were substantiated; and of these, over a thousand involved fatalities.[346] It has been estimated that about 5,000 children are killed as a result of child maltreatment every year.[347]

The trend has been continuing unabated for many years. Between 1980 and 1986, the number of children who experienced demonstrable harm as a result of child abuse or neglect increased 51%.[348] Between 1986 and 1993, the number of maltreated children nearly doubled.[349] By 1993, there were nearly 3 million reports of child maltreatment.[350] Between 1992 and 1998, while child sexual abuse (the variety of child abuse most often associated with male perpetrators) decreased substantially, physical child abuse and neglect (the kinds of maltreatment most often perpetrated by females) steadily increased.[351] Today, children are 3 times as likely as adults to be victims of assault, and every year thousands of American children continue to die as a result of maltreatment.[352] Between 1976 and 1994, more than 37,000 children were murdered in the United States.[353]

Given the level of violence to which children have been subjected in our country, it should not come as a surprise to learn that the majority of young women entering college today have used physical violence in their dating relationships and nearly half have physically abused their male partners at least once during the year just prior to their entry into college.[354]

The conclusion is inescapable that women, or at least most American women, are getting more violent.

Who are these violent women?

Unfortunately, very little is known about violent women. Whenever researchers discover numbers suggesting that women may be violent, all of the basic tenets of responsible research are suddenly suspended. Instead of conducting additional controlled research to test hypotheses and isolate causes, the response among most researchers appears to be to do everything possible to rush to the defense of these women, at whatever cost. "Well, yes," the researchers will say, "We did find that women are at least as violent as men, but they only do it in self-defense or to defend their children; it's still only the men who are the real aggressors." Then, when that argument is proven incapable of holding water any longer, the researchers will say, "Well, all right, maybe it's not always self-defense, but when it's not, well, it's not like it really hurts the guy or nothin'." Then, when some smart-aleck points out that it often does hurt the guy--severely--the name-calling starts: the smart-aleck must be an anti-feminist, a misogynist, a warrior against women, a backlasher, or perhaps even a closeted woman-batterer himself. And these are just the tactics that government officials and educated social scientists use. At the other extreme are the radical feminists who threaten to bomb, injure and kill anyone who dares reveal any fact about domestic violence that might tend to call the "patriarchy" model into question.[355]

In such a politically charged atmosphere of fear and intimidation, it is little wonder that very few researchers have been brave enough to climb the zealously guarded pedestal upon which women have been enthroned and take a hard, *honest* look at female violence.[356]

We have had thousands of international studies about male violence but there is very little about why or how women are violent. There seems to be a blanket of silence over the huge figures of violence expressed by women.[357]
-- Erin Pizzey

Ironically, the one researcher who has undertaken this task also happens to have been a pioneer in the field of advocacy on behalf of battered women: Erin Pizzey. Years ago, Ms. Pizzey founded and operated a battered women's shelter in Chiswick, England, the first modern battered women's shelter in the world. For many years, she was a prolific author and leader in the movement for recognition of woman-battering as a serious social problem. Later, she would be ostracized by her colleagues for calling attention to the fact that women can be violent, too. Noting that 62 of the first 100 women at her shelter were physically violent themselves, and after having worked with over 5,000 women, Ms. Pizzey came to the conclusion not only that women are sometimes capable of violence themselves, but that they are capable of *extreme* violence even in situations where it cannot be claimed that the violence was necessary for self-defense. For example, she recalls working with a woman who became so angry at another woman during an argument that she bit the other woman's finger off.

I have come to recognise that there are women...who express and enact disturbance beyond the expected (and acceptable) scope of distress. Such individuals, spurred on by deep feelings of vengefulness, vindictiveness, and animosity, behave in a manner that is singularly destructive; destructive to themselves as well as to some or all of the other family members, making an already bad family situation worse. These women I have found it useful to describe as "family terrorists."[358]

According to Pizzey, the "family terrorist" uses violence as a means to an end, an instrument of control to attain a specific goal. The goal may be to ensure that the children remain under her control, or it may be to reunite a dissolving family, or, in cases where dissolution is inevitable but undesired, it may be simply to destroy the other partner (or ex-partner) emotionally, physically and financially.

Ms. Pizzey makes some extremely insightful observations about the psyche of the violent female. In her view, female terrorists are usually "violence prone" women, which she defines as "a woman who, while complaining that she is the innocent victim of the malice and aggression of all other relationships in her life, is in fact a victim of her own violence and aggression."[359] Pizzey suggests that women who have been abused or neglected as children, or who believe that they were abused or neglected as children, actually become *addicted* to violence. As an adult, the woman may actually feel a compulsion to seek out and, if necessary, create situations and relationships characterized by further violence. In some cases, she contends, such a woman might even go so far as to distort reality in order to convince herself, and possibly others, that she is in an abusive relationship.

While I believe there is merit in what Ms. Pizzey says, I am not any more certain that all women who abuse men fit the "family terrorist" profile than I am that all men who abuse women fit the "patriarchal terrorist" description. Since many different typologies of male batterers have been identified, I suspect there are probably many different typologies of female batterers as well. Unfortunately, because most researchers do not have the courage to ascend the sacred pedestal and honestly study the phenomenon of female violence against men, precious few studies of female batterer typologies exist.

It is intriguing that Pizzey's insights about the psyche of women who batter caused such an uproar. I suspect that feminists became violent toward her because she was exposing data that tends to refute the feminist gospel that domestic violence is all about male privilege. It threatened the sacred teachings of Gloria Steinem, who had asserted that domestic violence, or the implied threat of it, is how the patriarchy sustains itself.[360]

It is unfortunate that feminists have chosen to excommunicate Ms. Pizzey and disregard everything she has said and done, as her description of the "family terrorist" comes closer to capturing the essence of the true batterer--whether male or female--than any other I have seen:

> *The terrorist, and the terrorist's actions, know no bounds....Intent only to achieve the goal (perhaps 'hell-bent' is the most accurate descriptive phrase) the terrorist will take such measures as: stalking a spouse or ex-spouse, physically assaulting the spouse or the spouse's new partners, telephoning all mutual friends and business associates of the spouse in an effort to ruin the spouse's reputation, pressing fabricated criminal charges against the spouse (including alleged battery and child molestation), staging intentionally unsuccessful suicide attempts for the purpose of manipulation, snatching children from the spouse's care and custody, vandalising the spouse's property, murdering the spouse and/or the children as an act of revenge.*[361]

Pizzey notes that in her experience, "both men and women are equally guilty of the above behaviour, but on the whole, because it is men's dysfunctional behaviour that is studied and reported upon, people do not realise that to the same extent women are equally guilty of this type of violent behaviour."[362]

9. Domestic violence against men is the most under-reported crime

Virtually every book and article that has ever been written on the subject of domestic abuse declares that the full extent of violence against women cannot really be known because women who are victims of domestic abuse are significantly less likely to report the crime than any other category of crime victims is. There is some reason to believe that this may have been true at one time in history, but recent research suggests that it is no longer true today.

It has been estimated that overall, only about one-third of all crimes of *any* kind are reported to police.[363] Yet, it has also been found that the majority of women who are victims of domestic abuse report the incident to police.[364] What this means is that women claiming to be victims of domestic abuse are not only "just as likely" to report it as other crime victims are, but they are actually *significantly more likely* to report it to the authorities than victims of other kinds of crime are.

In 1993, about one-half of the female victims of domestic violence reported the incident to police, and female willingness to report has been increasing ever since. In 1997, 58% of female victims reported the incident to police, and in 1998, 59% of the alleged incidents of domestic abuse against a woman were reported to police. *And this has all been happening at a time when the actual incidence of domestic violence against women has been declining.* (See Chapter 6.)

Although studies of domestic abuse against men are sparse, what data there is suggests that the rate at which male victims of abuse report the incident to police is not only lower than the rate at which female abuse victims report the crime to police, but that it is even lower than the overall rate at which crimes of *any* kind against *either* gender are reported to police. This low level of male reporting has remained fairly constant over the years.[365]

That female victims are substantially more likely than male victims to report that they have been victims of domestic abuse is well-known.[366]   In fact, male victims of abuse are at least *four times as likely* to decline to report domestic abuse to police out of a desire to protect the abuser from having to face the consequences of his/her actions as female victims are.[367] Male victims are also substantially more likely than female victims to regard domestic abuse as a "private" problem of no legitimate concern to anyone but themselves. A majority of the male victims who don't report an incident in which they have been abused cite this as one of their principal reasons for not reporting the incident.[368]

Some indication of the disparity between men and women concerning their relative likelihood of reporting violent victimizations can be gleaned from medical emergency room records. For example, in 1994, the majority (61%) of hospital emergency room patients treated for intimate-violence-related injuries were men, while nearly half as many (39%) were women.[369] Yet, the vast majority (more than 90%, according to some authorities) of the reports to authorities of violent victimizations by intimates were made by women.

If, as all the reliable data suggests (see above), males are at least as likely to be victims of domestic abuse as females are, yet only 10% of those who choose to report the incident to authorities are male, then we must conclude not only that women are more willing than men to report the incident to authorities when they are abused, but that women are *about 9 times more likely than men to report* when they have been victims of abuse. The survey research tends to corroborate the hypothesis that women are indeed 9 times more likely than men to report it to police when they have been assaulted by their spouses.[370]

What evidence there is suggests that most men have to be pretty severely injured before they will even consider reporting an incident or threat of domestic abuse to the authorities. And even then, it is doubtful that they will. Unlike most women, it would not even cross most men's minds to report their partners to authorities or take any other kind of legal action because they have been pushed, grabbed, shoved, slapped or had their hair pulled. And unlike most women, most men do not choose to make a report even after they have been so severely wounded that they have to be transported to the hospital in an ambulance--or indeed, even after they have had their penises lopped off.[371]

Reasons for under-reporting

That incidents of domestic abuse against men are vastly under-reported as compared to incidents of domestic abuse against women is clear. What has not been studied in any depth is *why*. Despite the paucity of scholarly research on this topic, a number of reasons why it would make sense for a male victim to keep it to himself can be identified.

1. *Socialization for self-reliance.* There is a grain of truth in the old stereotype that men won't stop and ask for directions when they are lost. Most American men are trained to fend for themselves, never to ask or rely on others for help with their problems. The idea of seeking law enforcement or judicial protection would never even cross most men's minds as a way of dealing with violence or a threat of violence to their own person.

2. *Courage (a.k.a. fear of being regarded as a wimp.)* Think about it. If you were to hear some guy complaining to police or a judge that his girlfriend grabbed him or slapped him or pulled his hair, would you hail him as a hero or think of him as a wimp? Though some men are working hard to change their attitudes, even liberated men have confessed that "wimp" would still be the first word that pops into their heads upon hearing of such a guy. I suspect there are also a lot of women who, though they may fight hard to suppress it, would nevertheless have this kind of reaction to such a guy, as well. In our society, complaining about being picked on by a woman is just not considered a manly thing to do.[372]

3. *Low self-esteem.* Many men define themselves in terms of their wives or female partners. That is to say, they measure their value in terms of how well they can provide for a woman and/or

children. They may not show it, but inside they do not believe that they have any inherent value or worth in and of themselves. If, as is often the case, the abuser is inflicting verbal abuse along with physical abuse, the victim's self-esteem is lowered even further. He may come to believe that due to his low income, small physical endowment, advanced age, poor physique, looks, weight, personality or whatever, the woman he is with is the best he will ever be able to get.

4. *Self-blame.* If a woman becomes agitated enough at a man to strike him, it is generally inferred that the man must have done something really bad to deserve it. Although our society has done a good job of training both women and men to understand that no woman "deserves" to be abused, nobody has made any effort to deliver the message that men don't deserve to be abused, either. To the contrary, many marriage counselors and domestic abuse treatment providers teach that men are responsible for *all* violence in a relationship--both their own and their partner's. As a result, male victims, and those who deal with them, are much more likely to believe that they are somehow responsible for provoking or causing their partners to become violent--that they somehow "deserve" to be punished--even if they can't articulate why. Unfortunately, many people who occupy positions of power and influence in our society are only too eager to reinforce that belief. To many people in our society, the oft-repeated credo that "No one deserves to be abused" is really means "A person deserves to be abused if and only if that person is male."

5. *Feelings of powerlessness.* It may seem strange to think of men as powerless, but there are many reasons why a man may feel this way.[373] In fact, a Canadian study found that 100% of abused men expressed feelings of powerlessness.[374]

6. *No advocate.* In our grandparents' day, battered women had no one to encourage them, no one to speak for them, no one to intervene on their behalf. As a result, few people knew about the problem, and therefore nothing much was done about it. The situation now is dramatically different. Today, women's advocates abound. Thousands of people across the country work as women's advocates, and many of them work exclusively for battered women. Seen many battered men's advocates lately?

7. *Emotional dependence*. Abusive women, like abusive men, can be very loving and affectionate between bouts of violence. Men who are starved for affection or social acceptance may consider an occasional hug or "high-five" from a woman a sufficient benefit to justify the cost of being abused.

8. *Economic dependence*. It is generally believed that the principal reason that women do not leave abusive relationships is that they are financially dependent on the abusive partner for their survival.[375] It is true that in our parents' generation, women were often dependent on men for their financial support. This was due to the fact that the normative family model was for the woman to stay at home and raise children while the man earned wages in the workplace for his family. All of that has changed. As a result of equal opportunity and affirmative action programs, women today comprise a larger share of the workforce than men do. That being the case, it is entirely possible--indeed, it is *probable*--that a substantial number of *men* are financially dependent on *women* now.[376] Some men today may have the same economic disincentive to report their abusive partners to authorities as women thirty years ago had.

It should also be noted that even an employed man who is not financially dependent on his wife may nevertheless be economically dependent on *the marriage*. When a man leaves a relationship with a woman, he has a continuing obligation to support the woman and any children they may have had. Although many states have gender-neutralized their alimony and child support laws, it is still primarily men whom the courts order to pay these things. Even a man who is able to maintain a household for himself independently if he leaves the marriage may reasonably fear that he may not have the resources to maintain two households.[377]

9. *Sex addiction*. A man may enjoy--and need--sex with his partner so much that he is willing to tolerate abuse in order to get it.

10. *Comparative lack of influence*. Wealthy or influential abusers can sometimes pressure decision-makers to show them leniency, but sometimes simply being of the female gender can carry a lot of clout, too. A woman can often accomplish more with a smile,

or by shedding a few tears, than a man who has enough money to buy the most expensive lawyer in town.

11. *Threats.* Threats can come in many different shapes and sizes. They may be directed at the victim, the victim's children, or even the perpetrator herself. It is not uncommon for abusers to threaten to harm or kill themselves if the victim calls the police or leaves the relationship.

Threats do not always need to be expressly stated. In fact, an implied threat can often be a better deterrent than an express one. For example, since it is common knowledge that women nearly always are awarded custody of the children in a divorce, a reasonable man could interpret the statement, "Go ahead and call the police, but if you do I'm going to file for divorce" as a threat to separate him from his children if he doesn't keep his mouth shut.

12. *Protection of children.* Many men believe it is better for a man to put up with being abused than to permit a child to come from a broken home. In addition, a man may reasonably believe that if he leaves (as he will almost certainly have to do if he reports his wife to the police for abusing him), the woman may use the children as the outlet for her anger. He may believe that without his presence in the home, no one will be there to intervene and protect the children from their mother's violence.

13. *Pressure from children.* "You aren't going to make mommy go to jail, are you, daddy?"

14. *Cultural diversity.* In the United States, it is culturally acceptable for women to hit, slap, push, shove and berate their husbands, and many men today are being trained to be tolerant of such "cultural diversity."

15. *Denial.* A victim who doesn't know what to do about it, and can't find out what to do about it, may be inclined to simply deny that it ever happened.

16. *Minimizing.* "It's just a flesh wound."

17. *Disability.* Disabled persons have their own reasons for dependence on others. They may also have more difficulty accessing resources for help.

18. *Belief in the abuser's excuses* (premenstrual syndrome, postpartum depression, stress of balancing family and career, under the influence of alcohol or drugs, rough day, etc., etc.)

19. *Belief in the sanctity of marriage and the marriage vow.* Some men genuinely believe that marriage is a sacrament until death, and therefore are unwilling to leave the relationship even if they are being abused. A husband might fear that if he reports his wife to the authorities, she will retaliate by divorcing him.

20. *Pressure from family, friends and relatives.* Even if a man does not himself have a strong belief in the sanctity of the marriage vow, he may be inclined to succumb to pressure from his parents, siblings, other relatives, and his friends, to refrain from reporting to the police that he has been beaten up by a woman. In addition, family, friends and relatives are often duped or charmed by the abuser into denying the existence of abuse or minimizing its severity. Family, friends and relatives typically have a variety of reasons for pressuring a man to stay in an abusive relationship. Misguided though it may be, this kind of pressure is often very effective in deterring a victim from reporting abuse to police.

21. *Fear of retaliation.* A woman doesn't need to make a threat in order for a reasonable man to fear retaliation. She doesn't even need to engage in conduct that implies a threat. An abused man can reasonably fear that if he reports it to the authorities, she will tell them (and/or other people) that he was the one who abused or threatened her and that she was only acting in self-defense. Therefore, he may reasonably fear that if he reports the incident to police, he will be the one who is arrested, taken to jail, and stigmatized for being an abuser. Even if she hasn't said as much, he can also reasonably fear that if he reports her to authorities, she may retaliate by filing for divorce and "taking him to the cleaners."

22. *Gratitude* (not for the abuse, but for something else she may have done for him at some time.)

23. *Bigger problems to worry about.* A person who is focused on basic survival needs for himself and his children, for example, may not have the luxury of figuring out what to do about being slapped around.

24. *Too many problems to worry about.* A person who has a lot of other major issues to deal with may not have time to worry about the problem of being abused.

25. *Belief that the abuse will eventually subside on its own, without outside intervention.* Sometimes abuse does subside on its own, without outside intervention. Without intervention, however, it almost always gets worse, not better. Unfortunately, the men who adhere most tenaciously to the hope that things will get better without outside intervention tend to be the ones who end up being dismembered, permanently disfigured or killed.[378]

26. *Isolation.* An abuser may try--and often succeeds--to cut "her man" off from his friends, which makes it much less likely that he will seek help or see his situation from other points of view besides the abuser's.

27. *Illiteracy.* Like lack of financial resources, illiteracy can force a person to be dependent on his partner for everyday survival. It can also prevent him from learning about domestic abuse and what resources, options and help, if any, may be available.

28. *Criminal record.* A man with a criminal record knows he will have no credibility at all if he claims to be a victim. He also knows that he will only get jeers, not help, from police. Having a criminal record causes everyone involved in the legal system--prosecutors, advocates, judges, court clerks, and so on--to perceive one as a perpetrator rather than as a victim. Moreover, the general feeling is that people who have committed a crime more or less "deserve" to have bad things happen to them for the rest of their lives. Thus, a prosecutor will be likely to assign such cases low priority, or will simply exercise his prosecutorial discretion not to file charges against the abuser at all. Likewise, a judge may be unwilling to grant a protection order to this kind of victim, may refuse to find the abuser guilty of any crime, or may impose a lighter sentence on the abuser than he would if the victim did not himself have a criminal record. Court clerks may show indifference to a victim with a criminal record, may decline to provide information or offer assistance with forms, and may erect arbitrary and capricious procedural obstacles in the victim's way if he is a male with a criminal record.

29. *Abuser is a judge, prosecutor, police officer, probation officer or women's advocate.* Police will be reluctant to arrest a fellow police officer; a prosecutor will be reluctant to prosecute a fellow prosecutor; and so on.

30. *Victim is bisexual or gay, or has had such an experience.* A gay or bisexual man may be afraid of being "outed" if he reports an incident. Also, a heterosexual man who has confided to his wife or girlfriend that he has had such an experience may fear that she will retaliate against him by disclosing this information to other people.

31. *Love.* Love can make a person blind to many things. It includes an element of loyalty, under the influence of which a person is inclined to come to the defense of the person loved rather than to report to other people that she has done something wrong. A person who is being abused often applies a perverse interpretation of acts of violence-- "she must really love me to treat me this way."[379]

32. *Counseling or mediation.* If the couple is going through marriage or couples counseling, or mediation, the victim may fear that reporting an incident of abuse will only cause the abuser to become less cooperative or less willing to compromise.

33. *Hope for reconciliation.* If the parties are separated or divorced, the victim may harbor a secret (or maybe not so secret) hope for reconciliation, and may believe that reporting an incident of abuse will only drive the couple further apart.

34. *Mental illness.* Mental illness can cloud a victim's judgment and cause him not to report something that a rational person would. In addition, a person with a history of mental illness may fear that because he is "insane" nobody will believe him even if he does report it, particularly since everyone "knows" that domestic abuse is entirely "a male phenomenon."

35. *Low intelligence, mental retardation or developmental delay.* These characteristics can make a person dependent on others for his survival. They can also make the victim susceptible to verbal manipulation. And they may also result in a lack of knowledge about what abuse is and how to report it, even if the victim were otherwise inclined to do so.

36. *Victim is in the military service.* A man who is in the military is being trained to be a "fighting machine." Since joining the military means that he is assuming the role of *protector*, it would be irrational to expect him to seek help and protection from someone other than himself. If he did, he would be the

subject of immediate ridicule, hazing and harassment. Most servicemembers are smart enough to figure out that if they make such a report to their commanding officer they will most likely be met with hostility and anger, and will be considered an embarrassment and disgrace to the service.

37. *Victim is a police officer or security guard.* For the same reason, a law enforcement officer or security guard who is a victim of violence at the hands of a woman is not likely to seek help and protection from others for the problem. Men are not likely to report abuse if it might hurt their careers.

38. *Victim is in one of the helping professions.* People in the helping professions (doctors, therapists, etc.) are often trained to think only of other people's problems and needs, and to ignore their own.

39. *Fear of damage to professional reputation.* A marriage counselor, therapist, mediator or similar professional may rationally fear damage to his professional reputation if it becomes known that he is having severe marital or relationship problems. He may fear that clients will doubt his ability to help them with their problems if he can't even handle his own.

40. *Victim is a minister, pastor or other religious leader.* Because religious leaders are expected to set an example for others, they generally prefer to avoid the risk of having their personal or relationship issues aired in public. In addition, the qualities of self-sacrifice, compassion and forgiveness that are central to virtually every religion may make a clergyman appear hypocritical if, instead of forgiving his wife, he presses criminal charges against her.

41. *Religious or spiritual beliefs.* One of the principal teachings of Jesus Christ is to "turn the other cheek." Even while nailed to the cross, he begged forgiveness for the people who were persecuting him. His example inspires many people to adopt a spirit of forgiveness toward those who trespass against them, even when the trespass is severe.[380]

42. *No place to go.* Battered women's shelters sometimes turn a woman away, but a woman can usually find a sympathetic friend or relative to take her in. A man who says he wants to move in because he's afraid of his wife or girlfriend is not likely to get

much sympathy. And unless you're counting alleys, bus depots, cardboard boxes and jails, there are no battered men's shelters in this country.[381]

43. *Assumption that no options or resources are available for abused men.* In many areas, this assumption would be valid.

44. *No knowledge of options and resources, even if they exist.* To my knowledge, no public education campaign has been initiated to educate battered men about their resources and options, and it does not seem likely that any such program is likely to come out of the federal government's Violence Against Women Office anytime soon.

45. *Victim has himself been accused of abuse.* A person who has been accused of abuse before may reasonably assume that he will not be believed if he now reports that *he* is a victim of abuse. A previous accusation that he has been abusive--even if completely untrue--can so damage a man's credibility that he may reasonably believe that reporting that he has been or is being abused would be futile, at best; and at worst, may cause him to be arrested again.

It is not uncommon for a perpetrator of abuse--whether male or female--to attempt to blame the victim. The difference is that when a male perpetrator attempts to blame the victim, he is rarely believed. Because of the enormous propaganda campaign to convince everybody that domestic violence is exclusively a "guy" thing, a female perpetrator who attempts to deflect attention from herself by blaming her victim will generally succeed, particularly when her audience consists of law enforcement officers who have arrived with either the intention or a strong predisposition to arrest a man rather than a woman.[382]

46. *Victim has been abused before.* A second incident of abuse against the same victim reinforces the victim's (and others') belief that he is somehow causing, or provoking, other people to be violent toward him.

47. *Negative court experiences.* A man who has been convicted despite his innocence, or who has experienced anti-male prejudice in family or criminal court, may reasonably believe that the legal system will not accord him any safety or protection at all.

48. *Feelings of guilt*. Men in the United States are socialized to feel guilty for things they haven't done. White males are educated, trained and socialized to feel guilty for the wrongs done by other white males to women and minorities in general, for the wrongs done by dead white males to women and minorities in the past, and even for the wrongs against women that are committed in countries other than the United States. In short, men are socialized to accept responsibility for everyone else's wrongs. Even if he is completely without personal blame, a man may not be inclined to report somebody else's wrongs if he *feels* that he himself does not have "clean hands."

49. *Socialization for tolerance and forgiveness of women*. Even men without religious backgrounds are usually socialized to adopt a forgiving and understanding attitude toward women.

50. *Abuser's promises to change*. The classic flowers-apologies-and-more-abuse pattern, a.k.a. the cycle of violence.

51. *Lack of transportation or access to services*. This factor may be of particular importance in the case of victims who live in rural or remote geographical areas.

52. *Embarrassment; shame*. There are many reasons why a male might feel embarrassed about being the victim of abuse. Sexual abuse--such as penetration of the anus with a physical object-- would be extremely embarrassing to a male, as would the torture or mutilation of his genitalia. Embarrassment is probably the principal reason that verbal and emotional abuse are not reported, either. In order to report these forms of abuse, the victim would have to repeat the very things the abuser said about him, things which have likely been said with the specific intent of making the victim feel ashamed and bad about himself. Physical abuse may be embarrassing to a male victim because it tends to indicate that he is incapable of defending himself, something a man is expected to be able to do. Indeed, the very definition of masculinity in our culture includes the ability to defend oneself and protect others.

53. *Fear of escalating the abuser's level of anger*. Reporting a person to the police may make her even madder than she was before.

54. *Fear of losing partner's trust/expectation of confidentiality.*
Marriage is a *confidential* relationship. Husbands and wives say
many things to each other that they don't expect to be repeated to
others. The law generally respects this confidentiality because
it is believed that without the ability to speak freely and openly
with each other a marriage will fail. A person who "tells tales
out of school" about the things his spouse has said or done to
him may reasonably fear that his spouse will become reluctant to
openly and honestly "speak her mind" or show her true feelings
in the future.

55. *Fear of violating a code of honor.* Unwritten codes of honor
exist in many different settings. For example, there is an
unwritten code of honor in nearly every school pursuant to which
it is considered disgraceful for one student to "rat out" or "tell
on" another. This code is most noticeable in elementary school
settings, but it is also present in secondary and postsecondary
school settings. Even when such a code isn't in place, or is only
weakly enforced, a student may have other motivations for not
wanting to report another student's misconduct. For example, a
person may not want to report a student's abusive and/or criminal
conduct for fear that it may affect the abusive student's academic
career.

56. *The Stockholm Syndrome.* Named for an incident in which
hostages came to sympathize with and support their captor's
cause, the Stockholm Syndrome is another possible reason
why an abuse victim might not want to report the abuse. A
feminist male, for example, might sympathize with and support a
woman's act of violence against him because he has been taught
to perceive violence against men as an act of empowerment for
womankind. There have been plenty of media examples since
Thelma and Louise that could reinforce the belief that acts of
violence against men by women are righteous because they
symbolize the empowerment of women.

57. *Fear of arrest.* A male who is being abused may reasonably
fear that he himself will be arrested if he reports the incident
to police. The fear may be based on the victim's involvement
in some criminal enterprise of his own (e.g., fear that if the
police are called they might discover the stash of marijuana in

his dresser drawer), or it may be based on the knowledge that when police are called to the scene of a domestic disturbance, they have been trained to arrive with the intention of taking a man to jail. Many police have been trained to believe that when men commit domestic abuse, they do it for control or because of "male privilege," but that when women perpetrate domestic abuse it is in self-defense. Since it is believed that women only become violent in self-defense, it is inferred that any man who reports that he has been abused by a woman must have "started it" by abusing or threatening to abuse her first. By the time the police arrive, then, the victim has already been tried and convicted, in their minds; the only thing remaining to do is to execute the sentence, i.e., take the man to jail. Although the actual frequency with which this occurs is not known, the law enforcement practice of arresting male victims who report abuse to police is sufficiently well-known to deter male victims from expecting help from them.[383]

Usually, a man who is a victim will try to report it only once. He calls...and they say, "What did you do to provoke her?"[384] -- Mel Feit, executive director, National Center for Men

58. *Alcohol and drugs.* Alcohol and drugs can affect reporting in a number of ways. It can directly affect it by diminishing the victim's mental capacity to make a report. It can affect reporting in less direct ways, too, as where the victim is under the influence of an illegal drug and fears that he will be arrested for that offense if he reports the abuse incident to police. If he is under the influence of alcohol or a medication (whether legal or illegal), he may fear that a police report containing that information may cause him to lose custody or the right to have unrestricted visitation with his children. If he was in a public place at the time of the incident, he may fear that he will be arrested and prosecuted for public intoxication, disorderly conduct or a related offense. If he had been driving shortly before the incident occurred, he may fear being arrested for driving while intoxicated. If it was his wife or girlfriend that was

intoxicated, he may fear that the arrest of the wife will result in removal of the children from the home. If he is a juvenile, he may fear that he or his girlfriend will be charged with underage consumption or possession of alcohol, and/or that his parents will find out that he has been drinking. Even if he has no reason to fear any of these things, he may nevertheless fear that his state of intoxication will cause him to lose his credibility--an asset that he probably knows is already in short supply simply by virtue of the fact that he is a male claiming to be a victim of a violent female.

59. *Lack of awareness that domestic abuse laws now protect men, too.* Until recently, domestic abuse was a gender-specific crime. Many jurisdictions had laws specifically prohibiting wife-beating and providing protections for female victims of male violence, while not prohibiting husband-beating and not providing any equivalent protections for male victims of female violence. Although many states have now gender-neutralized their domestic abuse laws, terms that used to be utilized in these laws--such as "wife-beating" and "battered women"--are still commonly used interchangeably with "domestic violence" in our society. This, along with the repeated pronouncements by government officials that domestic abuse is exclusively a "male phenomenon," helps reinforce the belief that domestic abuse is a gender-specific crime; that is to say, the belief that it is illegal for a man to beat his wife but not illegal for a woman to beat her husband.

60. *Fear of deportation.* An alien may fear (rationally or not so rationally) that he might be deported (and/or that his partner might be deported) if he reports an incident of abuse to police.

61. *Police and domestic abuse service agency personnel refusal to take reports from male victims seriously, or refusal to believe them.* Battered men who call domestic abuse hotlines or the police to report the crime are often told to get off the line in case a "real victim" (codeword for *woman*) might be calling for assistance--even before they have had a chance to describe how they have been victimized.

62. *Personal reluctance to acknowledge that females are capable of committing criminal or violent acts.* This is similar to, but not the

same thing as denial. Denial is a mental process that may occur when a person does not have the present ability or wherewithal to deal with a certain fact, so he simply behaves as if the fact does not exist. Reluctance to acknowledge something, on the other hand, may or may not involve denial. To some extent, we have all been socialized to resist the notion that women are as capable of violence or wrong-doing as men are. To some extent, we all want to believe that "women are made of sugar and spice and everything nice."

A person who is reluctant to acknowledge that females are capable of committing criminal or violent acts may deal with a female's perpetration of a criminal or violent act not by denying that it happened, but by coming up with some way of explaining it so as to make it appear aberrational. He may do this by male-blame ("women are only violent in self-defense, or when they are provoked"), by minimizing ("they were able to reattach my penis, so what's the big deal?"), by finding an excuse for her (job stress, PMS, abused as a child, etc.), or in some other way.

63. *Societal reluctance to acknowledge that females are capable of committing criminal or violent acts.* It has been noted that "even professionals may be reluctant to report female disclosure of [crimes they have committed]" because of this general societal desire to believe that females are incapable of doing any wrong.[385]

64. *Cultural view of males as property.* Cultural and legal norms in our country permit the use of physical violence (spanking, corporal punishment) by parents (and their designated hitters) to control the behavior of their children. These norms were developed at a time when children were regarded in law as the *chattel* (property) of their parents.[386] There may be a parallel cultural norm pursuant to which it is considered permissible for women, as the "owners" of their male "property," to use physical violence to control the behavior of what they regard as their chattel.

65. *Victim's inability to distinguish discipline from abuse.* The line between abuse and permissible corporal punishment may be difficult to draw in particular cases. For example, it is clear that our cultural norms are such that while a man who slaps a

woman on the face would clearly be guilty of abuse, it may be considered an appropriate method of behavior modification for a woman to do this to a man. But what if she uses a piece of cardboard instead of her hand? What about a stick or a ruler? How hard or sharp would the stick have to be? Figuring out where along the continuum of physical assaults to draw the line between acceptable corporal punishment and abuse can be an exceedingly complex and difficult task even for a professional to perform, much less a layman.

66. *Age*. Children and the elderly have a wide range of impediments to reporting: immaturity; senility; no knowledge of how to report or of the resources and help available; inability to distinguish between "discipline" and "abuse"; dependence on adults for nurturing; faith in parents/belief that parents know best; dependence on adults for protection; low self-esteem; love; loyalty to family; fear of getting parent into trouble; perceived unavailability of services (e.g., for sexually abused adolescent males); distrust of authorities; rebelliousness; embarrassment; fear of publicity; peer pressure; intimidation, threats or fear of retaliation; shame, guilt, self-blame ("I must have screwed up really bad for her to hit me like that"); no advocate; absence of moral, emotional, social or institutional support.[387] Due to these factors, abuse of children and the elderly is almost certain to go unreported unless detected and reported by someone else (such as a doctor.) Yet, mandated reporters have their own reasons for failing to report, such as: lack of training; fear of liability if wrong; fear of losing client, or damaging doctor-patient relationship if wrong; cultural acceptance of the use of physical force to control male behavior; perceived or believed unavailability of services for abused children; lack of faith in the child protection system; inability to distinguish "abuse" from "discipline"; view that children (especially male adolescents) are responsible for their own problems because they are trouble-makers or have behavioral problems; sympathy, empathy or desire to protect parent for some other reason; belief that women are not capable of violence; disbelief of child's or male's statements; belief in abuser's lies and excuses; refusal to acknowledge that a male child (especially an adolescent male)

can be a victim of abuse; belief that male adolescents are big and strong enough to take care of themselves.[388] In addition, a male child who has been sexually molested by a male adult generally will not voluntarily report it, particularly if he is an adolescent, due to the fear of being perceived as homosexual.[389] These factors, combined with the general male tendency to avoid seeking medical treatment for their injuries, make reporting of abuse of male children highly unlikely.[390]

67. *Report is ignored and/or victim believes it will be ignored.* Several years ago, when domestic abuse laws were first gender-neutralized in order to provide legal protection to men as well as women, I advised a male client who was being severely abused by his wife that he could report it to the police and obtain a protection order. Nevertheless, he was afraid of being arrested if he showed up at the police department alone, so I agreed to accompany him. The police officer who interviewed him jotted down the man's name and address and listened politely while the man told his story. When the interview was over, I inquired about getting a copy of the report, but was told that there would be no report because it was a "civil" matter. I provided citations to the statutes defining the wife's conduct as criminal, and pointed out that the laws had recently been gender-neutralized. Reluctantly, the officer finally agreed to file a report, but said that a copy of it would not be available until the next day. I checked back the next day and the report wasn't ready yet. I checked back a few days later and was told they had no record of any such report. The officer had never filed one. Since then, I have heard and read about other men who have had similar experiences. In one case, the only police response to a man's report that his wife had attacked him with a knife was to tell the man to buy plastic knives.[391] I have no idea how often this kind of thing happens. I would like to believe that it happens less frequently now than it did ten years ago, but I have no way of knowing that. What I do know, based on comments I hear from my male clients, is that a great number of male victims of abuse *believe* their reports will be ignored. Why bother reporting something to someone if you believe you are just going to be ignored?

68. *Belief that men are and/or should be big and strong enough to handle these problems themselves.* This may be a belief that has

been internalized by the victim, or a societal belief of which the victim is aware.[392]   Whether the belief is a societal one or one that has been internalized by the victim, in either case it is a barrier to reporting.[393]

69. *Chivalry.* Men are socially conditioned to *protect* women, including women's reputations. The conditioning is so strong that many men would rather endure abuse than subject a woman to the shame and embarrassment of a criminal record or the public exposure of her aberrant behavior.[394] This is why it is that in joint criminal enterprises it is usually the man, rather than the woman, who agrees to "takes the rap" for the couple's crimes.

Some say chivalry is dead, but it really isn't. True, many men no longer demonstrate the traditional outwards signs of servitude to women that were once the hallmarks of chivalry. Most men today would probably not be willing to engage in a duel with pistols just to "defend the sacred honor" of a woman, and some men today no longer engage in the etiquette of servitude, either (opening doors, etc.) The reason that many men no longer display the outward signs of servitude that used to be associated with the notion of chivalry is not because men are becoming more callous, but because women objected to them, complaining loudly and bitterly that such behavior is demeaning and patronizing to women. The fact that men stopped doing these things almost immediately upon learning that women no longer wanted them to is pretty good evidence in itself that the male desire to serve women is still very much alive and well in this country.

70. *Battered men's syndrome.*

71. *Absence of screening.* "Screening" in this context means the process of being alert to signs that an injury may have been the result of abuse. Health care professionals are trained to screen injured female patients for evidence of abuse, but are not often trained to screen male patients for it. Yet, since male victims are not likely to voluntarily divulge the fact that they have been assaulted by a female, the role of professionals in screening for it is critical. If the victim doesn't report it, and it is not detected by health care professionals, it will simply continue to go unnoticed and, therefore, unreported.

72. *Fear of change.* Reporting a woman for abuse will change a man's life forever. Most of these changes (incarceration, loss of job, social stigmatization, etc.) will be negative. Even in the absence of such considerations, however, many people simply have a fear of the unknown. It is not uncommon for people to prefer to deal with a known variable than an unknown one, even when the known variable is not a very good one.

73. *Fear of failure.* Our culture defines a man as a person who is a good provider for his wife and family. Traditionally, this meant being a good financial provider. Today, it means being *both* a good financial provider *and* a good emotional provider ("nurturer.") A man who believes a woman is dependent on him may fear that the woman will be unable to support herself if he leaves her. Even if he has no reason to believe this, however, an abused man may nevertheless be reluctant to leave an abusive home because by doing so he will be "running out" on his family, shirking his paternal responsibility, becoming yet another one of those "absent fathers" and "deadbeat dads" who, we are told, are responsible for all the major social problems in our country today.[395]

74. *Lack of knowledge.* Women receive a considerable amount of education--both formal and informal--about domestic violence. It is a favorite topic in women's studies courses, and women's magazines are constantly running articles about it (what it is, how to recognize the signs, what to do about it, etc.) Agencies at every level of the government publish numerous books, magazines, brochures, pamphlets, videotapes and so on, for the purpose of educating women about domestic abuse. Meanwhile, there has been absolutely no effort to educate male victims at all. As a result, most men know very little about it. What they do know is usually second-hand information they have gotten from a woman. Almost all of my male clients who were abused by their female partners told me they had done nothing about it because their partner had told them that "it's not abuse if a woman hits a man." Many men today simply do not know that it *is* abuse if a woman hits a man. Given the lack of outreach and education for male victims, how could a man be expected to know that the law protects male as well as female victims, especially when laws have titles like "The Violence Against Women Act"?

Erin Pizzey describes a male client she encountered in her practice whose wife had been verbally insulting him on a daily basis for thirteen years and had made a death threat when he tried to get a divorce from her. She relates that the client thought this was simply the kind of treatment that every man should expect from a wife; that it's how all wives treat their husbands. He did not know that his wife's behavior was abusive because no one had ever bothered to educate him as to what domestic abuse is.[396]

75. *Fear of ridicule.* In France, battered husbands were once made to wear ridiculous costumes and ride backwards around town on a donkey.[397] Although this practice has been discontinued, there is still a very strong social stigma that attaches to being a male victim of domestic abuse, a stigma which appears to be international in scope. Even in the United States, where nearly every citizen will tell you that domestic abuse is not a laughing matter, domestic violence against men is considered uproariously funny.[398] While battered men may no longer be literally paraded around town backwards on an ass, the same effect is achieved in other ways.[399]

76. *Fear of stigmatization.* There are actually two ways in which men are stigmatized when they disclose that they have been victims of domestic abuse. The first one, relating to "letting" a woman beat up on him, has already been discussed elsewhere. Because of the widely held belief that "violence is a male phenomenon," however, male victims can *also* reasonably expect to be stigmatized for all the same reasons that men who batter women are stigmatized. Since as a society we believe that all domestic abuse involves a man beating up a woman, it is reasonable to expect that people will insist on categorizing a claim of victim status coming from the mouth of a male as something else. To explain it, people usually suspect that the man must simply be trying to cover up his own misdeeds by shifting the blame to the female (who, of course, must be the real victim, since that is supposedly how all domestic abuse works.) Consequently, he is viewed not only with the disdain that is owed to any man who beats up on women, but with additional disfavor for trying to "blame the victim" for his own supposed violence.

Note that this factor, in tandem with the stigma of "letting" a woman beat one up, effectively ensures that a male victim will be stigmatized *no matter what*. In most cases, the man will not be believed, and therefore he will suffer the dual stigma of being both a woman-beater and a man who tries to blame a poor, defenseless woman for his own wrongs. On the other hand, if he is believed, then he will be subjected to the ridicule and stigma of having "let" himself get beaten up by a woman.[400]

77. *Absence of any moral, emotional, societal or institutional support for male persons alleging they are victims.* Philip Cook has noted that the "exceptional isolation of the abused male may be the characteristic that distinguishes him most from his abused female counterpart."[401] It has also been observed that "[m]ale...aggression [is] regarded as normative behavior in many contexts, thus further diminishing supportive responses for victims."[402] As a result, a male victim is more likely to hear something like, "Oh no, not another category of people claiming to be victims!" than he is to receive help.

78. *Fear of loss or damage to relationship with children.* Most men know that if a couple splits up, the courts are almost always going to award custody of the children to the mother, and the father will almost always be relegated to the status of every-other-weekend "visitor" to their children. All too often, the custody award is simply the first step in a process that eventually culminates in phasing the father out of his children's lives completely. Many men are willing to put up with an inordinate amount of abuse simply to keep this from happening.[403]

In view of the foregoing, I have no doubt that the estimate that women who have been victimized by abuse are 9 times more likely to report it than male victims are is accurate. Or, as Suzanne Steinmetz has put it: "The most unreported crime is not wife beating...it's husband beating."[404] The next most unreported crime, of course, is the abuse of male children. It is estimated that at least 72% of violent victimizations of children, most of whom are male, are not reported to police.[405]

10. It is not impossible for a woman to lie about being a victim

A common reaction among members of the legal profession when the suggestion is made that a woman in a particular case might not be telling the truth is anger. I have heard both male and female attorneys, judges and other court personnel loudly proclaim that "A woman would never lie about being abused!" or "A woman would never lie about being raped!" and proceed to glare menacingly at anyone who might even be thinking about suggesting such a possibility. While it may be true that most women would not lie about such things, it is wrong--dangerously wrong--to insist that no woman has ever been tempted to stretch the truth.

Take Jane Roe, for instance. (Yes, the Jane Roe of *Roe v. Wade*.) After the Supreme Court handed down its decision in that case, she admitted that she had lied about being raped. Why did she lie? Because she believed that saying she had been raped would make a stronger case for establishing a woman's right to get an abortion.[406]

Or take Cathleen Webb. In 1977, at the age of sixteen, she had unprotected sex with her boyfriend. Fearing the wrath of her foster parents if she were to become pregnant, she tore her own clothes in order to make it appear as if she had been raped. Later, she falsely testified that a man she'd never met before had raped her. Her testimony resulted in a sentence of 50 years in prison for an innocent man named Gary Dotson. It wasn't until much later, after this man had spent 6 years of his life in prison, that Ms. Webb finally came forward and admitted she had lied.

The Webb story is instructive because it shows how dangerous the belief that "no woman would ever lie" can be. When Ms. Webb came forward to admit she had lied, nobody believed her! The judge who had sentenced Mr. Dotson refused to reopen the case. Ms. Webb had to enlist the aid of a team of attorneys, take a lie detector test, file petitions with the supreme court and the governor, and even then it took many months to get the legal system to even consider the possibility that maybe, just maybe, this woman might really have lied about being raped.[407]

In the interest of securing more rape convictions, women's groups in the 1970's and 1980's successfully lobbied for the passage of laws relaxing the evidentiary requirements for a rape conviction[408] and limiting the ability of a man accused of rape to present evidence in his own defense.[409] As a result, the past twenty years has seen an unprecedented number of men--both guilty and innocent--sentenced to prison, sometimes for life.

In a forensic study of 556 investigations of rape allegations, 33% were proven (by DNA and other evidence) to be false. In another 27% of the cases, the woman either failed a lie-detector test or admitted having lied when faced with the prospect of submitting to a lie-detector test. In other words, it was found that at least 60% of rape allegations are probably false.[410] Even the liberal *Washington Post* has admitted that at least 30% of rape accusations are false.[411]

In a review of 350 criminal cases in which a person who had been convicted was later proven (by DNA evidence) to have been innocent, it was found that 23 had already been executed and 8 had already died in prison. 100% of them were male.[412]

In a society that views sex as dirty and immoral, it really shouldn't be all that baffling that a woman might lie about being raped. A woman could have a variety of motivations for lying: fear of parents' wrath, fear of husband's wrath, fear of society's condemnation,[413] revenge, etc.

A woman can also have a variety of motivations for lying about other forms of abuse, as well. Munchausen's syndrome and Munchausen's syndrome by proxy motivate some women to make up stories simply for the sake of getting attention and having people care for them. The desire to be able to commiserate with other women, peer pressure, may also be a motivating factor in some cases. A desire for publicity, or to be touted as a champion for women, have been motivating factors for lies in some cases. A child's desire to damage her parent's relationship (e.g., by falsely accusing a stepfather of sexual abuse), or her anger at a parent or other adult for some other reason, sometimes motivates a child to make a false claim of abuse.

Psychotherapy is another potential source of false accusations of abuse. A common goal of psychotherapy is to center the patient on his or her personal feelings in a self-affirming, nonjudgmental way, identifying sources outside of herself as the cause of her current mental health problem. Typically, this is done by examining the patient's family of origin. While this kind of work can be important (perhaps even essential), it also entails significant risks, including the risk that the patient may try to manufacture incidents of maltreatment in her family of origin, either to ensure that she will continue to receive sympathetic treatment from the therapist or to alleviate personal guilt feelings ("blame-shifting.") Most psychologists are trained to test and correct for such things, and most of them probably do. Unfortunately, there are many documented cases of unskilled and/or unscrupulous therapists who have neglected to do this. Worse still, there are documented cases of unskilled and/or unscrupulous therapists who have actively conspired with the patient in this process by persuading the patient to believe that she has been abused when in fact she has not, sometimes even going so far as to suggest or implant false "memories" of abuse in the patient's mind.[414] Patients with mental health problems are especially vulnerable to this practice.[415]

The principal reason for most false claims of domestic abuse, however, is probably the simple desire to gain an advantage during the breakup of a relationship. A woman who claims she has been abused can expect, as a result, to win not only sympathy and support, but also the immediate right to the exclusive use and possession of the couple's house, custody of the children, child support, alimony, and a host of other legal and economic advantages. A woman with concerns about losing custody of her children in a contested divorce may try to ensure her success by claiming her husband abused the children.[416]

Are all claims of rape and abuse false? Certainly not. Many women really are raped. Many women really are abused. But those statements are radically different from the statements, "All women

who say they have been raped have been raped," and "All women
who say they have been abused have been abused," and "No woman
would ever lie about a thing like that." A lot of people--many of
whom, unfortunately, occupy positions of great power and influence
in our country--refuse to acknowledge the difference.

11. Many domestic violence researchers are gender bigots[417]

The implications of linking our research agenda with our political agenda and intentionality are profound for feminist research. Perhaps the most awkward rite of passage...is the ethics approval requirement...."[418] *-- Sandra Kirby, Chair of Sociology, University of Winnipeg*

Serious scientists who review research studies on the subject of domestic abuse are often amazed at the shoddiness of the research methods employed. As Jeffrey Fagan, Ph.D., of Columbia University's School of Public Health, politely put it: "The empirical literature is littered with weak evaluation designs."[419] That's putting it mildly. With the possible exception of political science in the mid-twentieth century, domestic violence research has been more severely crippled by deliberate breaches of ethics and logic than any other field of academic inquiry in recent history. Any one of these breaches should have shocked the conscience of the scientific community. Apart from an occasional murmur of protestation, however (such as Dr. Fagan's remark, quoted above), the silence of the scientific community has been deafening.

The weaknesses in many of the studies that have been conducted on domestic violence in recent times are so numerous that it would be impossible to catalog them all in one book. It can be said, however, that every single principle of responsible research has been violated, all for the sake of "proving" that women are good and men are bad.

Lack of independence

> *There are as many violent women as men, but there's*
> *a lot of money in hating men, particularly in the United*
> *States.*[420] *-- Erin Pizzey*

With the possible exception of research commissioned by tobacco companies to prove that cigarette smoking does not cause cancer, few other areas of research are as rife with conflicts of interest as is research on violence and gender issues. Even feminist activist Erin Pizzey, who founded the first shelter for battered women in England and wrote the groundbreaking exposé about violence against women, *Scream Silently or the Neighbors Will Hear*, acknowledges that "The activists...[are] there to fund their budgets, their conferences and their statements against men."[421]

For example, the widely-publicized study[422] that reported an astonishing number of women had been subjected to "unwanted" sexual activity (the "new and improved" definition of rape) was funded by the feminist magazine, *Ms.* Similarly, the "gender bias" studies that report on how unfair the legal system is to women[423] are often controlled or at least heavily influenced by feminist organizations. It was the National Organization for Women (NOW) and the National Association of Women Judges that lobbied for them and that framed the issues for them to study.[424] As Warren Farrell has put it, "A feminist government commission on gender bias is the equivalent of a Republican government commission on political party bias."[425]

> *I feel that man-hating is an honorable and viable*
> *political act*[426] *-- Robin Morgan, former editor-in-chief of*
> *Ms. Magazine*

Domestic abuse researchers have themselves acknowledged that domestic abuse research as it is conducted today has become inextricably intertwined with advocacy for women. "[R]esearchers are immersed in the advocacy community and function both as advocates and researchers, serving...on boards of directors, or as activists in the larger community."[427]

Indeed, many feminists[428] openly regard bias, lack of objectivity and conflicts of interest as *good* things.[429] Some social scientists have forthrightly acknowledged that domestic abuse researchers have "a vested interest in the analysis of program data to demonstrate the need for additional financial support...."[430]

Edleson and Bible are among those who believe it is a good thing for domestic abuse researchers to be beholden to women's advocates. They maintain that "accountability to battered women and their advocates" is an appropriate goal of scientific research in this area.[431] According to them, the goal of researchers should be to develop research data that "support the assertions of battered women and their advocates."[432]

In reporting the experience of researcher Beth Richie, Edleson and Bible unwittingly give a stark example of what is wrong with this approach. According to Edleson and Bible, Ms. Richie reported that because she considered herself part of the women's advocacy community, "I didn't want to feel that I couldn't go back...I didn't want to be faced with that."[433] According to Edleson and Bible, "Research conducted collaboratively [with women's advocates] has the potential to transform...the researcher..."[434] That's true. It transforms the researcher into someone who is terrified of reporting findings and conclusions that women's advocates do not want to hear.

Selection bias[435]

Selection bias refers to the process of excluding certain categories of information from a study in order to produce a figure that more closely approximates the conclusion a particular researcher wants to reach. It is one of the more common test design flaws in domestic violence research. Here are some examples of how researchers have used selection bias to skew results:

Exclusive reliance on law enforcement data while ignoring scientific studies. Feminists and other policy-shapers almost uniformly rely exclusively on law enforcement statistics, ignoring scientific research on the subject. This is not surprising, since scientifically conducted research shows that women are more violent toward men than men are toward women, while law enforcement reports seem to indicate just the opposite. Yet, in view of what we know about domestic violence from the scientifically conducted research, the only thing that the disproportionate rates of arrest and conviction of men demonstrates is that men have long been, and continue to be, victims of discriminatory enforcement of the laws.[436]

Exclusion of violence by ex-girlfriends. Studies of violence by intimates almost always include violence committed by spouses, ex-spouses and those who are currently involved in a boyfriend-girlfriend relationship, but they almost always exclude violence by ex-girlfriends.[437] Since no reliable data have been collected on the incidence of violence by ex-girlfriends, I have no idea how often it occurs. I know it has happened to me, though, so I suspect there may be other men out there to whom it has happened, too.

Exclusion of youthful victims. Since most youthful victims are male and most perpetrators of violence against youthful victims are female, the exclusion of this category of victims will produce a finding that fewer females commit violence against members of the opposite sex than is actually the case.[438]

Multiple-offender killings. If a woman hires or conspires with someone else to kill a man, the data will not show that a woman has killed a man. This is true even if the person the woman hires or conspires with is also a woman. Why? Because contract-killings are recorded as "multiple offender killings," not as cases involving a woman killing a man.[439] This is significant because criminological research shows that women are substantially more likely to enlist the aid of another person to commit a murder than men are.

Censorship and attrition

Outright censorship and attrition have been known to occur in research studies on domestic violence.[440] For example, in one research survey[441] that asked respondents about whether and how they had been victimized by an intimate, most of the responses from females were counted, but only the responses from about a third of the males were. In fact, more male survey respondents were "screened out" than were accepted--and that isn't even taking into account the 7,552 males who declined to participate at all! The opposite was true of the female responses. No explanation was given for why the responses of such extraordinarily high numbers of men were excluded (8,828 men--nearly twice the number of female respondents who were screened out--were "screened out," and that's *on top of* the 7,552 males who declined to participate.) Do you suppose the fact that the report was prepared by a government agency called the Violence Against Women Grants Office might have had anything to do with it?

Series victimizations

Researchers and reporters do not always distinguish between the number of *victims* and the number of *victimizations*.

> *Example*. Suppose that Jane Jones is the only woman in Anytown who is being abused, and her husband has abused her 200 times. Suppose, further, that 100 men in Anytown are being abused, but each one is being abused by a different woman. This would mean that there are 100 women abusing 100 men, but only 1 man who is abusing a woman. If an incident-reporting system is used, the data will only reflect that there have been 200 incidents of abuse against women and 100 incidents of abuse against men. Unscrupulous researchers would then conclude from this that women are two times more likely to be abused than men are, when in truth what the data really shows is that the probability of being abused is 100 times greater for men than it is for women.[442]

The distinction is particularly relevant to domestic abuse research because the rate of series victimizations is known to be significantly higher for female victims than it is for male victims.[443] Studies that base their findings on incident-based reporting systems (and most of them do) will therefore make it seem as if women are more likely to be victims than they actually are. It is when studies (such as the Dunedin study) are based on the *number of victims* rather than the number of *incidents* of abuse that it is found that men are more likely to be victims of domestic violence than women are.

According to the U.S. Bureau of Justice Statistics, 57% of domestic abuse victimizations are series victimizations (victimization of the same person by the same person.) And since the government defines *series victimizations* as 6 or more victimizations of the same person, the 57% figure does not even take into account the number of incidents that may have been a second, third, fourth or fifth victimization of the same person. Therefore, although 57% is a high number, the percentage of incidents involving revictimizations is probably even much higher than that.[444]

It is also worth noting that the number of *perpetrators* may be substantially lower than the number of victimizations, because it is entirely possible--indeed, it is highly probable--that the same man may be responsible for victimizing two or more different women.

Advocacy researchers always seem to forget to mention these things.

Insufficient forensic investigation

Data obtained from law enforcement agencies and conviction records are often unreliable due to failure to perform an adequate criminal investigation. It is well known that among persons who commit premeditated murder, women are considerably more likely than men to use poison as the instrumentality of choice. Yet, the cause of death in poisoning cases is often recorded as "heart attack." There have been many reported cases in which a woman was discovered to have poisoned a child or a husband after the cause of death had been officially recorded as "natural causes." In some cases, the woman had poisoned dozens of her children and husbands before police even began to consider her a possible suspect.

Sudden infant death syndrome (SIDS) is another example. A significant number of investigators and coroners have demonstrated an inclination to record a baby's death as SIDS without considering the possibility that the child may have been deliberately killed, such as by asphyxiation.[445]

> *I want to see a man beaten to a bloody pulp with a high-heel shoved in his mouth, like an apple in the mouth of a pig.*[446] *-- Andrea Dworkin, feminist philosopher*

Gender-specific reporting laws

Some governmental and law enforcement agencies are required by law to keep records or maintain statistics about domestic abuse or violence against women, but have no corresponding duty to keep records of domestic abuse or violence against men. A government agency with limited resources is not likely to voluntarily maintain special records concerning the incidence and characteristics of abuse or violence against men when it doesn't have to.

Gender-specific crimes

Although many states have gender-neutralized their domestic violence laws, there are still states in which certain kinds of crimes are defined in such a way that only a male could be guilty of them; that is to say, the crimes are defined in such a way that it would be legally impossible for a woman to commit them even if she wanted to. For example, rape is defined at common law as sexual *penetration*. Since women do not have penises, and since a clitoris is not normally large or firm enough to penetrate a vagina or anus, it is virtually impossible for a woman to "penetrate" another person with her sex organs. Hence, it is legally impossible for a woman to be guilty of this crime. Of course, many states have recently enacted laws intended to broaden the range of prohibited sexual conduct beyond the act of penetration of the female by the male, but because "penetration" has been an element of the crime for so long, many victims, mandated reporters, law enforcement officials and prosecutors still think of a sex crime as something only a male is legally capable of committing.

It should be noted that even in states that have broadened their criminal sexual conduct laws, gender bias is still prevalent in both the law and its enforcement. For example, despite the fact that a kick to the testicles or other intentionally inflicted wounds to a man's external sexual organs can be just as painful and humiliating as the penetration of a sexual organ, law enforcement officials will generally charge the latter out as a sex crime and the former out as a simply assault; prosecutors, juries and judges generally follow suit.

Gender-biased interviewing

Questions asked during victimization surveys are often phrased in gender-biased ways. Consider, for example, the following questions from The National Violence Against Women Survey[447]:

"Has a man or boy ever made you have sex by using force or threatening to harm you or someone close to you? Just so there is no mistake, by sex we mean putting a penis in your vagina." Wording the question this way rules out, from the inception, even the possibility that a man might be coerced into having sexual intercourse with a woman.

For purposes of questions about oral sex, researchers informed participants that "by oral sex we mean that a man or boy put his penis in your mouth or someone, male or female, penetrated your vagina or anus with their mouth." Note that this definition excludes even the possibility that a woman or girl might put her vagina or anus on a male's mouth. It also excludes even the possibility that a man or woman might perform unwanted fellatio or analingus on a male. Since this is a serious crime--and a favorite practice among pedophiles--it strikes me as highly inappropriate to exclude it from the definition of oral sex.

"Has anyone ever made you have anal sex by using force or threat of harm? Just so there is no mistake, by anal sex we mean that a man or boy put his penis in your anus." Again, this rules out even the possibility that a female might coerce a male to have sex with her.

"Has anyone, male or female, ever put fingers or objects in your vagina or anus against your will or by using force or threats?" This rules out even the possibility that a male or female might touch a boy's or man's genitals against his will.

Note how these questions are all permeated with the concept of *penetration*. That is to say, they are all gender-biased. To see this, consider why abuse of an anus with a physical object would be considered a sex crime, while abuse of an exclusively male sex organ (e.g., kicking, grabbing or cutting a man's penis or testicles) is not. There is no explanation for it other than gender bias.

Gender-biased definitions of abuse

Originally, domestic abuse was understood to mean battering, that is, a pattern of repeatedly beating up one's partner in order to maintain power and control over her. Over the past thirty years, however, there has been a largely successful movement to expand the meaning of domestic abuse to cover a much broader range of conduct. Although legal definitions vary from state to state, most states now have laws that provide at least some form of protection from three basic forms of abuse: physical abuse; sexual abuse; and emotional or verbal abuse. Definitions of emotional and verbal abuse vary widely. Most include things like threats of physical or sexual abuse, verbal insults, and causing a person to feel embarrassed in front of one's friends or family. The expansion of the definition--especially its expansion into the realm of emotional conflicts--has generated enormous grey areas. These grey areas are all too often vulnerable to exploitation by people who have an axe to grind against members of the opposite sex.

For many years, the domestic violence field has been informed almost entirely by feminist literature that focuses exclusively on the woman as victim, such as Gloria Steinem's oft-repeated intonation that "the patriarchy requires violence or the subliminal threat of violence in order to maintain itself."[448] Despite the modern tendency to deify Ms. Steinem and accept as gospel anything she says, this particular proclamation of hers is just not true.

To begin with, the statement assumes that the United States is a patriarchy. Given the denial of rights to women in the nineteenth century, it is clear that patriarchal ideologues played a significant part in the early history of the United States. Whether or not our culture is still as strongly influenced by patriarchal ideologues as it once was, however, is not as clear. Patterns discernible from the legal system, especially family and criminal courts, suggest that the United States has actually become a matriarchal system, not a patriarchal one, and indeed that it has been a matriarchal system for many, many years. The extraordinary, unquestioning deference that the media gives to every statement made by a person who attaches the "feminist" label to himself or herself--together with the intense desire among the majority of the population to be classified as a "feminist"--suggests that it is feminist ideologues, not patriarchal ideologues, who have the most power and influence in our culture today.

The second part of Ms. Steinem's assertion, that violence is the tool by which the patriarchy subjugates women, is also dubious. Even supposing the United States was a patriarchy at some time in its history, it simply is not true that violence was ever required to maintain it. Before there were technological advancements and legal protections to make factories, railroads, mines and other workplaces safer, women consented to the notion that the workplace should be the exclusive domain of men. Men didn't need to beat up or subliminally threaten to beat up women to come to dominate the economic sphere; women voluntarily consented to it because very few of them wanted to endure the rigors and risks of injury and death themselves. Even today, many women still believe that it is a man's responsibility to support women, even if it means working a demanding, demeaning and/or dangerous job, while it is a "woman's prerogative" to work only if she wants to and only at the kinds of jobs she wants to. That is to say, many women today believe that it is a woman's right to be financially supported by a man if she wants to be, or not be supported by a man if she doesn't want to be, but that men's only option should be to support women.

While it is true that some men with deviant mental health problems might use violence or the "subliminal threat" of violence to maintain power in their relationships, it doesn't follow from this that "the patriarchy" uses violence to maintain itself, much less that it *requires* it--or even that there is such a thing as "the patriarchy" in the United States today.

Despite all of this, devotion to Mr. Steinem and her teaching is pernicious, particularly among domestic violence researchers and policy-formulators. This has resulted in gender-biased definitions that obscure the full dynamics of domestic abuse.

For example, surveys sometimes classify "withholding money" as a form of emotional abuse. This kind of behavior is commonly perceived by female victims and their advocates as one of the ways that an abusive male attempts to maintain power and control in a relationship. The surveys, however, never classify "withholding access to children" as a form of emotional abuse, even though male victims of female-perpetrated domestic violence commonly cite this as one of the most common techniques that abusive women use to maintain power and control over their male partners.[449]

Just as some men might use domestic violence to control women in the interest of furthering some personal vision of a patriarchal utopia, so some women, I think, may be using control of the domestic violence issue itself as a means of furthering some personal vision of a matriarchal utopia.

Kill your fathers, not your mothers.[450] *-- Robin Morgan, former editor-in-chief of Ms. Magazine*

Manipulation of definitions

Feminist researchers are notorious for stretching the meanings of words in order to obtain the results they want. The *Ms.* magazine study of college "rape"[451] is a good example of this technique. By defining rape to include situations where the "victim" appeared to want to have sex, and said she wanted to have sex, but secretly didn't really enjoy it, researchers were able to conclude that a remarkable number of women had been "raped."

I claim that rape exists any time sexual intercourse occurs when it has not been initiated by the woman[452] *-- Robin Morgan, former editor-in-chief of Ms. Magazine*

If we define cancer as having monkeys fly out of our noses, then it will be pretty easy to prove that smoking cigarettes bears no correlation at all to cancer.

Inadequate control of variables

Survey-based research on the subject of violence often makes some rather serious blunders with respect to controlling for the effect of extraneous variables.

Example. Jill has served two years of a ten-year sentence, but is up for parole in another month. The warden informs her that someone calling herself a researcher from the United States Department of Justice wants to interview her. She agrees. The researcher asks her if she has ever assaulted anyone. Thinking it will hurt her chances for parole if she admits that she has, she denies it. The researcher then asks if she was abused as a child. She says yes, believing it might cause a parole board to view her in a more sympathetic light. Both of her responses are false. Nevertheless, the researcher tabulates her responses and, based on similar responses from a few hundred other female prisoners, concludes that women do not commit assaults and that most women who commit crimes were themselves victims of abuse as children.

Failure to control for extraneous variables is one of the most common defects of research on domestic violence. Most studies obtain their data either from law enforcement reports or from victims' self-reports. We have already seen how extraneous variables (such as under-reporting) can make law enforcement reports unreliable, but uncontrolled extraneous variables are also a problem in some of the self-report surveys.

Example. John is being abused by his wife. One day, while he and his wife are sitting in the living room watching television, the phone rings. John answers it. "Hello, my name is Ms. Gloria Steinham," the person on the other end says, "I am from the Violence Against Women Office and I'd like to ask you a few questions." Knowing his wife can hear him, John proceeds to tell the woman on the phone that he has a perfectly wonderful wife who has never laid a hand on him. "Of course she hasn't," the woman says, "Now, what about other women? Has there ever been any other woman that you have been afraid of?" John puffs out his chest and strikes a Superman pose. "Me? Afraid of a woman? You've got to be kidding!" "Thank you for your time," the researcher says, adding one more man to her growing list of men who have never been abused by a woman.

Most studies based on self-reports make no attempt to control for lying. Data is usually compiled solely on the basis of the victim's uncorroborated statements. The only time when researchers seem to become concerned about lying is when they obtain data suggesting that men and women abuse each other at roughly equal rates.

The Dunedin longitudinal study[453] is one of only a small number of studies I have come across that makes an intelligent and responsible effort to control for extraneous variables such as lying. It also happens to be one of the studies that comes to the conclusion that a man is more likely to be abused by a woman than a woman is to be abused by a man, and that men are more likely to be victims of severe abuse than women are.

The Dunedin study was unusual because it demonstrated a high probability of accuracy based on statistical correlates, by virtue of the fact that *both* members of a couple were interviewed and were interviewed separately, at the same time but in different rooms, neither one knowing what the other said. Further controls were provided by ensuring that couples were not informed what the interviews would be about so that no prior planning or coordination of responses could occur, and no one would have a motivation to lie or feel afraid to tell the truth. Confirmation of validity was obtained by finding a strong correlation between the male and female responses notwithstanding these controls.

Scorn for and/or inability to use, logic

Many studies of domestic violence suffer from illogic. The feminist (or "patriarchal") theory of abuse suffers from this defect inasmuch as it involves the following reasoning: "Most people who abuse are male; therefore being male is what causes abuse."

The numerous studies that are used to "prove" that witnessing domestic abuse between one's parents causes one to engage in abusive behavior as an adult are also examples. The reasoning goes something like this: "Many adults who abuse their partners witnessed abuse between their parents when they were children;

therefore, witnessing abuse is what causes children to become abusive as adults." Since we've all been repeatedly drilled to believe (and in the state of Washington, it's the law) that men are the exclusive perpetrators of non-self-defensive partner abuse, the conclusion can then be made that domestic violence against women is what causes children to grow up to be abusers themselves.[454]

Of course, the same reasoning could be used to "prove" that drinking milk causes heroin addiction: "Most heroin addicts drank milk when they were children; therefore, most children who drink milk will grow up to be heroin addicts." Most children who drink milk will not grow up to be heroin addicts.

Studies that test for other explanations besides gender usually find them. For example, the Dunedin study found that poverty has significantly more to do with the probability of abuse than gender does.[455]

In 1994, lawyers were informed by their leadership that "Studies show that abusive fathers are far more likely than nonabusive parents to fight for child custody...."[456] Not exactly. It may be true that fathers who are involved in custody disputes are more likely to be accused of abuse than fathers who are not, but this is a vastly different thing from saying that abusive fathers are more likely to fight for custody. In my practice, I have had to disprove false allegations of abuse in child custody cases many times. The same data that is used to support the theory that fathers who seek custody do it as part of a systematic plan to abuse and harass their ex-partners can just as well support the theory that women are far more likely than men to use a false or embellished accusation of abuse as a litigation tactic in custody cases.

Overgeneralization is another major problem in the field of domestic violence research. Overgeneralization is the logical fallacy that goes like this: "Some A are B; therefore all A are B." It is a favorite practice among racists ("Some black people eat watermelon; therefore all black people eat watermelon") and female supremacists ("Some men are rapists; therefore all men are rapists.")

The numerous attempts to infer generalizations about the incidence of domestic violence from data about the societal response to it (that is to say, the practice of using law enforcement records to "prove" that violence is a male phenomenon) are also examples of the resistance to logic in this field.

Circular reasoning

A related problem is *circularity*. Consider, for example, this explanation of why researchers tend to exclude male victims from their studies: "[In] research on partner violence...the emphasis is on giving first attention to wives as victims...because men's [violence] results in more clearly defined consequences for women. The impact of violent acts on males or associated costs of such violence have not received as much study."[457] To sum up: We study female victims more because we know more about them. Why do we know more about them? Because we've studied them more.

Inadequate scholarship

Some domestic abuse researchers have not done any reading or investigation into the scientific theories pertaining to violence in general, and/or they simply refuse to integrate these theories into their thinking about domestic violence. The failure to do this is often rationalized by saying that domestic abusers are different from other criminals. Of course they are different, in some ways. But there are also many ways in which they are similar. A responsible researcher should acquaint herself with the causes and correlates of violence in general so that she can then reach a better understanding of the true nature of the phenomenon in all its variations, rather than myopically focusing on "men who hate and the women who love them too much."[458]

Stereotyping

[R]esearch on...domestic violence has treated batterers as a homogeneous group. This obscures potentially important subgroup differences in the effects of legal sanctions. Moreover, failure to distinguish analytically among subgroups may mask potential iatrogenic effects from legal sanctions that elevate risks for victims of more

*serious assaults....The social and ideological constructions
of battering have limited the types of variables considered
in research on domestic violence. Assuming that patriarchy
and power relations alone cause domestic violence leads
us toward conclusions that do not consider a full array of
explanatory variables from other disciplines.*[459]

One of the most widely disseminated stereotypes about domestic
violence is that it always follows a cyclical pattern. As originally
described by Lenore Walker,[460] the pattern is said to go like this:
tension, violence, remorse, tension, more violence,...,with the
violence becoming more frequent and severe over time. This
might be a characteristic typical of those abusers whose victims
end up seeking refuge in shelters, but it is not typical of all
abusers. "In fact, intimate violence which is relentless, cyclical...or
which becomes progressively more severe over time may not be
characteristic of the majority of intimate violence...."[461]

Responsible researchers have identified at least 14 different
typologies of men who abuse, finding the typologies differ
dramatically in terms of background, characteristics and
implications for treatment.[462] Unfortunately, because the field has
been dominated for so long by anti-male ideologues who insist
that blaming and shaming men for being part of "the patriarchy" is
the only correct approach to the treatment of abusive men, all men
are simply lumped together as "batterers." As a result, "controlled
studies examining different treatment strategies for the various
offender typologies have rarely been conducted."[463]

Misleading comparisons

Domestic violence advocates, researchers and advocate-
researchers have a marked proclivity for comparing apples and
oranges. The best example of this I have come across is the
"finding" that "there are nearly three times as many animal shelters
in the United States as there are shelters for battered women and
their children."[464] The conclusion we are supposed to draw from
this is that people care more about animals than they do about
women.

Why is this like comparing apples and oranges? Well, to begin with, animal shelters do not discriminate against animals of the male gender. To my knowledge, there are no animal shelters in the country that accept only female animals. Animal shelters house both male and female animals.

More to the point, most animal shelters accept *all* kinds of animals, irrespective of whether they have been battered or not. It has been estimated that there are about 1,200 shelters for battered women.[465] To my knowledge, there are 0 shelters exclusively for abused female animals. Since other shelters are available for abused women besides those that discriminate against abused men, the appropriate comparison should be between animal shelters and all of the various kinds of shelters that accept homeless human females (whether or not they are specifically designated as "battered women's" shelters) The 1996 Survey of Homeless Assistance Providers and Clients shows that there were over 10,000 homeless shelters in the United States in 1996, not including subsidized housing programs, rent assistance, Section 8, voucher programs, etc.[466] The U.S. Census Bureau counted 170,706 people living in shelters (other than battered women's shelters)--40% of whom were female--in the year 2000.[467] Yet, according to the National Council on Pet Population Study and Policy, there are only 4,700 animal shelters in the United States[468]

Comparing animal shelters to human shelters is inappropriate for another reason. Although they both use the word "shelter" in their names, they are not really the same kind of thing. In many respects, animal shelters are more analogous to prisons than to battered women's shelters. Animals that are placed in shelters are typically kept in cages and, if no one posts sufficient "bail" for their release, they are put to death after a specified period of time. Women in battered women's shelters are not kept in cages, nor are they euthanized by shelter staff. A human being who bit another human being, or injured another person's livestock, or trespassed onto another person's property, would not be sentenced to stay in a battered women's shelter; he or she would be sentenced to jail. Any meaningful comparison with animal shelters would therefore need to include not just homeless shelters and battered women's shelters, but also jails and prisons. For the same reason, it would also need to include orphanages, halfway houses, group homes, hospitals, residential treatment facilities, nursing homes, and so on.

Misrepresentation

The Emergency Room Hoax. A classic example of misrepresentation in this field is the survey research conducted on women receiving treatment for injuries at emergency rooms. In this kind of research, women are typically asked whether they have been abused (which, depending on the survey in question, might be emotional or verbal abuse, not necessarily physical or sexual abuse) at any time in their lives. The survey question may not necessarily inquire into whether the injury for which the woman is seeking treatment in the emergency room was actually a result of the domestic violence, but may simply ask whether she has ever been abused at *any* time in her life. Based on this survey, it is then possible to conclude that "X% of women treated in emergency rooms are victims of domestic abuse." Technically, the only truly logical inference that can be made is that "X% of women *say* they have been victims of domestic abuse." Even if we assume, though, that all of these women were telling the truth, it still would not follow logically from this that X% of women surveyed in emergency rooms were being *treated* for injuries caused by domestic abuse. Yet, this is the proposition for which these kinds of studies are most often cited.

> *Example.* During a heated argument, Jack and Jill call each other a bad name. The argument eventually subsides and there are no further altercations between them. Later that year, the neighbor's dog bites Jill and she goes to the emergency room for treatment. While she is there, she is asked if her partner has abused her at any time in the past year. Since verbal insults are a form of emotional abuse, Jill answers affirmatively. The researcher tabulates her response, along with a number of other women's responses, and reports her finding that Jill and a number of other women being treated in emergency rooms were victims of domestic abuse. Unscrupulous statisticians, lobbyists,

politicians and journalists then report that the survey shows that more women require emergency medical treatment after an incident of domestic abuse than for any other kind of injury. Although the statement might technically be true, wording it in this way creates the false impression that Jill and a great many other women received treatment for domestic-violence-related injuries when in fact they had not.[469]

One such survey, which was reported in the otherwise highly reputable *Journal of the American Medical Association*, "found" that 36.9% of the women surveyed in an emergency room had been victims of domestic abuse. On this basis, politicians, women's advocates and the media immediately began reporting that "36.9% of women treated in emergency rooms were abused by their partners" or "36.9% of women who are abused by their husbands or boyfriends require emergency room treatment" and the like. These kinds of statements are fraudulent for several reasons: (1) No data about the number of males seeking emergency room treatment who had been victims of emotional or physical abuse was gathered or reported; (2) The reports falsely state or imply that the emergency room treatment was for domestic abuse injuries, when in fact many women were there for completely unrelated reasons (dog bites, etc.); (3) They falsely assume that all domestic violence against women is perpetrated by men (some domestic violence against women is perpetrated by a lesbian lover, a female parent or a female sibling); (4) They fail to mention that many of the women surveyed had only been victims of emotional abuse, not physical abuse, yet one does not ordinarily require emergency medical treatment for emotional abuse; (5) By including the broad term "emotional abuse" (which has been defined to include things like "made you feel embarrassed in front of your friends or family"), the percentage of women who were able to claim they were "abuse" victims was tremendously inflated. Since the vast majority of survey research shows that women are at least as likely to be emotionally abusive toward men as vice versa, it is likely that if men had been surveyed in emergency rooms, it would have been found that a huge number of men treated in emergency rooms had been victims of domestic abuse, too.

In reality, only about 1% of women who are treated in emergency rooms are being treated for injuries that resulted from domestic violence.[470]

"A woman is beaten every 9 (or 15) seconds." Another misleading assertion that is repeated in mantra-like fashion these days is the one according to which the FBI has supposedly found that a woman is beaten every 9 (or 15) seconds. I have seen various versions of this statement, some claiming that a woman is beaten every 9 seconds; others saying it's every 15 seconds, or every 18 seconds.

These statements are false and misleading for several reasons. To being with, the FBI does not maintain data about the incidence of domestic violence. It is true that an FBI publication did comment on findings presented in a book by independent researchers Straus, Gelles and Steinmetz[471] that made it appear that an act of domestic abuse is committed against a woman every 18 seconds. The FBI itself never made any such finding, though.

More to the point, it is both false and misleading to say that anyone has ever found that a woman is "beaten" every 9 seconds. This particular statistic is derived from the Commonwealth Fund study that was conducted in 1993. The Commonwealth Fund defined "abuse" to include every physical act, even those that are not likely to result in injury (such as pushing, shoving, slapping a wrist, taking car keys from someone's hands, etc.) It is false and misleading to say that a woman who has car keys taken from her hands to prevent her from driving drunk is being "beaten."

Finally, it is a bit fraudulent to only present one-half of the statistic, while concealing the other half of it. The same studies that show that a woman is abused every 15 or 18 seconds *also* show that a *man* is abused by a woman every 14 or 15 seconds.[472] We never hear the second half of that statistic.

Lying

The Birth Defects Hoax. Sometimes researchers, advocates and advocate-researchers simply lie. The Super Bowl Sunday hoax discussed earlier[473] is one example of this. Another example is the "birth defects" hoax perpetrated by the media and the president of the National Women's Studies Association a few years back.

In November, 1992, Deborah Louis, then president of the National Women's Studies Association, wrote that "According to [a] March of Dimes report, domestic violence (vs. pregnant women) is now responsible for more birth defects than all other causes combined."[474] In fact, no such report existed. Indeed, no such finding has ever been made. If anyone had bothered to check with the March of Dimes, they would have been told that the March of Dimes had no knowledge of any such study. Nevertheless, the story was published in nearly every major news outlet in the country.[475] *Time* magazine used the alleged "report" as a basis for an article decrying the "grotesque brutality" that men reserve for pregnant women.[476] Journalists and editors who usually follow a strict policy of checking sources didn't bother to check a single source before publishing this story. Obviously none bothered to actually read the supposed "report" they wrote about in their "news" articles, either, since no such report existed. Christina Hoff Sommers ultimately traced the source of the "birth defects" story to Sarah Buel, a founder of the domestic-violence advocacy project at Harvard Law School. Ms. Buel had included the false information in a manuscript which was then circulated, as if it were true, among family-violence professionals.[477]

"4,000 women killed each year." "4,000 women each year are killed by their husbands, ex-husbands, or boyfriends." I traced this statement to a report issued by the Congressional Caucus for Women's Issues in 1992 as part of a lobbying campaign to ensure passage of the Violence Against Women Act.[478] The report cited no authority for the statistic. The statistic started showing up in gender bias and domestic violence task force reports at about the same time, usually citing either the women's caucus report or no authority at all.[479] It has appeared in both popular literature[480] and in scholarly journals,[481] is still called a "fact" by law enforcement and other government officials,[482] and has even been relied upon by courts in making sentencing decisions in domestic abuse cases.[483]

It is repeated in the *Domestic Violence Training Manual,* even though the same manual states, at other places, that the number of women killed by men every year is 3,000 and that only 40% of female homicide victims are killed by male partners.[484]   40% of 3,000 does not equal 4,000.

In truth, nowhere near 4,000 women per year are killed as a result of domestic violence. According to the FBI, the figure is closer to 1,000.[485] Perhaps the people who proliferate the "4,000 women" myth are confusing statistics about female fatalities with the statistics on child fatalities resulting from abuse and neglect. Estimates of the number of children who die as a result of abuse or neglect have ranged as high as 4,000 per year.[486] Most of these children, however, were killed by women, not men.

"50% of homeless women." "50 percent of all homeless women and children are on the streets because of violence in the home." This statistic appears to have originated with Senator Joseph Biden.[487] In a survey of the mayors of major cities in the United States, however, the majority did *not* cite domestic violence as one of the principal reasons for homelessness.[488] The National Coalition for the Homeless puts the figure at 22%.[489]

Teenagers serving time for killing their mother's abuser. "63% of the young men between the ages of 11 and 20 who are serving time for homicide have killed their mother's abuser." This alleged statistic has been published by various agencies of the government, including the Hamilton County, Tennessee District Attorney's office, and the police departments of New Castle County, Delaware and the City of Orange, California, to name but a few. It also appears on the web site of Chicago's Loyola University. Sources cited for this "fact" include the March of Dimes, the U.S. Department of Justice, the Hazelton Foundation, and the FBI's Uniform Crime Reports. The Hazelton Foundation is a drug and alcohol rehabilitation program and does not collect or publish this kind of information. The March of Dimes is a nonprofit organization concerned with baby and infant health care, with a special concern for the detection, prevention and treatment of birth defects; it neither collects nor publishes juvenile justice statistics. The FBI's Uniform Crime Reports do not report on prison populations, nor do they break down data on homicide convictions by age of offender and relationship to victim.[490] The U.S. Department of Justice does publish data about the ages of offenders and their relationships to their victims; however, it has never made any findings or published the results of any studies having to do with the percentage of convicted teenage boys who have killed their mother's abuser.

Data that really has been published by the U.S. Department of Justice actually tends to refute the "63% kill mother's abuser" claim. A 1999 Department of Justice report on juvenile offenders and victims states that between 1980 and 1997, 37% of the homicide victims of male juvenile offenders were strangers (completely unknown) to the offender. This means that in 63% of juvenile homicides committed by males, the victim was known to the offender, either as a family member, a friend or an acquaintance.[491] It does *not* mean that 63% of the victims were abusing the offenders' mothers. Given that the median age of the victims of juvenile perpetrators of homicide is 17,[492] many are between 13 and 16 years old, and nearly two-thirds of the victims are not older than 24,[493] it seems highly unlikely that the majority of the victims were committing acts of domestic abuse against the offenders' mothers. While it is possible that some teenage boys' mothers are romantically involved with, married to, or molesting male children or men who are substantially younger than they are, it seems highly unlikely that *most* of them are. In this connection, it should also be noted that only 9% of the homicide victims of male juvenile offenders were related to the offender--and this 9% includes *all* relatives (fathers, mothers, husbands, wives, siblings, aunts, uncles, grandparents, etc.), not just fathers.[494] It is not known what portion of this 9% were men who were abusing the offenders' mothers, but even if all 9% were, this would still be 7 times lower than the "63%" figure routinely recited by district attorneys, police departments and other women's advocates.

"More women are treated for injuries caused by domestic violence than any other kind of injury." This statements has appeared in various forms--e.g., that "more women are treated for domestic violence injuries than for all other kinds of injuries combined," or that domestic violence is "the leading cause of injuries to women ages 15 to 44," more common than automobile accidents, muggings, and cancer deaths combined.[495] Yet, according to the Centers for Disease Control (CDC), the leading causes of women's injury-related emergency room visits are motor vehicle accidents and other kinds of accidents unrelated to domestic

violence. In fact, more women are treated for animal bites and injuries from venomous plants than are treated for injuries from domestic violence. As it turns out, domestic violence not only isn't the "leading cause," but among all the known causes of injuries to women, it is actually one of the *least* common causes of injury to women.[496]

Worse than the Vietnam War. "Family violence has killed more women in the last five years than Americans killed in the Viet Nam War."[497] This statistic is usually attributed to a 1992 American Medical Association publication.[498] It is an outright lie. 58,135 American men died in the Viet Nam War[499] The 1992 Statistical Abstracts for the United States show that the total annual number of female victims of homicide (whether by a husband, boyfriend, or someone else) at that time was 5,045.[500] Even assuming this number has remained constant (it hasn't; it's been decreasing)[501] and even assuming all women who are murdered are killed by their husbands or boyfriends (the majority of them are not),[502] the number of women killed by husbands and boyfriends would still be less than half the number of men killed in Vietnam. Adjusting the annual homicide figure to exclude killings of women by people other than husbands and boyfriends, we find that the truth is that something like *ten times more* American men died in the Vietnam War than women who are killed as a result of domestic violence over the course of a five-year period.

The thing that makes this particular spin on the Vietnam War tragedy so disturbing is that it was obviously nothing less than a shameless effort to co-opt a growing national concern for veterans of an unpopular war--a deliberate attempt to shift the national spotlight back to women's issues quickly, lest anyone might start to care about men. Female supremacist literature often claims women are superior to men because men are selfish and competitive by nature while women supposedly are cooperative and other-oriented by nature, but this "we deserve more sympathy than war veterans because our gender has more victims than your gender does" business is one of the basest manifestations of selfishness and competitiveness I have ever seen.

Violence against researchers

When researcher Suzanne Steinmetz published the findings of her study showing that wives initiate as many attacks against husbands as husbands do against wives, she was immediately met with angry protests. Threats from female supremacists to harm her children eventually forced her to leave the field.[503]

Later, when Erin Pizzey (the founder of the first battered women's shelter in England) wrote a book[504] that provided some support for Steinmetz's thesis, her publisher received a telephone call threatening to smash the windows at the publisher's office and kill him. Ms. Pizzey herself received death threats, including bomb scares at her personal residence. On her book tour, she was met with so many angry female supremacist protestors that police insisted on escorting her everywhere she went. The protestors invariably carried signs smeared with the familiar declamations that "ALL MEN ARE RAPISTS"[505] and "ALL MEN ARE BATTERERS."

The brave examples of Steinmetz, Straus and Pizzey notwithstanding, researchers operating in such an atmosphere of fear and intimidation cannot necessarily be trusted to tell the truth in an honest, straightforward way, not when doing so could cost them their reputations, their careers, their lives, and the lives of their children.[506]

Domestic violence is a problem that deserves serious attention, but revictimizing male victims and those who would try to help them is not the way to solve it. Exaggerating, distorting, suppressing and making up statistics vilifying an entire gender simply for the selfish purpose of owing and controlling "victim" status not only does a disservice to abused men but, as is discussed at more length in Chapter 13, it ultimately does a disservice to abused women, too.

12. Males are the primary targets of gender bias in the American legal system

The "Rule of Thumb" Myth

Wife-beating has never been legal or condoned in American law. The punishments for wife-beating in early America were severe, including not only imprisonment, but also public whippings. In addition to penalties inflicted by the legal system, suspected wife-beaters were regularly excommunicated from their churches and abducted and whipped by relatives and neighbors.[507] Despite this history, one of the most persistent urban legends of our time is the one according to which the phrase "rule of thumb" supposedly originated from a man's right to beat his wife so long as the stick was no wider than his thumb. In truth, there is absolutely no basis in either law or fact to support this origin of the phrase; nor is there any basis for believing that any such rule ever even existed at all.[508] Yet, it continues to be repeated over and over again, sometimes even by people who are otherwise highly responsible and respected leaders and policy-makers.

The obvious purpose of this myth is to draw attention to the legal system's supposed patriarchal condonation of the use of violence and "male privilege" as a means of subjugating women. It also helps deflect attention away from the uncomfortable truth that it is actually *women*, not men, who receive preferential treatment in the American legal system.

Invisible Victims

Due to the history of racial prejudice in our country, research on discriminatory enforcement and administration of the laws typically breaks down the categories for comparison along racial and ethnic lines in order to determine the extent to which discriminatory enforcement of the laws is currently taking place in our country. The possibility that gender may have even more to do with it than race or ethnicity is rarely even considered a possibility.

Despite the enactment of civil rights laws and widespread activism to raise consciousness about race prejudice, I have no doubt that racial discrimination in the enforcement of facially neutral laws still happens in America, at least in some areas, at some times and for some kinds of offenses. The "dirty little secret" of the American criminal justice system, however, is not racial discrimination; it's gender discrimination. And I don't mean discrimination against women, as the "gender bias task forces" would have you believe. I mean discrimination against men.

Discriminatory investigations

On a fairly regular basis, for as long as I can remember, a newspaper will publish an article about yet another child who was killed by his mother even though she had been reported to child protection authorities many times before. Each time, the article comes to the same conclusion: the child protection agency isn't really at fault; it's just that they are so gosh-darned overworked and understaffed. I'm sure that the directors of these programs would like to have more money thrown their way to help them do their jobs, but I'm not buying this "overworked" excuse for one minute.

Yes, child protection agencies have a lot of reports of maltreatment to deal with. Yes, child maltreatment reports are on the rise.[509] Yet, these agencies don't seem to encounter any problems with short-staffing when it comes to investigating reports of alleged sexual abuse of a female child by a male adult. They handle these kinds of cases with extraordinary zeal. If they can manage to handle these cases with such devotion and expertise, then it's not lack of resources that's the problem; it's *allocation* of resources. The figures bear this out.

Only about 8% of the child maltreatment cases investigated by the average child protection agency involve allegations of sexual abuse.[510] Yet, *the majority* of the cases--over 50%--that are referred by a child protection agency to the police or prosecutor for criminal charges are cases in which a male is alleged to have sexually abused a female child.[511]

When we look at what happens to other kinds of criminal child maltreatment cases, we see a vastly different pattern. Although about a third of all criminal maltreatment cases are substantiated--i.e., there's a finding of probable cause to believe that a crime has occurred--children are removed from the home in only 10% of the cases. 29.2% of the substantiated cases are closed almost immediately upon being substantiated! That is to say, in 29.2% of the cases in which it has been substantiated that a serious crime has been committed against a child, not only does the child protection agency fail to report the crime to the police or a prosecutor, but the agency does not even provide any kind of protection or services for the child at all.[512]

In many states, child protection agencies freely admit to feeling that there is no need for any action at all on their part in the majority of the cases in which it is found that the crime of physical assault has been perpetrated against a child.[513]

Statistics reveal that about half of the children who are killed as a result of physical abuse were known to the authorities well before the assault that caused their deaths.[514] Disabled children fare a little better, but still, over 42% of the cases involving maltreatment of a disabled child are "repeat" offenders--parents who had been reported to Child Protective Services for maltreating the child at least once before.[515]

Reports of alleged sexual abuse frequently come from mothers who are afraid of losing custody of their children to their fathers, and from daughters and stepdaughters with a variety of motivations for getting their fathers or stepfathers into trouble. Only a tiny fraction of the reports of child sexual abuse come from physicians and day care providers. Yet, 44% of the reports of sexual abuse are actively investigated.

Just a coincidence? Not based on gender animus? Maybe, but consider this statement appearing in a United States Department of Justice training manual for child protection workers: "A [child] abuse case might involve a child who has been victimized by a father, stepfather, uncle, or family friend...."[516] The manual does not even mention the possibility that it might involve a mother, stepmother or aunt, despite the fact that it is well-known that the vast majority of the most severe forms of child physical abuse--up to and including infanticide[517]--is perpetrated by women!

Don't get me wrong. Sexual abuse of a child is something that child protection and police investigators should take very seriously. But it doesn't justify simply standing by and shrugging while children--one every 2 hours, according to one estimate--are being snuffed out of existence altogether by their mothers.[518]

Discriminatory arrest policies

A U.S. Justice Department handbook for law enforcement officers on how to approach and help crime victims advises officers who appear on the scene of a domestic dispute to provide the victim with a referral to a battered women's program.[519] The message that is given, of course, is that domestic abuse is a gender-specific crime, that it is something of which men are guilty and women are victims, never vice versa.

Studies show that this kind of indoctrination is having the intended effect on police practices: police are very likely to arrest and charge an alleged abuser when the alleged victim is female, but it is extremely rare that police will take a female abuser into custody when the victim is male.[520]

Inadequate police response to women's reports of domestic abuse is also a myth. It may have been a problem a couple of generations ago, but it is not a problem today. A 1996 study shows that police respond to about 90% of the calls for assistance from women alleging to be victims of domestic abuse within 10 minutes of the call.[521] This is a much quicker response rate than for other kinds of crimes.

About half of all spouse killings are committed by women, but men are arrested for this crime about six times as frequently.[522]

In 89% of arrests for violent crimes, a male is arrested.[523] This is radically disproportionate to the rate at which males are committing violent crimes. (See the discussion in previous chapters.)

Perhaps the most damning of all the statistics, however, is this one: When probable cause exists to charge a juvenile with a sex offense, the offender is *46.5 times* more likely to be arrested and charged with a crime if he is male than if she is female. I don't mean juvenile sex offenders are 46.5 times more likely to be male. I mean that if a female offender commits a sex offense, she is *46.5 times less likely to be arrested* for it than if a male commits the very same crime. Juvenile offenders receive counseling and therapeutic services if they are female; underage males are handcuffed and taken to jail.[524]

Even the National Center for Juvenile Justice admits that "regardless of offense, males [are] more likely to be detained than females....[M]ales are overrepresented in the detention caseload, compared with their proportions in the overall delinquency caseload."[525]

The fact that the victim is male also substantially decreases the probability that the perpetrator will be arrested.[526] This rule applies to all male victims--children and adult victims alike.[527]

As has been previously noted, most victims of child maltreatment are male. The National Study of the Incidence and Prevalence of Child Abuse and Neglect conducted in 1980 found that police, coroners and sheriffs did not even report 58% of the children whose conditions suggested child abuse.[528] Ten years later, nothing had changed. A 1991 study reports that 58% of the child abuse cases for which police had probable cause to arrest did not result in arrest.[529] The same study found that although only a tiny fraction of all child maltreatment investigations involved sexual abuse, nearly 80% of the cases in which an arrest was made involved allegations of sexual abuse. By contrast, arrests were made in only 20% of the cases in which a finding of probable cause to arrest for criminal physical assault was made. *Not a single arrest was made for criminal neglect*, even though criminal neglect comprised the largest category of crimes against children.[530] Almost all cases of criminal neglect are perpetrated by mothers, and a substantial majority of child physical abuse and child killings involve a female perpetrator. The only category of maltreatment in which men comprise the majority of offenders is sexual abuse. In other words, despite the fact that women comprise the vast majority of all categories of maltreatment except sexual abuse, the one category that contains the most men is the one that yields the most arrests, while the category that contains the most women yields no arrests at all. Putting it another way, although 92% of all substantiated maltreatment cases are in female-dominated categories, and although the vast majority of all criminal maltreatment of children is perpetrated by women, the vast majority of the people who are arrested for these kinds of crimes are male.[531] A clearer case of discriminatory enforcement cannot be made.[532]

In a U.S. Justice Department publication[533], Barbara Smith attempts to give five justifications for the disproportionate rates of arrest of men who sexually abuse their children as compared to the rate of arrests of women who physically abuse their children:

(1) Line between discipline and physical abuse isn't clear. True, but this would only explain a failure to investigate, or a failure to refer a case to police for arrest. It doesn't explain why a case of physical abuse *that has already been substantiated* does not result in an arrest. Remember, we are talking about disparate treatment in cases in which abuse has been *substantiated*, not cases involving bare allegations alone.[534]

(2) Difficulty of proving abuse in court.[535] Yet, it shouldn't be any harder to prove a *substantiated* case of physical abuse or neglect than it is to prove an allegation of sexual abuse. In some cases, it should be easier. For example, since many sexual abuse cases involve only "fondling" allegations, the sole evidence available is often the child's testimony--testimony which is highly susceptible to suggestion and manipulation by a parent or prosecutor. *Substantiated* cases of physical abuse, on the other hand, leave physical marks and bruises that a physician or forensics expert (and sometimes any ordinary person of reasonable intelligence) can positively identify as tangible evidence of abuse.

(3) Difficulty of identifying the perpetrator. Yet, it shouldn't be any more difficult to identify the perpetrator of physical abuse than it is to identify the perpetrator of sexual abuse.

(4) Treatment is a more effective approach to physical abuse than punishment.[536] Thousands of dead children would take issue with this one, if they were still alive enough to speak. The high rate of recidivism in physical abuse cases also belies this excuse.

(5) Prosecution will only further traumatize the child. This last one has got to be the lamest excuse I have ever heard. Can anyone honestly believe that making a child talk about her private parts and what was done to them is not traumatic? The fear of further traumatizing children is precisely why so many innovative techniques are being introduced in sexual abuse prosecutions--videotaped testimony, accompaniment by mother while testifying, etc. Furthermore, being subjected to additional physical abuse--in some cases eventually resulting in permanent disfigurement or death--can hardly be regarded as merely minor annoyances in a child's life.

None of these excuses makes any sense, and they all mask the real reason that police arrest sexual abusers but not physical abusers. The real reason that over half of the children who are killed as a result of child abuse every year were known to the authorities to be victims of physical abuse is not that enforcement agencies are overworked and understaffed, either. The real reason is simply that nobody wants to arrest a mother. Motherhood is sacred.

Discriminatory prosecution policies

> *Nationally, prosecutors process many more cases of child sexual abuse than physical abuse and only a few neglect cases....91% of 600 prosecutors interviewed stated that they prosecuted fewer physical abuse cases than sexual abuse cases, with 80 percent reporting that they prosecuted 'substantially' fewer numbers of physical abuse cases than sexual abuse cases.* [537]

It is a well-documented fact that cases involving female victims of child abuse are much more likely to be prosecuted than cases involving male victims.[538]

It is also a well-documented fact that among juvenile offenders, district attorneys are more likely to prosecute male arrestees for their crimes than female arrestees. That is to say, even females who make it all the way to the prosecution stage are more likely to receive more lenient treatment than males who have made it that far for committing the same offense.[539]

The same thing is true in adult prosecutions. For example, it is a documented practice among prosecutors, in cases involving joint male-female criminal enterprises, to seek imprisonment of the male but not the female.[540] As Assistant Prosecutor J. Dennis Kohler put it:

> *In plea bargaining with a married couple, often we say, 'Well, let's get the man.' We're satisfied with getting the husband to plead guilty and dropping the charges against the woman. Of course, then he has a criminal record, she doesn't. If they both repeat the crime, he can 'legitimately' receive a longer sentence.*[541]

Every year, hundreds of thousands of female domestic abuse victims receive some kind of assistance from a victim service agency.[542] These agencies are usually run out of or in cooperation with the prosecutor's office, or by some other government agency. This further reinforces the perception that the legal system is designed for the benefit of women, not men. Not a lot of men feel very comfortable about walking into a "battered women's" office to ask for help, no matter how badly they have been abused. It would be comparable to expecting a woman to go to a "men's health club" for hormone replacement therapy.

The greatest evidence of discriminatory enforcement, though, comes from the mouths of the prosecutors themselves. It was California's chief prosecutor, Attorney General Daniel E. Lungren, who issued the proclamation that "Violence is primarily a male phenomenon in American culture."[543] We would consider it evidence of an established governmental policy of discriminatory enforcement (not to mention an egregious example of overt racism) if the chief prosecutor of the most populous state in the country were to publicly declare, "Violence is primarily a black phenomenon." We should consider it evidence of discriminatory enforcement policies against males when the same is said about them.

Discriminatory defense attorneys

Unfortunately, a lot of defense attorneys have bought into the whole "men bad, women good" way of thinking. In some cases, this can have extremely dangerous consequences for their male clients. For example, out of loyalty and deference to mothers, attorneys for juveniles facing capital charges sometimes refrain from introducing as a mitigating factor evidence that the child had been (or is being) severely abused by his mother.[544] It is not really surprising that an attorney might behave this way, since it is usually the parents who pay for their minor children's lawyers. In my opinion, any defense attorney who would fail to introduce potentially exculpatory evidence in a capital case for *any* reason--whether to protect a mother from embarrassment or otherwise--should be immediately and permanently disbarred.[545] Not a lot of people share this view, however. As a result, there are abused children on death row right now, waiting for the day when they will finally be snuffed out of existence altogether--if not by their mothers, then by the state.

Discriminatory judges and juries

Studies have shown that judges are more likely to release a female defendant on her own recognizance (no bail required) than male defendants who are charged with the same crime. It has also been shown that when bail is required to be posted, a lower amount is set for women than for men accused of the very same crime.[546]

Judges and jurors, reflecting as they do the values and mores of the broader society of which they are a part, often apply the "women good, men bad" prejudice in their deliberations, too. As Barbara Swartz, [former] director of the Women's Prison Project, observed, "people in the criminal justice system basically look at women as incapable of committing some of the crimes they are charged with. They therefore try to find rationales as to why the woman wasn't really involved."[547]

When Josephine Mesa killed her 23-month-old son with a toilet plunger, she was exonerated because she claimed to have been the victim of child abuse herself.[548] When 16-year-old Heath Williams was found to have been a victim of child sexual abuse, though, he was nevertheless sentenced to death for being a coconspirator in a murder. The other coconspirator, an adult female, went free.[549]

In cases where a man's credibility is pitted against a woman's, judges and jurors invariably believe the woman rather than the man. Remember that Gary Dotson spent six years of his life in prison because judges would not grant requests for a new trail made on his behalf by the "victim" herself after she finally came forward to confess that she had lied out of fear of parental wrath. So strong is the American desire to believe that women never lie that she had to introduce the results of a lie-detector test, along with other physical evidence proving Mr. Dotson's innocence, and wage a massive media campaign before anyone in the legal system would even consider the possibility that a woman might actually be capable of lying about rape.[550]

Unfortunately, men are not always able to exonerate themselves until it is too late.

In a review of 350 cases in which a person had been convicted and then later conclusively proven to have been innocent, it was found that 23 had already been executed, and another 8 had already died in prison. All 350 were men.[551]

> *Men who are unjustly accused of rape...gain from the experience.*[552] *-- Catherine Comins, Assistant Dean of Student Life at Vassar College*

Discriminatory sentencing

Gender bias task forces claim that sentencing practices discriminate against women. The usual reason cited for this conclusion is the observed fact that women are placed on probation more frequently, or for longer periods of time, than men are.[553] Might there be a few things these people are sort of overlooking? For example, could it be that more women receive probation simply because men are much more likely to be sentenced to hard time in prison rather than merely slapped on the wrist with probation? Well, let's take a look at the statistics and find out.

Currently, about 1% of the adult male population of the United States is a sentenced prisoner, as compared to 0.06% of the adult female population. In other words, if you are a U.S. citizen who was born male, you are over 15 times more likely to be sentenced to prison than if you were born female.[554]

Of course, this statistic could be interpreted simply as evidence that men commit more crimes than women do. Other statistics, however, show that there is no direct correlation between the comparative rates at which men, as compared to women, are committing crimes and the gender composition of American prisons.

To begin with, data from the U.S. Department of Justice show that a male who has been arrested, charged and convicted of a felony has about a 50% chance of being sentenced to prison, while a female who has been arrested, charged and convicted of the very same crime has only about a 33% chance of being sentenced to prison. For every kind of offense (burglary, larceny, murder, assault, etc.), men who are convicted are substantially more likely to receive a prison sentence than are women who have been convicted of the exact same crime.

A man convicted of felony aggravated assault is over twice as likely to be sentenced to prison as a woman who is convicted of felony aggravated assault. Women who are convicted of murder or felonious aggravated assault are about 3 times more likely than men to be sentenced only to probation or a small jail sentence instead of prison for their crimes.[555]

The differences are even more stark when *lengths* of sentences are compared. The average length of sentence imposed on a male convicted of murder is *over 6 years longer* than the average length of sentence imposed on a female who has been convicted of murder. The average sentence imposed on a male who is convicted of felony aggravated assault is nearly *4 times as long* as the average sentence imposed on a female convicted of the same crime. The average length of sentence imposed on a male convicted of any felony is 43 months (about 3.5 years); the average length of sentence imposed on a female convicted of a felony is 25 months (about 2 years.)[556] The average sentence imposed on a male convicted of burglary is 70% longer than for women convicted of the same crime; for sexual assault, the male sentence is 74% longer; and for larceny, the sentence imposed on males is 75% longer than the sentence imposed on females for the same crime.[557]   Nationwide, jail and probation sentences, on average, are also longer for males than for females.[558]

When a male felon is sentenced to prison, the average *maximum* length of sentence imposed is nearly 7 years; the average maximum length of sentence imposed on females convicted of felonies is 4.6 years. The average maximum length of jail sentences for men is 7 months; for women who receive a jail sentence, the average maximum length is 5 months. The average maximum length of sentence imposed on men who are convicted of felony aggravated assault (assault with a deadly weapon or causing serious bodily harm) is over twice as long as the average maximum length of sentence imposed on women for the same crime. The average maximum length of sentence imposed on a man convicted of murder is 6 years longer than the average maximum length of sentence imposed on a woman who is convicted of murder.[559]

The average length of sentence imposed on women who are jailed for murder is merely 3 months![560]

In North Carolina, a man who is convicted of second-degree murder receives, on average, a sentence that is 12.6 years longer than a woman who is convicted of second-degree murder.[561]

Overall, the average length of sentence imposed upon a man in the United States for killing his wife is 17.5 years. The average length of sentence imposed upon a woman in the United States for killing her husband is 6.2 years.[562]

Even in states that have attempted to eliminate discrimination in sentencing by adopting sentencing guidelines, sentences imposed on men are still 23% longer than those imposed on women. When criminal histories and the severity level of the crime are exactly identical, women are still 57% more likely than men to be ordered into treatment rather than imprisoned for their crimes, and they are 59% more likely to be made eligible for release and released after they are imprisoned than men are.[563]

In California, only 1.5% of the third-time convicts that are sentenced to mandatory life sentences with no possibility of parole for 25 years are female; 98.5% are male. Only about 25% were for violent crimes; the vast majority of men who are serving time under California's "three strikes" law are there for possession or sale of drugs.[564]

The vast majority of perpetrators of serious maltreatment of children under 12 years of age are female. In an unbiased system, this would mean that the vast majority of inmates serving time for child maltreatment should be female. In reality, however, it's just the opposite. The vast majority of people serving time for child maltreatment are male.[565] In fact, not just 51%, not two-thirds, but a full _96.6%_ of the people serving time in prison for crimes against children are _male_![566]

Although sexual abuse comprises only 8% of all substantiated child maltreatment crimes, 66.8% of the people who have been sentenced to prison for child maltreatment were guilty of sexual abuse. Only 2.6% of the people who have been sentenced to prison for child maltreatment were convicted of physical abuse, and this statistic _includes_ the crime of homicide.[567] That is to say, _a man is over 25 times more likely to be sentenced to prison for inappropriately fondling a child than a woman is for killing or maiming one!_

Is this simply a reflection of general societal disgust with the idea of adults having sexual relations with children, or does it stem from the fact that men are substantially more likely to have sexual relations with children than kill them, while women are substantially more likely to kill children than have sexual relations with them? Ask any judge, lawyer or other criminal justice professional and he or she will tell you it has nothing whatsoever to do with discrimination and absolutely everything to do with disgust. But how certain can we really be about that?

Consider this: Although the majority of victims of crimes (including sex crimes) against children are male, about 75% of the people who are serving time in prison for victimizing a child are serving time for victimizing a _female_ child; only 25% are serving time for victimizing a male child.[568] If the disparity in sentencing were really only due to general societal disgust with the idea of adults having sex with children, then most (or at least half) of the people serving time for victimizing a child should be serving time for victimizing a male. That the ratio instead is 3 to 1 the other way means something else is going on.

Although crimes against children comprise about 33% of all crime, and although the rate of crime against children is between 2 and 3 times higher than the rate of crime against adults, only about 1 in 500 prison inmates is serving time for child abuse.[569] Might this have something to do with the fact that most women who commit crimes target children, while most men who commit crimes target adults?

It is often complained that the criminal justice system does not take domestic violence as seriously as other kinds of crime. Yet, about 25% of the jail population and 7% of the prison population consists of people who have committed violence against an intimate, and about 75% of these are serving time for assault.[570] And these are just the people who have been incarcerated in penal institutions for their crimes; it doesn't count the people who have been committed to mental institutions, treatment facilities or work release programs; it doesn't count people who have been placed on home monitoring; and it doesn't count people who have been sentenced to community service or some other alternative sanction.

Even more significant is the fact that the median prison sentence for assaulting one's spouse is actually *4 years longer* than the median prison sentence for assaulting any person other than one's spouse.[571]

It may have been true in our grandparents' time that the legal system did not take domestic abuse as seriously as other kinds of crime, but it certainly is not true anymore. Today, not only is domestic abuse taken as seriously as other kinds of crimes; it is actually taken considerably *more seriously* than other kinds of crimes. Could this possibly bear any correlation to the fact that virtually every participant in the legal system has been taught to believe the myth that domestic violence is strictly "a male phenomenon"?

The Death Penalty

Under international law, capital punishment is considered a human rights issue. Since the adoption of the U.N. Declaration of Human Rights, more than half of the countries in the world have abolished the death penalty. Outside of the U.S., there were only 22 documented executions of juvenile offenders (all males, by the way) in the world between 1985 and 1995. These occurred in Iran, Iraq, Bangladesh, Pakistan, Nigeria, Saudi Arabia and Yemen.[572]

In 1976, the U.N. adopted an International Covenant on Civil and Political Rights stating that the "sentence of death shall not be imposed for crimes committed by persons below eighteen years of age"[573] The United States refused to agree to this provision, declaring instead that it was "reserving the right" to kill children who commit crimes. 11 countries objected to this reservation and in 1995, the U.N.'s Human Rights Committee asked the U.S. to withdraw it. President Clinton refused.

In 1989, the U.N. Convention on the Rights of the Child[574] was passed. Article 37(a) thereof states that "neither capital punishment nor life imprisonment without possibility of release shall be imposed for offences committed by persons below eighteen years of age." President Clinton signed it, but made it subject to a reservation on the part of the United States of the right to kill its children.

In 1998, the U.N. Special Rapporteur on extrajudicial, summary and arbitrary executions again asked the United States to withdraw its reservation of the right to kill children. Again the United States refused.

152 of the 154 countries that are members of the United Nations have signed the Convention. The only members of the United Nations that have not signed it are the United States and Somalia. Even China, long the leader in imposing death sentences, has signed it.[575] It is largely for this reason that Amnesty International now lists the United States, once a leader in defending human rights, as one of worst violators of human rights in the modern world.[576]

What does all of this have to do with discrimination against men? A lot, when you stop to consider that as of June 2000, all 74 of the 74 people who are currently on death row in the United States for crimes committed while they were children are male.[577]

Furthermore, less than 2% of all prisoners who were sentenced to death during the twenty-seven years from 1973 to 2000 were female, and not a single one of them has actually had the penalty carried out on the basis of crimes committed while they were underage. During the same period, however, the United States did execute 17 people who were children at the time they committed their crime. All 17 were male.[578]

Among people who are actually convicted of murder (not just some lesser crime like manslaughter), men convicted of murder are *20 times as likely to receive the death penalty* as are women who are convicted of the same crime. Less than 1/10th of 1% of women convicted of unjustified, intentional, premeditated murder are sentenced to death.[579] And almost 100% of all the inmates on death row are male.[580]

Although women kill their husbands and boyfriends with some regularity, the last time a woman was executed for killing a man was nearly half a century ago, in 1954.[581]

Between the time the death penalty was reinstated in 1976, and 1990, 120 of the men on death row, and only 1 of the women on death row, have been executed.[582]

Between 1955 and 1990, over 70,000 women committed premeditated, unjustified homicides, and 90% of the victims have been male. Although hundreds of men have been put to death since 1955, only 1 woman has. It cannot be made any clearer that our criminal justice system simply does not regard the killing of men by women to be a particularly "heinous, atrocious or cruel" kind of crime, no matter how or under what circumstances it is committed.583[584]

Imprisonment

94% of the adults who are serving time in prison are male, and 96.7% of the children who are sentenced to adult prisons are male.[585] Among juvenile cases transferred to adult courts for prosecution, 95% are male. 97% of juvenile transfers to adult courts for trial of assault charges are male. Even the United States government has been forced to admit that "Given their proportion of transfers [to adult courts], females [are] underrepresented among assault cases (3%.)"[586]

Most American jurisdictions permit the imposition of a sentence of life imprisonment without possibility of parole for offenders younger than age 16; some even make it mandatory. In the state of Washington, children as young as 8 (eight) years of age can be sentenced to life imprisonment.[587] In Vermont, 10-year-olds can be.[588] In Kentucky, not long ago, a 14-year-old boy was convicted of rape and sentenced to imprisonment for life without possibility of parole.[589]

As a rule, judges are far less likely to impose criminal penalties upon female children who are arrested and found guilty than upon male children who are arrested and found guilty of the same crime; and for each category of crime, males are much more likely to be incarcerated for their crimes than females are; they are also more likely to receive much lengthier sentences than females are.[590]

Males as young as 13 and 14 have been sentenced to adult prisons. No female that young ever has.[591]

In those rare cases where a teenage girl is tried as an adult, her sentence is likely to be only one-half as long as the sentence served by a male of the same age upon conviction of the same crime.[592]

Curiously, male children who are tried as adults receive even longer prison sentences than *adults* who are sentenced to prison for the same crime.[593]

Study after study has shown that being male has more to do with receiving a harsher sentence in court than any other factor-- including race.[594]

Gender bias task forces sometimes complain that more money is being spent on male correctional facilities than on female ones. It is true that despite geometric rates of growth in violent crimes committed by females, and despite declining rates of violent crime committed by males, state governments are nevertheless busily going about the business of building more prisons for males and expanding the storage capacities of existing prison facilities for men. In most states, no new or expanded facilities for female offenders are being planned (apart from improvements designed to make the existing female prison population more comfortable.) Only a gender-biased task force could interpret this as discrimination against females, though. Anyone with any capacity to reason at all must be able to see that the reason more prison facilities are being built for males and not for females, at a time when females are committing more and more imprisonable offenses and males are committing fewer and fewer, is that government planners know that female offenders generally are going to receive much more lenient sentences than prison time, regardless of the kinds of crimes they commit.[595] Why build more prisons for women if judges aren't willing to sentence women to them?

The relative conditions of prisons to which men and women are sentenced also says a lot about the relative value our society ascribes to men and women. The prison units with the least amount of space per inmate are in facilities that house males; prison units with the greatest amount of space per inmate house females.[596] Prisoner density (overcrowding) is highest in male-only prisons.[597] Male prisoners are also confined to their units for a greater portion of each day than female prisoners are.[598]

There are substantially more self-improvement, support groups, counseling, arts and crafts, pre-release and community integration programs for female prisoners than there are for male prisoners.[599] Yet, a recent report from the U.S. Department of Justice states that "researchers and advocates are calling for correctional strategies that are gender specific and community based"[600]...*for the benefit of women only*!

Federal and state agencies already fund many special programs exclusively for female prisoners. The Women's Prison Association is just one example. This government-backed organization provides education, support and transitional services to females; offers emergency and transitional housing, individualized case management services, skills-building workshops, child care, counseling and other supports...*to women only*.[601] There is no comparable Men's Prison Association.

Incarcerated mothers often are provided special facilities in which to see their children, while incarcerated fathers are not.[602] In Minnesota, female prisoners are sometimes placed in battered women's shelters instead of prisons. Mothers in New York's Bedford Hills Corrections Facility even have a live-in nursery; fathers, of course, do not.

Due to the conditions of its men's prisons, the United States could meet neither the United Nations' nor the European Union's minimum standards for the humane treatment of prisoners.[603]

That females receive more favorable treatment at every stage in the American criminal justice system than males do should be beyond any reasonable doubt to anyone who has responsibly, objectively and unselfishly considered the issue.[604]

13. Conclusions and Recommendations

Domestic abuse is not "a male phenomenon."

There are two possible conclusions about domestic violence that one can draw from the research literature: (1) women are more violent than men; or (2) women are becoming as violent as men. Whatever else the research establishes, however, the one thing it most definitely does *not* support is the notion that violence is strictly "a male phenomenon."

That isn't to say that some people won't try to interpret the literature this way. For example, some people, upon learning that female violence is rising, react by contending that females are not really more violent or getting as violent as men, but that the criminal justice system is simply starting to hold them more accountable for their conduct.

A gender bias task force no doubt would argue that evidence of increasing female arrest rates is simply "proof" that women are being discriminated against in the criminal justice system, that the rise in female crime rates is a result of selective enforcement of the criminal laws, a "backlash." As we have seen, though, the research does not support this conclusion. True, women historically have not been held accountable for their conduct to the same extent that men have. True, some law enforcement officials no longer adhere to the view that women should never be held accountable for their criminal conduct. These things can hardly be taken as evidence of discrimination against women, though. If anything, they are signs that women are beginning to achieve true equality with men. Even

so, every aspect of the criminal justice system--from investigation to
sentencing--is still heavily weighted against men, not women.

The fact that women (or at least *some* women) are beginning to
be held accountable for their conduct in ways that men always have
been has been offered as a possible explanation for the data showing
that female arrest rates are rising.[605]   There is a certain appeal to
this notion. On the other hand, given the voluminous data showing
that women are still treated much more leniently by the criminal
justice system than men are, the theory seems dubious, at best. It
also ignores the recent development of a wide range of special
defenses ("battered women's syndrome," etc.) specifically designed
to improve a woman's chances of *avoiding* accountability for her
actions. Finally, it ignores the data obtained from sources other than
incident-based reporting systems; that is, the scientific research that
shows that women are becoming either more violent or equally as
violent toward their intimate partners as men are.

Application of a rational-choice model yields a more plausible
explanation for why women have become more violent toward their
intimate partners than men are:

> *For [females], it was not an irrational choice to hit when*
> *they were angry because they knew they probably would*
> *not...get arrested. Men, on the other hand...were likely*
> *to...be arrested. Under a rational-choice model, men would*
> *have good reason to control their anger.*[606]

> *[W]omen know that...their partners...[are] unlikely to*
> *call for help, and the police are unlikely to intervene. Thus,*
> *there is little to deter an angry young woman from hitting*
> *her partner. As such, women of all sorts may be apt to hit*
> *their partners, not just women whose judgment is clouded*
> *by stress, mental illness, or intoxication.*[607]

The empirical evidence tends to support this conclusion. Simply
put, the extreme measures that have been taken in our society to
curb male violence against women are having their intended effect:
they are deterring men from beating up women. Because violence

is always framed as "a male phenomenon," however, there has been no corresponding deterrent of female violence against men. [608] Furthermore, the perception that only male violence is bad naturally leads to the perception that female violence is not a bad thing. Since the opposite of "bad" is "good," people are prone to interpret the statement that "violence by women against men is not a bad thing" as roughly equivalent to the statement, "Violence by women against men is a good thing." People with a firm understanding of the finer points of linguistics might see the difference, but a member of a generation that grew up watching several hours of television per day probably would not..

We are living in a society that encourages people to believe that violence against women is bad, while violence against men is good.

By defining violence as a "male phenomenon" and refusing to acknowledge the existence of female violence, by insisting that anytime a woman acts violently it must be in self-defense, women's advocates have succeeded in convincing an entire generation that violence by a man against a woman is always bad, while violence by a woman against a man is always good.

An Australian researcher presented a hypothetical scenario to mixed groups of men and women. The scenario involved either a husband or a wife perpetrating domestic violence against his or her spouse, under identical circumstances. It was found that participants were significantly more negative in their evaluation of the husband than the wife, were angry at the husband but sympathetic to the wife, and believed that the husband deserved a harsher penalty for his behavior than the wife did--even though they had both perpetrated the very same crime under exactly the same circumstances.[609]

In a 1994 poll conducted jointly by the Minneapolis *Star Tribune* and WCCO Television, it was found that people are 6 times more likely to condone the use of violence by a woman against a man than the use of violence by a man against a woman under the exact same circumstances. Almost 100% of those surveyed said a man is absolutely never justified in hitting a woman, while a substantial number of both men and women (in fact, more men than women!) said they believed it is a good thing for women to abuse men as a way of getting the upper hand in a relationship.[610]

In experimental studies, it has been found that both men and women exhibit greater readiness and willingness to inflict pain on men than on women, under otherwise identical conditions.[611]

According to a survey conducted by the U.S. Department of Justice, Americans rank stabbing one's wife to death as a substantially more serious crime than stabbing one's husband to death--nearly twice as serious, in fact. Indeed, the Survey found that *Americans regard stabbing one's husband to death as a less serious crime than selling marijuana!*[612]

Anyone who is really concerned about helping battered women should also be working to end violence against men, not promoting it.

So who cares if men are victimized? Battered women and those who care about them should. Because violence is a learned phenomenon, violence *against* men begets violence *by* men. If for no other reason than this, a person who is truly concerned about violence *by* men is eventually going to have to acknowledge the need to do something about violence *against* men.[613]

The American tradition of abusing children must stop.

Violence against men in our society begins on the day they are born. Almost immediately upon entry into this world, most American males are subjected to a primitive scarification ritual politely referred to as *circumcision*. Genital mutilation of male babies is usually rationalized as a prophylactic health measure, but this hypothesis isn't borne out by the facts. If the reason for removing the male's foreskin is to prevent the accumulation of smegma, as is usually claimed, then we should also be removing the clitoral hood of female babies.[614] We don't. Instead, we enact laws specifically prohibiting that sort of thing.[615] The performance of circumcisions on dead male infants--a practice which, though rare, occurs with more frequency in this country than any form of female genital mutilation ever has--also belies the "health" theory. A dead baby's health cannot be improved by cutting off a piece of his penis. In view of the growing evidence of a causal relationship between circumcision and subsequent male violence, the adamant refusal of legislators to acknowledge that cutting into a baby's penis with a knife for purely cultural or religious reasons is genital mutilation is difficult to understand.[616]

Circumcision, however, is just the beginning. While they are growing up, male children are subjected to even more violence--an incredibly enormous amount of violence, in fact. As we have seen, the research data clearly show that most of this violence comes from mothers.

As long as we cling to the need to believe that mothers are sacred and can do no wrong, as long as we deny the truth that mothers are capable of hurting their children, we really have no right to object to the pervasiveness of violence in our society. If, by our examples, we teach our children that problems can be solved by beating up those who are weaker and more vulnerable than we are, then we have no right to complain if, as adults, our children believe that problems can be solved by beating up those who are weaker and more vulnerable than they are.[617] As Lynn Cothern, of the U.S. Coordinating Council on Juvenile Justice and Delinquency Prevention has expressed it:

> *Public investment in early intervention programs for children at risk of abuse,...and positive involvement with caring adults will go a long way toward eliminating violent crimes....*[618]

The true causes and correlates of domestic violence need to be acknowledged.

Too many women's advocates and researchers (and advocate-researchers) are so concerned about vindicating a pet theory about patriarchy or "male privilege" that they either cannot see or adamantly refuse to see any other factors that may be contributing to the problem.[619] But a bruised, battered or dead woman (or child or man, for that matter) is too high a price for our society to keep paying for such blind devotion to a creed.

Those involved in the treatment of offenders need to honestly and openly acknowledge that not all batterers are alike; that "patriarchy" and "male privilege" usually have very little to do with it; and that things like low self-esteem,[620] dependence,[621] poverty,[622] unemployment,[623] lack of education,[624] alcoholism,[625] drug abuse,[626] mental illness,[627] stress,[628] biological and neurological factors,[629] cohabitation at an early age,[630] parentage at an early age;[631] parental rejection, abusive childhood[632] weak parent-child attachment,[633] tolerance of corporal punishment (a.k.a. child abuse),[634] marital dissatisfaction,[635] and yes, even female violence,[636] do in fact have a lot to do with male violence.[637] Unless these issues are addressed honestly and objectively, the real causes of violence will never be treated.

For the same reason, adamantly denying that women ever initiate violence, and insisting that all female violence is in self-defense, accomplishes about as much toward teaching a violent man how to deal with conflict as sticking one's head in the sand helps one avoid being trampled by a stampede of elephants.

Treatment programs should be for treatment, not the proliferation of ideology.

For many years, the content of domestic abuse treatment programs has been controlled by women's advocates--either directly, or indirectly through research and development funded by feminist organizations. As a result, screeds about the gender inequities in society that women suffer pervade these programs. Studies have shown, however, that assaulting and shaming men with broad feminist accusations and negative generalizations and stereotypes about men not only is ineffective as a means of changing behavior, but it is actually counter-productive. The approach can actually incite a man who is already prone to violence to commit further acts of violence. Perhaps it is time to consider the possibility that persons with a zealous dedication to a singular point of view should not be treating or conducting research on the treatment of men who batter. As long as these "treaters" insist on causing men to stray from the paths they need to follow toward true recovery, they are only helping to perpetuate and exacerbate the problem of violence against women.[638]

The traditional approach to domestic violence always begins by insisting that participants accept that violence is "a male phenomenon." In other words, in order to complete a domestic abuse program, a man must begin by agreeing to believe a lie. Why is this always the first step in treatment programs? Evidently, the belief is that change can be effected through shame; in this case, gender shame. By making a man feel ashamed of himself for being a member of the gender that uses violence to control and subjugate other people, the theory goes, it will be easier to persuade him to accept the feminine ideal. To many women's advocates, the feminine ideal involves the assumption by men of a position of servitude and subservience to women. Hence, the Marriage Relationship Counseling Center's conclusion that men who are battered essentially had it coming to them because they failed to change their personalities to fit their wives' needs. Changing one's personality to meet someone else's needs may work for a while, but human nature is such that eventually it will demand respect for its own dignity. A man may become a nice little "Stuart Smalley" for a while, but the effect will wear off eventually.

Psychiatrist James Gilligan has observed that "[s]hame in the absence of guilt stimulates anger and a desire to destroy people or force their respect...."[639] Lectures and teaching materials designed to "correct" the supposed male perception that his position of "superiority" in society gives him a "male privilege" to use violence to control women may temporarily shame him into stopping his violent behavior, but in the long run they will only serve to make him more angry and more violent.

The reason that abusive men are likely to feel shame without guilt as a result of treatment programs that are based on feminist theories about patriarchy is that most men who are violent are not in fact using some sort of "male privilege" for the purpose of controlling a woman. To the contrary, studies have found that the desire for control over one's *own* life is a much more significant predictor of violent behavior than the desire for control over one's partner is. That is to say, if "privilege" has anything to do with it, then male violence has more to do with the "female privilege" to control men's lives than it does with any supposed "male privilege" to control women's lives. To put it bluntly, shaming a man for trying to control his wife's life, when in fact it is the wife who is controlling the man's life, won't change his ways; at most, it will only cause him to become even more frustrated and angry. Any domestic abuse "treater" who insists that a man believe things which the man knows from his own personal experience are not true is diminishing his or her own credibility and, therefore, the effectiveness of the entire "treatment" program.

Perhaps the single most important thing that women's advocates and man-treaters refuse to "get" is that men who abuse usually do not do it because they are powerful; they do it because they feel *powerless*.[640] It is well-known that men are more likely to become depressed, self-medicate by consuming alcohol and drugs, commit acts of violence (domestic or otherwise), and commit suicide following the break-up of a relationship than women are. All of these things are evidence that *men, on the whole, are more dependent on women than women are on men.*[641] That is to say, men are generally weaker--emotionally, at least--than women, because they are more likely than women to believe that they are of no intrinsic value in and of themselves; they measure their worth in terms of their value to someone else. Just as lack of self-esteem makes a woman feel powerless, so lack of self-esteem makes a man feel powerless. To compensate for these feelings of powerlessness, some men may resort to physical violence.[642]

That is why it is ironic, and entirely counterproductive, that while women's advocates, researchers, educators and legislators are busily developing programs to enhance girls' and women's self-esteem and make them more independent, coercion and shame are the only things on the menu for boys and men.[643] Programs that focus on the goal of improving women's and girl's self-esteem, while doing nothing but tearing down men's and boys', are misguided, not to mention more than a little mean-spirited.[644] By exacerbating men's and boys' emotional and psychological dependence on women, intensifying their feelings of powerlessness, and increasing the experience of shame without guilt, those who shape these policies are actually cooking up a recipe for an eventual *increase* in violence on the part of men. They therefore share part of the blame for the perpetuation of male violence in our society.[645]

Don't get me wrong. Programs designed to foster independence and build self-esteem among girls and women are laudable. We need them. All I am saying is that it is a serious mistake to fail to foster and build these same qualities in boys and men. Maybe it isn't politically correct to think of males as victims of low self-esteem and dependent personalities; maybe it serves our supremacist inclinations better to express nothing but condemnation and focus exclusively on retribution whenever the male gender is involved; maybe allowing even a sliver of sympathy to show through for any person of the male gender leaves an unpalatable taste in our mouths; nevertheless, it is something that we are simply going to have to start to do if we are really serious about reducing male violence and rage. As Dr. Gilligan has put it:

> *Many [violent men] desperately want to feel that they are big, tough, independent, self-assertive, self-reliant men, so as not to feel needy, helpless, frightened, inadequate, unskilled, incompetent and often illiterate. It is essential that we understand this psychology. For we will never understand violence and violent criminals until we see through what is, in truth, a defensive disguise; and until we understand violence, we cannot prevent it.*[646]

Teach peace, not war.

The statement that "violence is a male phenomenon" is essentially war propaganda. It is propaganda because it is something that is stated and repeated over and over again for the sole purpose of getting people to believe it, irrespective of the fact that it is not true. It is war propaganda because its purpose is to incite outrage against a person or class of persons who have been identified as "the enemy."

Feminists speak of an undeclared war against women. I don't believe there is any war against women, declared or otherwise. Maybe some men are at war with women, but I do not believe that most men are. It is clear, however, that there is currently a declared war against men in this country. I'm not going to give female supremacists the benefit of republishing here all the vicious slanders and attacks that have been hurled at men for the past thirty years. I'll just say that I know they exist, and I believe that anyone who is honest with himself or herself (assuming he or she has been living in America for any length of time) knows they exist, too.[647]

.   Attorney General Daniel E. Lungren's Policy Council on Violence Prevention's "Vision of Hope"[648] is a classic example of war propaganda. After defining violence as "a male phenomenon" and covering up the existence of violence against men by women, the Council then has the *chutzpah* to chastise *the media* for portraying women as victims! Only two paragraphs after complaining about media stereotyping of males as aggressors and females as victims, the very same Report goes on to opine that males are more violent than females because males play video games and females do not.[649]   Later, the same report declares that "Acceptance and respect for all people should be instilled...*by countering stereotypes and cultural misconceptions in every possible context.*"[650] (emphasis added.) It reiterates the party-line that "schools and youth-serving organizations should expand programs that build independence, self-esteem and leadership skills among young women and girls," while directing them to teach boys and men to be nonviolent--as if fostering self-esteem and independence has nothing to do with teaching boys and men to be nonviolent![651] Like every other publicly-funded report on domestic abuse policy, it urges the government to become even more involved in helping women leave abusive men, without urging any corresponding governmental involvement in helping men deal with abusive women.[652] And what is perhaps most telling of all, it talks about "increasing reports of...men assaulting women," at a time when both the scientific research and incident-based statistics were clearly showing that the incidence of male violence against women had been steadily decreasing for years.[653]   In fact, the only thing that was increasing at the time the Policy Council's findings and recommendations were being formulated was the *incidence of violence by women against men.* No mention of that well-documented fact can be found anywhere in the report. Why? Because it its intent was not to address the problem of domestic violence; its purpose was to proliferate more propaganda in the joint feminist and governmental war against men.

It has been observed that:

> *Females and the elderly generally express a greater fear of crime than do people in groups who face a much greater risk. The Reactions to Crime project found that such impressions are related to the content of information about crime. Such information tends to emphasize stories about...female victims. These stories may influence women and the elderly in judging the seriousness of their own conditions....This behavior would account...for their high levels of fear and their low levels of victimization.*[654]

Whether intentionally or not, those who proliferate false propaganda about supposedly soaring rates of violence against women are not only inciting violence against men; they are needlessly causing a lot of women to live their lives in desperation and fear. Why are they doing this? The desire to assure a steady stream of public funding for the promotion of female supremacist ideology is obviously a major part of it. Another part of it may simply be the desire to play the role of knight in shining armor. Protecting and saving defenseless women makes men and some women feel good about themselves. Unfortunately, these "knights in shining armor" are just about the only people who really benefit from any of this. Lesbian victims are marginalized because they do not fit the "patriarchy" theory of violence; male victims are marginalized for the same reason; and those women who really are victims of male batterers continue to be battered because resources that could be used to effect real changes in batterer behavior are being diverted instead to the cause of proliferating feminist propaganda in the ongoing war against men.

Domestic violence is a *human* phenomenon.

When the Violence Against Women Act was under consideration in Congress, men were not permitted to testify.[655]

It was not the first time Congress had taken a step like this. In the early nineteenth century, Congress forbade Quakers from testifying in favor of the abolition of slavery.

Why do people try to suppress the expression of alternative points of view? There is nothing to fear from a mistaken point of view. One can deal with it simply by countering it with the truth. Alternative points of view are not prohibited out of fear of falsity; they are prohibited out of fear of the truth. Congress deliberately turned a deaf ear to male victims because it had more important matters at hand to deal with than the truth.

Of course, special legislation exclusively for the protection of women is not without precedent. Occupational safety and health laws were originally enacted only for the protection of female workers; male workers were specifically excluded from those protections.[656] Still, the fact that "equal protection" has been interpreted in the past to mean "some are more equal than others" should not have been taken to mean that "equal" must *always* be interpreted to mean unequal.

Moreover, the argument that special laws are appropriate because most victims (supposedly) are female does not even make sense. Assuming, for the moment, that there are fewer male than female victims of violence, how does this justify a refusal to protect those males who are victims? The only way to justify that conclusion is by adhering to the premise that people are not entitled to legal protections if they belong to a minority group. Yet, the fact that a person is a member of a minority group is not normally regarded as a good justification for denying her the equal protection of the laws. To the contrary, in American law, being a member of a minority group is usually regarded as a justification for *greater* legal protections, not fewer.

Some people argue that violence against women is a "more serious" problem than violence against men. Shelter employees demonstrate this belief when their response upon hearing a male voice on a telephone help-line asking for help is to tell the man to get off the line in case a "real" victim (i.e., a *female* victim) might be trying to get through.

Some people say violence against a woman is a more serious problem because women are more likely than men to feel "locked into" a marriage or an intimate relationship. Yet, the vast majority of divorce petitions in the United States are initiated by the wife, not the husband. Overall, it is men who most often seem to feel compelled to cling to relationships; women seem to have comparatively fewer inhibitions about leaving their marriages or other intimate relationships.

When it was the norm for women to stay home and depend entirely on men for their financial support, the notion that women had fewer alternatives than men made some sense. Today, however, most women work and earn incomes rather than staying at home and relying on men for financial support. In many areas of the United States, there are actually more women in the workforce than men.

It is also important to remember that when a man leaves a relationship, he is more likely to be held responsible for alimony and child support than a woman is. In this sense, he may be regarded as being economically dependent on *the marriage* even if he is not otherwise financially dependent on his wife.[657]

In interviews with abused men, researchers have found that men are at least as likely as women to feel "locked into" a marriage or intimate relationship. A common reason cited by these men is that they believe that if they leave the relationship they will lose contact with the children.[658] This is not an unreasonable belief. Until recently, the law of custody expressly recognized the maternal preference doctrine, a rule of law according to which custody must always be awarded to the mother unless she is shown to be completely unfit to be a parent. As a result, custody was awarded to fathers only about 5% of the time.[659]

The maternal preference doctrine has recently been replaced, in most states, with the "best interests of the child" standard, under which custody is supposed to be awarded according to what is in the child's best interests, not on the basis of the parent's gender.

Although courts can no longer expressly rely on the maternal preference doctrine, it is clear from the decisions they issue that they are still heavily influenced by it. Although one often comes across a reference to a gender-biased task force report that supposedly has "found" that men are awarded custody "70%" of the time, the latest U.S. Census Bureau figures show that in reality fathers have custody of only 5% of the children of divorced or separated parents in the United States.[660] In an extensive study of custody decisions nationwide, researchers Maccoby and Mnookin found that fathers are awarded sole physical custody 9% of the time. Among cases that were resolved through mediation, sole custody went to the father 6% of the time, and in cases in which a custody evaluation or trial was conducted, sole custody went to fathers about 11% of the time.[661] Men who are relegated to the position of "visitor" in their children's lives may also reasonably fear losing even this modest level of contact with their children, since studies have shown that custodial mothers are more likely to interfere with visitation rights than custodial fathers are.[662]

Then there are those who maintain that domestic abuse is worse for women because it is more frightening for women than it is for men. Could it be that bombarding women with exaggerated figures and fabricated statistics designed to make it appear as if every man in the country is hell-bent on dominating and controlling women by brute physical force might also be frightening women?

Perhaps more to the point, is it really wise public policy to discriminate against an entire class of victims of violence (men) simply because they have been socialized almost from the day they were born to conceal their fears?

Unfortunately, the prospects for change at this time appear to be dismal, at best. In view of the nature of the recommended agenda for domestic abuse education in law schools that the American Bar Association recently published, it looks like the next generation of lawyers and judges is going to be trained to be at least as prejudiced as the current one is. The ABA treatise adopts the traditional sexist approach of first insisting that everyone believe the lie that domestic violence is "a male phenomenon." Despite special sections addressing the unique problems encountered by specific categories of victims (elderly women, black women, Latina women, gays, lesbians, etc.) nowhere at all does it acknowledge or address the kinds of problems males are likely to encounter in the legal system when they have been victims of abuse at the hands of a female. Given the otherwise extensive detail and breadth of the treatise, it is impossible to believe that this omission was merely a careless oversight. The conclusion is inescapable that a significant purpose of this project was to ensure that male victims of female violence will continue to be invisible to succeeding generations of attorneys, judges and lawmakers; that is, that they will continue to be re-victimized by the legal system in the future just as they are being victimized by the legal system right now.[663]

There is no indication that this agenda will not be adopted in more and more law schools as time goes on. If that happens, then it will likely take years--maybe decades--to undo the damage.

Does any of this mean we should just resign ourselves to the fact that males are forever going to be abused with impunity in this country? Not at all. It simply means that we will need to strengthen our resolve to stop it. We will just need to think of it as something which, although perhaps not achievable in our lifetimes, may be achievable in the lives of our children, and if not in theirs, then in those of our children's children.

Appendix. Methodological Issues: Archival Data vs. Scientific Research

Archival vs. Survey Data

Archival data means information that can be obtained by reviewing records kept by organizations and governmental entities in the ordinary course of their business or operations. With reference to domestic violence, *archival data* includes such things as law enforcement records; court records; emergency room records; and information obtained from battered women's shelters. The reliability of archival data is a function of the sample size, the randomness of the sample selected, the manner in which the inquiry is formulated and communicated, the absence of factors that may affect reporting, and the manner in which information from records is communicated and interpreted.

Survey data is information obtained by soliciting information from a sample population. Like archival data, the reliability of survey data depends on the size and randomness of the sample selected; it also depends on the kinds of questions asked and the manner in which they are asked.

It has been pointed out that the utility of archival data is inherently more limited than that of survey data because the samples from which archival data are obtained are never randomly selected. Data from battered women's shelters, for example, by definition exclude one-half of the population (males) right from the start. Similarly, data from medical facilities will mostly involve people who have not been socialized to suppress their pain, to "take it like a man." Law enforcement records will exclude data about male victims for this reason, too--as well as for a host of other reasons discussed at more length in Chapter 9.

These kinds of considerations are what led Lenore Walker, in her treatise on battered women, to state that archival data cannot be considered a legitimate database from which to make generalizations about domestic violence.[664] For that, survey information obtained from random samples of the population at large is needed.

The Conflict Tactics Scale ("CTS")

The *Conflict Tactics Scale* is a survey-based measure of domestic violence that was originally developed by Murray Straus over twenty years ago. It has been revised several times since in the intervening years since then. The measure assesses how parents react in conflicts with their children, as well as how people react in conflicts with their partners.

Criticisms of the Conflict Tactics Scale ("CTS")

Context and Meaning. The CTS has been criticized on the grounds that it only measures the incidence and severity of violent acts, not the causes or motivations behind the acts.[665] Criticisms of this kind usually cite as examples the woman who "playfully" punches her husband or "jokingly" kicks her husband in the groin without really meaning any harm by it, the premise being that not all violence is equally motivated by malice. This shortcoming is kind of a strange criticism to hear from the mouths of those who would urge reliance on archival data instead, since archival data are also simple tabulations of acts (and alleged acts) that do not usually entail the making of fine distinctions along motivational or contextual lines.

It is true that surveys employing the CTS are not always accompanied by psychoanalysis of the survey participants to ascertain the true motivations for and significance of each of their violent acts. Still, there are reasons why it can be expected that CTS-based survey data would be more reliable than archival data in this respect. Most of the items that the survey classifies as "severe" are by their very nature not likely to be things that are done in jest. It would be hard to imagine how stabbing someone with a knife, or shooting a gun at someone, or slamming someone against a wall, or beating someone up, could ever be regarded as "playful" acts. By distinguishing these kinds of acts from "mild" acts, such as pushing and shoving, the CTS gives us a better approximation concerning malicious intention than a record of a conviction for battery does. "Battery" is legally defined in such a way that it can include everything from tickling a person with a feather to beating a person senseless with a baseball bat. Thus, simply by building in measures of severity, the CTS provides a much more accurate estimate of malicious intention than archival data does.

It should also be noted that although the CTS does not delve deeply into the underlying causes of violence, other studies have been specifically designed for this purpose. For example, Fiebert and Gonzales[666] have specifically studied the motivations underlying female violence as measured by the CTS scales. They found that female violence is motivated by the same kinds of things that motivate male violence--jealousy, control, etc. Other researchers have reached the same conclusion.[667]

Self-Defense. Critics of the CTS sometimes contend that it doesn't provide accurate information about domestic violence because it only tells about the number of acts of domestic violence, without distinguishing which of these acts were committed in self-defense and which were committed with malicious intent.

This criticism could just as easily be made about the archival data, too. Law enforcement records also only tell about the number of reports of violence, not motives. Indeed, one of the primary criticisms of the data showing that the rate of arrests of women for domestic violence is catching up to the rate of arrests of men is the fact that arrest data do not necessarily reflect which of the two parties was "the primary aggressor" and which one was acting in self-defense. This is why women's advocates have secured the passage of legislation in some states (and are lobbying for similar legislation in other states) requiring police to make detailed findings concerning which party to a mutually combative domestic dispute is "the primary aggressor" before they may take the female combatant into custody.

Data obtained from emergency room records are also subject to this criticism. Findings about domestic violence that are based on emergency room records tally the number of patients who respond positively to what is essentially a survey-type of question: "Have you ever been a victim of domestic violence?"[668] This is the same type of question that the CTS asks. Neither question can tell us for certain whether the subject was acting in self-defense or with malice aforethought.

Information from battered women's shelters also does not provide reliable information about self-defense. Battered women's shelter services are usually provided only to women, not men, so one-half of the population is selectively excluded right from the start. In addition, battered women's shelters can only provide information about one small subcategory of abuse victims--women who are victims of life-threatening abuse. Even the archival data shows that the vast majority of domestic abuse is not life-threatening. Women seeking shelter in a battered women's shelter comprise the one category of victims that is most likely either to have been victims of lethal (or threatened lethal) violence--and therefore most likely to have been acting in self-defense if they themselves were violent, or to have a motive to claim self-defense in order to qualify for services. In short, it is impossible to draw any meaningful conclusions about domestic violence from information obtained from battered women's shelters.

Actually, the best source of information that is available, so far, about whether or not particular acts of domestic violence were perpetrated in self-defense comes from CTS-based research. It is probably true that the earliest versions of the CTS did not contain adequate measures for determining whether violence was perpetrated in self-defense or not. The CTS was subsequently revised, however, in ways that provide more information about the extent to which self-defense may have been involved.

Contrary to popular belief, a considerable amount of research has been conducted into the motives for domestic violence. The research goes well beyond simply tabulating the number of acts of violence committed by members of each gender. Research studies that have tested and disproved the hypothesis that female violence is always in self-defense are set out in Chapter 3 and include, among others: Billingham and Sack, *supra*; Bland and Orne, *supra*; Bookwala, *supra*; DeMaris, *supra*; Fiebert and Gonzales, *supra*;

Gonzales, *supra*; Mann, *supra*; Mason and Blankenship, *supra*; McCarthy, *supra*; McKeowan, *supra*; Morse, *supra*; O'Keefe, Brockopp and Chew, *supra*; Sommer (1994), *supra*; Sorenson and Telles, *supra*; Stets and Pirog-Good, *supra*; Stets and Straus, *supra*; Straus (1996), *supra*; Tyree and Malone, *supra*; and the National Youth Survey, *supra*. Some researchers, such as Sommer (1994), *supra*, have found that in domestic violence cases, it is actually men who are most likely to be acting in self-defense when they are violent toward a member of the opposite sex.

Chronicity. One of the most oft-repeated criticisms of the CTS is that it only tallies up the number of acts, without distinguishing between "occasional" perpetrators and "repetitive" perpetrators. This may have been true of the earliest version of the CTS, but for several years now the CTS has contained a variable that specifically tests for chronicity.[669]

Severity/Injury. Critics of the CTS sometimes claim that it only tabulates the number of violent acts, without telling anything about how severe or injurious the acts were. Again, this criticism could also be made about law enforcement and court records. Law enforcement and court records are rife with records of men who were reported for "abuse" for things like slamming a door in anger, or taking a woman's keys from her hand to prevent her from driving drunk.[670] In one documented case, an overzealous child protection caseworker who observed a man in a restaurant open his arms to invite a hug from his six-year-old daughter pursued charges of child sexual abuse against him on this basis alone.[671]

The claim that the CTS does not distinguish between the number of acts committed and their relative severity is completely unfounded. The CTS, both as originally constructed and as subsequently revised, has always measured both the incidence *and* the severity of violence. In addition, Dr. Straus has always taken these kinds of criticisms to heart and has made revisions to the CTS from time to time, in an effort to improve its efficiency for distinguishing between mild and severe forms of violence. For example, after receiving criticisms of the CTS on the grounds that "throwing something" doesn't distinguish between throwing something relatively harmless (such as a pillow) and throwing something that could be more dangerous when thrown (such as a glass or a plate), Dr. Straus revised this particular item, so that it would instead ask respondents to tell whether they or their partner had "thrown something *that could hurt.*" (emphasis added.) The revised CTS includes even more specific measures of the kinds of injuries that have resulted from the specific acts of violence about which the survey asks.[672]

Research studies that have specifically tested for and confirmed the severity of female violence include, among others: Arias, Samios and O'Leary, *supra*; Brinherhoff and Lupri, *supra*; George, *supra* (1999); Greenfeld, *supra*; Headey, Scott and De Vaus, *supra*; Kalmuss, *supra*; Langhinrichsen-Rohling and Vivian (1994), *supra*; Magdol, et. al., *supra*; McKeowan, *supra*; McLeod, *supra*; McNeely and Mann, *supra*; Russell and Hulson, *supra*; Rollins and Oheneba-Sakyi, *supra*; Rouse, *supra*; Stets and Henderson, *supra*; Steinmetz (1981), *supra*; Straus (1996), *supra*; Straus and Gelles (1986), *supra*; Straus and Gelles (1990), *supra*; *and* Vivian and Langhinrichsen-Rohling (1996), *supra*. The National Crime Victimization Survey (1994) also reached a similar conclusion.

Choking. Several writers have criticized the CTS on the grounds that it supposedly fails to measure the incidence and frequency of choking.[673] Perhaps these critics are confusing the CTS with the All-Alberta study.[674] The All-Alberta study did not include choking. Then again, the All-Alberta study also did not include wife-against-husband assaults as a possible category of violence, either![675] The CTS included choking, as have most studies that have concluded that male and female rates of violence are similar (including the National Family Violence Survey), long before the 1996 expansion of the CTS.[676] The CTS still includes choking. Appropriately, the CTS not only includes choking, but has always classified it as a "severe" form of violence.[677]

Scratching. Given that scratching is a behavior more often engaged in by women than men, its supposed omission from the CTS seems an odd complaint to hear from those whose ultimate mission is to discredit CTS-based findings that women are as violent as men. Yet, the same people who criticize the CTS because it supposedly omits choking also criticize it for failing to include scratching.[678] According to Vera Mouradian, Ph.D., of the National Violence Against Women Prevention Research Center at Wellesley

College for Women, however, studies using the CTS and other instruments have, in fact, measured scratching[679] as a specific form of domestic violence.

Moreover, even if "scratching" isn't specifically mentioned in a CTS-based survey, questions 11 and 12 of the CTS2 specifically ask whether the respondent ever received or inflicted even a small cut because of a fight with an intimate partner.[680] A "small cut" strikes me as being pretty much the same thing as a "scratch."

Rape and Sexual Assault. The original version of the CTS covered only physical, verbal and emotional abuse. Consequently, it was sharply criticized for failing to specifically include measures of rape and sexual assault.[681]

Given that the CTS was originally constructed thirty years ago, the omission of this category of violence is understandable. Historically, rape was a crime that was defined in such a way that it was only possible for a man to commit it, and the only victims of this crime could be female. This is because one of the essential elements was *penetration of the female sexual organ by the male sexual organ.* Therefore, any survey that included "rape" as a form of domestic abuse would necessarily find that 100% of the perpetrators are male and 100% of the victims are female--not because men are more violent than women, but because male sexual organs are constructed in such a way that they can be used to penetrate, while female sexual organs are designed in such a way that they cannot be used to penetrate. We don't need a survey to tell us that a penis is more likely to penetrate something than a vagina is. Such data would tell us only about anti-male gender biases in the definitions of crimes, not about the relative propensities of each gender for violence.

Between the time the CTS was originally constructed and its subsequent revision, the legal definition of rape was broadened and new categories of sex crimes were created that did not necessarily require the penetration of a vagina by a penis. After the concept of sexual assault was thus expanded, the CTS was revised to include measures of sexual assault, defining the term in this broader sense.[682]

For the past several years, the CTS has included measures of sexual assault and has classified such an assault as a "severe" form of violence. This is as it should be. The CTS should classify an assault on one's sexual organs as a more "severe" form of violence than things like slapping, pushing, shoving, or calling someone a name. There should be no question but that inserting something (whether it's a penis, a physical object, or something else) into another person's vagina or anus against that person's will should be classified as a "severe" form of violence. By the same token, kicking, hitting, yanking or cutting a man's penis or testicles should also be considered "severe" forms of sexual abuse. For reasons having only to do with a deeply-rooted tradition of gender bias, however, the latter acts are normally classified--both in the law and in social science research--as "physical," not "sexual" assaults.[683] As a result, the CTS classifies assaults on male sexual organs as sometimes "mild" and sometimes "severe," whereas *all* assaults on (or "unwanted" contacts with) female sexual organs are automatically classified as "severe." In this respect, the CTS, as it is currently constructed, is actually gender-biased in favor of women, not men.

The current version of the CTS measures behavior that is intended to cause one's partner to engage in unwanted sexual activity and covers three ranges of coercion: force, threats of force and verbal insistence. Thus, the revised CTS adopts the broad feminist definition of sexual coercion, under which "verbal insistence" resulting in sexual activity is considered a form of sexual assault, even though neither force, threat nor even an implied threat is employed. Even worse, the revised CTS specifically adopts the same gender-biased definition of sexual abuse that is employed by the Violence Against Women Grants Office, a definition that is couched in terms of violative penetrations of a vagina, anus or mouth, while omitting violent assaults upon penises and testicles.[684] The incorporation of the broad feminist definition of sexual abuse, while at the same time defining terms in a manner that arbitrarily excludes a significant category of male victims, can be expected to make it appear that the ratio of female-to-male victims of sexual abuse is far higher than is actually the case.

Despite the obvious anti-male gender bias in the current version of the CTS, it is important to keep the actual incidence of sexual abuse in perspective. Non-CTS studies on the incidence of sexual abuse show that it occurs with far less frequency than other forms of physical abuse. The most reliable survey data show that less than 1/10th of 1 percent of women are victims of rape, attempted rape, or some other form of sexual assault. If archival data is used, the figure would be 1/20th of 1 percent.[685] If, as the survey data, the National Organization for Women, the Violence Against Women Office and hundreds of other organizations claim, more than 3 million women are victims of domestic abuse each year--or if between 5% and 100% of all women are victims of domestic abuse[686]--yet less than 1/10th of 1% of all women are victims of sexual abuse, then mathematically it necessarily follows that sexual abuse must be involved in only an extremely tiny fraction of all domestic abuse.[687]

None of this is meant to trivialize the experience of rape, attempted rape or sexual assault. These are serious offenses, and those who commit them should be severely punished. Nor is it my intention to imply that domestic violence never involves sexual abuse. It most certainly can. My point is only that it does not happen anywhere near as frequently as other forms of domestic abuse do. As was noted in Chapter 1, the data show that the higher rates at which men are victimized relative to women do not change that much even when rape and sexual assaults are factored into the computations.

Murder. Critics have also complained that the CTS does not provide information about murder.[688] Of course the CTS does not provide information about murder. It's a survey. Dead people tell no tales; they also don't respond to surveys. This is why murder is the one type of violence that has to be measured by archival data, not survey data.

Having said that, it nevertheless should be noted that although the CTS does not specifically measure homicides, it does measure the propensity to use lethal forms of violence (shooting, stabbing and choking, for example.)

Stalking. Several writers have criticized the CTS for its omission of questions about stalking.[689] In defense of the CTS, it has been pointed out that some of the behaviors classified as "emotional abuse" may qualify as "stalking" behaviors as well.[690] Be that as it may, however, there are sound reasons for excluding data about stalking from the CTS.

The CTS is designed to measure violence between people who are currently involved in a relationship with each other. Inasmuch as stalking normally does not occur while a couple is together, and inasmuch as it is not necessarily an act that involves intimate partners,[691] it doesn't make much sense to include it in a study that is only designed to analyze the tactics that people who are involved in an intimate relationship use to deal with conflicts.

There are also significant definitional problems. In some states, simply existing in a public place with knowledge that one's presence there may be "unwanted" or "annoying" to another person who is also existing either in the same public place or in close proximity to the same public place where the first person is existing can make one guilty of "stalking." Some states include the exercise of First Amendment rights within the definition of "stalking" if done in a residential neighborhood with knowledge that at least one of the residents disagrees with one's point of view ("residential picketing.") Harmon, Rosner and Owens also adopt a broad definition of stalking, according to which anytime one commits two acts of *any* kind that are "unwanted" and "annoying" to another person, one is guilty of "stalking."[692] Under this definition, a man who, seeing an attractive woman sitting at a bar, sits next to her (1st act) and then asks her, "Do you come here often?" (2nd act) would be guilty of "stalking" if the woman doesn't happen to find him attractive, but would not be guilty of "stalking" if the woman did happen to find him attractive. Perhaps I'm missing something, but this just doesn't comport with my intuitive sense of what is meant by "domestic violence."

Following a person is also a form of stalking. Yet, is "following a person" really a conflict tactic? Perhaps in some cases it is. In many cases, however, people have entirely different reasons for following other people. Often, it is misguided courtship behavior (e.g., the women who have stalked members of pop groups such as the Beatles, or television personalities like David Letterman, and other wealthy and/or famous men.) In some cases, a person may follow another person to obtain information, not to harass, annoy or intimidate the person. Sometimes people follow other people simply for reasons of courtesy, as where one person follows another into a store or a theater rather than pushing ahead of him.

Moreover, since stalking is defined in terms of the subjective reaction to one's presence rather than the inherent dangerousness of the defendant's act, and since not all states require any proof of a specific intent to harass or frighten, it is essentially a strict liability, subjective thought-crime. In many states, being alive is the only overt physical act that is essential for a conviction.[693] A person may have a genuine interest in taking part in a public event, even though he knows that there's a chance he might run into someone who would prefer not to see him there. In some states, he may be guilty of "stalking" if he nevertheless decides to attend the event.

For all of these reasons, this particular kind of "violence" would be exceedingly difficult to measure by means of a survey. "How many times have you existed?" Would not provide a researcher with much useful information. Yet, "How many times has somebody felt fear as a result of seeing you or knowing that you were close by?" is not the kind of question for which we can expect to get a reliable answer, since most human beings are not telepathic.

Actually, some efforts have already been made to measure the prevalence of "stalking." What survey data there is on stalking wouldn't necessarily change the results of studies that are based on the CTS, though. For example, although some studies have shown a somewhat higher rate of stalking victimizations for women, surveys conducted by organizations that are not committed to the principle of gender-based discrimination,[694] such as the Statistics Profiles published by Statistics Canada each year, show that men and women are about equally likely to be victims of stalking.[695]

Reliability. As was discussed at some length in Chapter 11, the problem of over-reporting and under-reporting is a significant shortcoming of archival data, and the actual incidence of female violence against males could well be 9 times greater than what the archival data appears to indicate. Critics of the CTS have raised the same kind of complaint about findings based on CTS surveys, arguing that some people might deliberately lie, or might experience memory problems, when they take the survey, which could result in either over-reporting or under-reporting on the part of survey participants.[696]

Unfortunately, the problems of lying and mental incapacity are inherent in all data. As was discussed at length in Chapters 10 and

11, there are many reasons why people can be expected to have strong motivations to lie to police, prosecutors, medical personnel and shelter operators. It is also a well-documented fact that most acts of violence never even get reported to these archival sources of data in the first place.

To some extent, survey data, although intended to fill in the gaps left by archival data (by attempting to control for strong motivators like the desire to avoid going to jail, etc.) may themselves be vulnerable to participant dishonesty and faulty memory. Generally, there should be fewer motivations to lie, however, where responses are confidential and anonymous and cannot be used either for or against the respondent in any way, as compared to data gathered in contexts where strong motivations to lie are present, such as where one's responses may determine whether one will be taken to jail or not, or whether one will get custody of her children or not, or whether one will be able to obtain benefits like housing, support and money.   Nevertheless, it certainly is conceivable that even in the context of a confidential, anonymous survey, a male survey participant might be resistant to the idea of acknowledging that he has abused a woman. On the other hand, it is equally conceivable that a male participant may have difficulty admitting that he "let himself get beat up by a woman" or that he's "afraid" of a woman. Since men are trained to "blow off" the injuries they receive, a woman might be expected to have a better recollection of the times when she either victimized someone or was victimized by someone. At the same time, since women are trained to be on the lookout for signs of even *potential* violence, a woman might perceive a wider range of conduct as having violent connotations than may be objectively reasonable under the circumstances.[697] The combination of these factors could result in a tendency among some women to over-report, and a tendency among some men to under-report.

In light of these facts, the manner in which the CTS is administered is very important. If it is only administered to one gender, but not the other, the potential for either over-reporting or under-reporting is greater. For this reason, participation by both genders can be expected to heighten the accuracy of survey data, since the male tendency to under-report would then be counter-balanced by the female tendency to over-report.

CTS survey data attains the greatest degree of reliability when members of both genders participate *and* the male and female responses corroborate one another. In this respect, it can be said that some CTS-based studies may be more reliable than others, as there are higher levels of corroboration in some CTS-based studies than there are in others.

Some critics of the CTS have attempted to create the impression that there is *never* any agreement between male and female responses to CTS survey questions. This is not true. A few of the earlier CTS-based studies did have relatively low levels of agreement, but in subsequent CTS-based studies utilizing more refined administration methods, high rates of agreement were noted. For example, the Dunedin study found an extremely high rate of agreement between the male and female responses. The Dunedin study also happened to be one of the studies that found that females perpetrate significantly more violence--both mild and severe--against their intimate partners than males do.[698]

As a matter of fact, levels of corroborative agreement, and therefore reliability, seem to be higher among the studies that have found significantly higher rates of perpetration by females against males than the studies that merely show "equal" or "nearly equal" rates for both genders.[699]

Straus and Gelles have noted that even when male responses to the CTS survey were completely disbelieved, and reliance was placed entirely on female versions of events, the results do not change much. Even female-only responses to the CTS confirm that women are at least as violent toward men as men are toward women.[700]

There is one respect in which the CTS can legitimately be criticized for lack of reliability: the attempt to measure how an individual experiences a victimization; that is to say, the psychological consequences of victimization. By necessity, one can only obtain survey information about an individual's internal experience of pain by asking him or her about it. Yet, this is almost guaranteed to result in a false response. For example, asking a perpetrator, "Did it hurt your partner when you hit him/her?" invites the perpetrator to alleviate personal guilt feelings by minimizing the consequences of his/her actions: "Sure I punched him, but he

didn't cry about it, so it must not have hurt him much." Since
the perpetrator cannot be expected to provide reliable information
about the victim's internal experience, it would be necessary to
rely entirely on the victim's responses. Yet, the victim may have
his/her own motives for either exaggerating or concealing the extent
of the pain he/she suffered. A victim who has learned through
experience that her expression of pain is likely to be rewarded with
sympathy or other benefits, or who has learned that guilt feelings
can be exploited for personal gain, can be expected to over-report
the extent of negative consequences she has experienced.[701] On
the other hand, a victim who has learned through experience that
his expression of pain is likely to be punished, and/or that his
suppression of pain is likely to be rewarded, can be expected to
under-report the extent of negative consequences he experiences.
Without any way to cross-corroborate responses, there is no way
to control for over-reporting on the part of one gender and under-
reporting on the part of the other gender.

For this reason, CTS survey data about the nature and extent
of the psychological harm suffered as a result of violence, as
distinguished from the actual *incidence* of violent acts, is inherently
unreliable. Based on years of sex role-typing, the psychological
consequences of domestic abuse for women will generally be over-
reported, while the psychological consequences of domestic abuse
for men will generally be under-reported.

Ironically, the same people who attack the methodological
soundness of CTS-based research in connection with measuring
the incidence of abuse nevertheless cite it as reliable authority for
the proposition that domestic abuse supposedly has "more negative
outcomes" for women than it does for men.[702] Yet, the part of the
CTS that supposedly supports the latter conclusion is the only
aspect of CTS-based research that employs inherently unsound
methodology.

Ex-spouses and former intimates. The CTS only measures
violence between intimates. It does not measure violence between
people who are no longer involved in an intimate relationship with
each other. This is understandable, given that the purpose of the CTS
is to study the tactics people use to deal with conflicts with their
intimate partners. By definition, a person someone used to know

but with whom one is not involved in an intimate relationship is not a person with whom one is involved in an intimate relationship.

On the other hand, it is true that by limiting its focus to intimate relationships, the CTS misses some of the violence that occurs in our society. The archival data does suggest that a woman is more likely to be a victim of lethal violence after the termination of a relationship with a man than during one. A married woman does appear to be less likely to experience lethal forms of violence than a separated or divorced woman is. On the other hand, men may also experience a heightened risk of domestic violence during or after the breakup of a relationship. We cannot really know for sure, because what research has been done on the subject of domestic violence against men always seems to exclude inquiries into the subject of violence by ex-girlfriends.

The same reasons that justify the exclusion of information about violence by former girlfriends from U.S. government-backed studies of violence by intimates can also be cited as good reasons for the exclusion of information about violence by former intimates in the CTS. The best justification for excluding such information is that its inclusion would tend to undermine the reliability of CTS research. The very factors that lead to the breakup of a relationship typically cause a considerable amount of ill-will toward one's former partners, ill-will that can be expected to cloud both one's memory of past events and one's interpretation of current events. For example, there are documented cases in which former boyfriends and ex-husbands have had protection orders issued against them, and in some cases have been arrested, for things as simple as sending birthday cards to their children, simply because the former girlfriend or ex-wife interpreted the act as an effort to "harass" the mother by reminding her of the father's continued existence.

It's not just the women, either. In my practice, as well as among people I have known on a personal level, I have seen some pretty bizarre twists of logic and psychological self-protective devices being used by *both* genders when it comes to their perceptions about their former partners. Specifically, I have observed a strong tendency among members of *both* genders to demonize their former partners, to interpret everything the other person said or did in the past as an "abusive" act, and to interpret everything the other person now says or does as a "vindictive" act.

The termination of an intimate relationship is a deeply painful experience. The grief one experiences during a divorce has been compared to the grief one experiences upon the death of a family member. Some scholars have even gone so far as to say that a divorce is the most stressful event a person can experience in life, outranking all other setbacks life can throw one's way--being fired or demoted, changing jobs, moving, the death of a loved one, etc. It almost always involves a profound blow to one's self-esteem; and the risk of mental health problems is extremely high during and immediately following the breakup of a relationship. It is not a time when a person can be expected to give accurate, unbiased responses to survey questions about the relationship.

Including survey questions about former intimates would also compromise the reliability of CTS surveys in another way. As we have seen, CTS surveys depend for their reliability on cross-corroboration. Relying exclusively on the responses from only one-half of the couple is not likely to generate very reliable information. It is only when we are able to analyze the rate of agreement between the male and female halves that we can be certain of a high level of reliability in the results obtained from the survey. Data about former partners, which by definition must be based entirely on only one of the parties' recollection and interpretation of events, are not only inherently suspect but are not even capable of being tested for reliability through analysis of the level of agreement among responses given.

Those who would fault surveys on the grounds of insufficient measures of corroborative reliability should not fault the same surveys on the grounds that they do fail to include inherently unreliable, unverifiable data.

Conclusion

Despite the many valiant efforts to discredit the CTS, it is recognized by responsible scholars as the single best instrument available for accurately measuring the actual incidence, frequency and severity of violence among intimate partners, as distinguished from the societal response to domestic violence.[703] It also bears pointing out that findings based on CTS survey data have been replicated and corroborated by studies that do not use the CTS.[704]

There is a considerable amount of hypocrisy among critics of the CTS. Specifically, the same people who say it is "unreliable" and therefore should not be believed when it tells us that women commit as much or more violence than men, often rely on the same CTS studies for their figures about the rate of domestic violence against women! The statement that "2,000,000 wives are abused by their husbands every year" was derived from Murray Straus' 1977 CTS-based survey, as was the factoid that "a woman is abused by a man every 15 seconds." It is only when someone points out that the same study from which these figures were derived *also* shows that a man is abused by a woman every *14* seconds and at least 2,000,000 *husbands* are abused by their wives every year, that people then turn around and say the CTS is not reliable. You can't have it both ways.

Because it is well-documented that most domestic violence never gets recorded in the archival data, the CTS is the only reliable instrument that has been devised, to date, for determining the true extent of domestic violence. Archival data must still be relied upon for the collection of data concerning fatalities, but with respect to domestic violence in general it really only tells about the societal response to domestic violence, not its actual prevalence.[705] For the latter purpose, data obtained from surveys, such as the CTS, are essential.

The common practice among educators, women's organizations and members of the media, to cite survey data when talking about violence against women, but to cite archival data when talking about violence against men, is deceptive, manipulative and, frankly, irresponsible. It perpetuates myths and stereotypes about men and women that serve only to impede inquiry into and the development of knowledge about the phenomenon of domestic violence. Those who impede knowledge impede solutions.

Selected Bibliography

Aizenman, M., and G. Kelley, "The incidence of violence and acquaintance rape in dating relationships among college men and women, *Journal of College Student Development*, 29, 305-311(1988)

Aldarondo, E., "Cessation and persistence of wife assault: A longitudinal analysis," *American Journal of Orthopsychiatrics*, 66(1), 141-151 (1996)

Aldarondo, E. and Straus, M.A., "Screening for physical violence in couple therapy: Methodological, practical, and ethical considerations," *Family Process*, 33, 425-439 (1994)

Aldarondo, E. and D.B. Sugarman, "Risk marker analysis of the cessation and persistence of wife assault," *Journal of Consulting and Clinical Psychology*, 64(5), 1010-1019 (1996)

Alexander, P. C., S. Moore, S. and E.R. Alexander III, "What is transmitted in the intergenerational transmission of violence?" *Journal of Marriage and the Family*, 53, 657-668 (1991)

American Bar Association, *Legal Interventions in Family Violence: Research Findings and Policy Implications,* Research Report, NCJ 171666. Washington, DC: National Institute of Justice (1998)

American Bar Association, *Sexual Abuse Allegations in Custody and Visitation Cases: A Resource Book for Judges and Court Personnel.* Chicago, Ill.: American Bar Association (1988)

American Medical Association, *Diagnostic and Treatment Guidelines on Child Physical Abuse and Neglect.* Chicago, Ill.: American Medical Association (1992)

American Medical Association, *Diagnostic and Treatment Guidelines on Child Sexual Abuse and Neglect*. Chicago, Ill.: American Medical Association (1992)

American Medical Association Council on Scientific Affairs, "Adolescents as Victims of Family Violence," *Journal of the American Medical Association* 270(15): 1850-1856 (1993)

Ammerman, R. T. and M Hersen, eds., *Assessment of Family Violence: A clinical and legal sourcebook*, New York: Wiley (1992)

Amnesty International, *Betraying the Young: Human Rights Violations Against Children in the U.S. Justice System*, New York: Amnesty International USA Publications (1998)

Amneus, Daniel, *The Garbage Generation*, Alhambra, Calif.: Primrose Press (1990)

Archer, John, "Sex differences in aggression between heterosexual partners: A meta-analytic review," *Psychological Bulletin*, 126 (5), 651-680 (September, 2000)

Archer, John and N. Ray, "Dating violence in the United Kingdom: a preliminary study, *Aggressive Behavior*, 15, 337-343 (1989)

Arias, I., *A social learning theory explication of the intergenerational transmission of physical aggression in intimate heterosexual relationships*, doctoral dissertation, State University of New York (1984)

Arias, I., M. Samios, and K.D. O'Leary, "Prevalence and correlates of physical aggression during courtship,". *Journal of Interpersonal Violence*, 2, 82-90 (1987)

Arias, I., and P. Johnson, "Evaluations of physical aggression among intimate dyads," *Journal of Interpersonal Violence*, 4, 298-307 (1989)

Attorney General Daniel E. Lungren's Policy Council on Violence Prevention, *Violence Prevention: A Vision of Hope* (1995)

Bachman, Ronet, *Violence against Women: A National Crime Victimization Survey Report*, NCJ 145325, Washington DC: U.S. Bureau of Justice Statistics (1994)

Bagshaw, Dale and Donna Chung, *Women, Men and Domestic Violence*, University of South Australia: Pirie (2000)

Baker, Robert A., ed., *Child Sexual Abuse and False Memory Syndrome*. Amherst, N.Y.: Prometheus Books (1998)

Barling, et al., "Factor similarity of the conflict tactics scales across samples, spouses, and sites: Issues and implications," *Journal of Family Violence*: 2, 37-54 (1987)

Bates, R. E., "A Plea for the Battered Husband," *Family Law* 11: 92-94 (1981)

Beaupre, Becky, "No place to run for male victims of domestic abuse: Shelters, support groups rare for men," *Detroit News*, April 20, 1997

Bergen, R. K., ed., *Issues in Intimate Violence*, Thousand Oaks, Calif: Sage (1998)

Bergman, L., "Dating violence among high school students," *Social Work*, 37(1), 21-27 (1992)

Berk, R. A., et. al., "The differential deterrent effects of an arrest in incidents of domestic violence: A Bayesian analysis of three randomized field experiments," *American Sociological Review*, 87, p. 698-708 (1992)

Bernard, M. L., and J.L. Bernard, "Violent intimacy: The family as a model for love relationships," *Family Relations*, 32, 283-286 (1983)

Berrios, D. C. and D. Grady, "Domestic violence: Risk factors and outcomes," *Western Journal of Medicine*, 155(2), 133-135 (1991)

Besharov, Douglas J., ed., *Family Violence Research and Public Policy Issues*. Washington, D.C.: AEI Press (1990)

Besharov, Douglas J., ed., *Protecting Children from Abuse and Neglect: Policy and Practice*. Springfield, Ill.: Thomas (1988)

Besharov, Douglas J., *Recognizing Child Abuse: A Guide for the Concerned*. New York: Free Press (1990)

Besharov, Douglas J. and Marcia Robinson Lowry, "Four Commentaries: How We Can Better Protect Children From Abuse and Neglect," *The Future of Children*, vol. 8, no. 1 (Spring 1998)

Billingham, R. E., and A.R. Sack, "Courtship violence and the interactive status of the relationship," *Journal of Adolescent Research*, 1, 315-325 (1986)

Bland, R., and H. Orne, "Family violence and psychiatric disorder," *Canadian Journal of Psychiatry*, 31, 129-137 (March, 1986)

Bohannon, J. R., D.A. Dosser Jr. and S.E. Lindley, S. E., "Using couple data to determine domestic violence rates: An attempt to replicate previous work," *Violence and Victims*, 10, 133-41 (1995)

Bookwala, J., et. al., "Predictors of dating violence: A multi variate analysis," *Violence and Victims*, 7, 297-311 (1992)

Borkowski, M., M. Murch and V. Walker, *Marital Violence: The Community Response*, London: Tavistock (1983)

Bowker, L. H., *Beating Wife Beating*, Lexington, Mass.: Lexington Books (1983)

Bowker, L. H., ed., *Women and Crime in America*, New York: Macmillan (1981)

Brand, P.A. and A.H. Kidd, "Frequency of Physical Aggression in Heterosexual and Female Homosexual Dyads," *Psychological Reports*, 59:1307-1313 (1986)

Brassard, Marla R. and Stuart N. Hart, *Emotional Abuse: Words Can Hurt*. Chicago, Ill.: National Committee for Prevention of Child Abuse (1987)

Breiner, Sander J., *Slaughter of the Innocents: Child Abuse through the Ages and Today*. New York: Plenum Press (1990)

Briere, J., et. al., eds., *The APSAC Handbook on Child Maltreatment*. Newbury Park, Calif.: Sage Publications (1996)

Brinkerhoff, M., and E. Lupri, "Interspousal violence," *Canadian Journal of Sociology*, 13, 407-434 (1988)

Brockopp, Karen, "Violence in Adolescent Dating Relationships Common, New Survey Reveals" *Sexuality Today*, December 22, 1986

Brott, A., "The Facts Take a Battering," *Washington Post Weekly*, August 8-14, 1994, p. 24

Brown, David, "Women's shelters under veil of secrecy," *Ottawa Citizen*, December, 1998

Brown, Mareva, "Arrests of women soar in domestic abuse cases," *Sacramento Bee*, December 7, 1997, pp. A1 and A14

Browne, A., *When Battered Women Kill*, New York: Macmillan Free Press (1987)

Browne, A. and K.R. Williams, "Exploring the effect of resource availability and the likelihood of female-perpetrated homicides," *Law and Society Review*, 23(1), 75-94 (1989)

Browning, J. and D. Dutton, "Assessment of wife assault with the Conflict Tactics Scale: Using couple data to quantify the differential reporting effect," *Journal of Marriage and the Family*, 48(2), 375-379 (1986)

Brush, L. D., "Violent Acts and injurious outcomes in married couples: Methodological issues in the National Survey of Families and Households, *Gender & Society*, 4, 56-67 (1990)

Brutz, J., and B.B. Ingoldsby, "Conflict resolution in Quaker families," *Journal of Marriage and the Family*, 46, 21-26 (1984)

Buckley, Stephen, "Unfounded Rape Reports Baffle Investigators," *The Washington Post,* June 27, 1992: B-1 and B-7

Bullock, L. F. and J. McFarlane, "The birth-weight/battering connection," *American Journal of Nursing*, 89, 1153-1155 (1989)

Burke, P. J., J.E. Stets, J. E., and M.A. Pirog-Good, "Gender identity, self-esteem, and physical and sexual abuse in dating relationships," *Social Psychology Quarterly*, 51, 272-285 (1988)

Burns, N., C. Meredith, C. and C. Paquette, C., *Treatment Programs For Men Who Batter: A review of the evidence of their success*, Cambridge, Mass.: Abt Associate of Canada (1991)

Bushman, B. J. and H.M. Cooper, "Effects of alcohol on human aggression: An integrative research review," *Psychological Bulletin*, 107(3), 341-354 (1990)

Buzawa, Eva and Thomas Austin, "Determining Police Response to Domestic Violence Victims: The role of victim preference," *American Behavioral Scientist*, 36 (5) (May 1993), 610-623

Buzawa, Eva and Carl Buzawa, *Domestic Violence: The Criminal Justice Response*, 2d. ed. Thousand Oaks, Ca.: Sage Publications (1996)

Buzawa, Eva and Carl Buzawa, "The impact of arrest on domestic violence," *American Behavioral Scientist*, 36 , no. 5, 1993

Caesar, P. L., "Exposure to violence in the families-of-origin among wife-abusers and maritally nonviolent men," *Violence and Victims*, 3(1), 49-63 (1988)

Campbell, J. C., ed., *Assessing Dangerousness: Violence by sexual offenders, batterers, and child abusers,* Newbury Park, Calif.: Sage (1995)

Campbell, Terence W., *Smoke and Mirrors: The Devastating Effect of False Sexual Abuse Claims.* New York: Insight Books (1998)

Carlson, B. E., "Dating violence: a research review and comparison with spouse abuse," *Social Casework*, 68, 16-23 (1987)

Carrado, M., et. al., "Aggression in British heterosexual relationships: a descriptive analysis, *Aggressive Behavior*, 22, 401-415 (1996)

Cascardi, M., J. Langhinrichsen, and D. Vivian, "Marital aggression: Impact, injury, and health correlates for husbands and wives," *Archives of Internal Medicine*, 152, 1178-1184 (1992)

Caulfield, M. B., and D.S. Riggs, "The assessment of dating aggression: Empirical evaluation of the Conflict Tactics Scale," *Journal of Interpersonal Violence*, 4, 549-558 (1992)

Chesanow, Neil, "Violence at Home," *New Woman*, February 1992, pg. 96-98

Chicchetti, D. and V. Carlson, eds., *Child Maltreatment: Theory and Research on the Causes and Consequences of Child Abuse and Neglect*. New York: Cambridge University Press (1989)

Coleman, V.E., "Lesbian Battering: The Relationship Between Personality and the Perpetration of Violence,"" *Violence and Victims*, 9(2):139-152 (1994)

Coney, N. S., & Mackey, W. C., "The feminization of domestic violence in America: The woozle effect goes beyond rhetoric," *Journal of Men's Studies*, 8, (1) 45-58 (1999)

Conger, R. D., et. al., "Linking economic hardship to marital quality and instability," *Journal of Marriage and the Family*, 52(3), 243-656 (1990)

Cook, Philip W., *Abused Men: The Hidden Side of Domestic Violence*. Westport, Conn.: Praeger (1997)

Corry, C. E., and M.S. Fiebert, "Controlling domestic violence against men," *Sixth International Conference on Family Violence*, San Diego, Calif., September, 2001

Crary, David, "In the gender wars, another flashpoint: battered men," *Seattle Times*, June 16, 2001

Crary, David, "Domestic Violence Strikes Men," *Amarillo Globe-News* (Associated Press), June 18, 2001

Deal, J. E., and K.S. Wampler, "Dating violence: The primacy of previous experience," *Journal of Social and Personal Relationships*, 3, 457-471 (1986)

DeKeseredy, Walter S., *Four Variations of Family Violence: A Review of Sociological Research*, Ottawa, Ont., Canada: National Clearinghouse on Family Violence (1993)

DeMaris, A., "The efficacy of a spouse abuse model in accounting for courtship violence," *Journal of Family Issues*, 8(3), 291-305 (1987)

Dibble, U. and M.A. Straus, "Some social structure determinants of inconsistency between attitudes and behavior: The case of family violence," *Journal of Marriage and the Family*, 42(1), 71-80 (1980)

Dobash, R. E. and R.P. Dobash, *Violence Against Wives*. New York: Free Press (1979)

Dobash, R. P., et. al., "The myth of sexual symmetry in marital violence," *Social Problems*, 39(1), 71-91 (1992)

Douglas, H., "Assessing violent couples," *Families in Society*, 525-535 (1991)

Downs, W. R., B.A. Miller and D.D. Panek, "Differential patterns of partner-to-woman violence: A comparison of samples of community, alcohol-abusing, and battered women," *Journal of Family Violence*, 8(2), 113-135 (1993)

Dunn, Katherine, "Just As Fierce," *Mother Jones* (November/December, 1994)

Dutton, Donald G., "Patriarchy and Wife Assault: The Ecological Fallacy," *Violence and Victims*, 9(2):167-82 (1994)

Dutton, Donald G., "Profiling of wife assaulters: Preliminary evidence for a trimodal analysis," *Violence and Victims*, 3(1), 5-29 (1988)

Dutton, Douglas G., "The origin and structure of the abusive personality," *Journal of Personality Disorders*, 8(3), 181-191 (1994)

Dutton, D. G. and A. J. Starzomski, "Borderline personality in perpetrators of psychological and physical abuse," *Violence and Victims*, 8(4), 327-337 (1993)

Eagly, A. H. and V.J. Steffen, "Gender and aggressive behavior: A meta-analytic review of the social psychological literature," *Psychological Bulletin*, 100(3), 309-330 (1986)

Easton, Steven A., *Abuse of Men in Families and the Interacting Legacy of Abuse in the Justice System*, testimony before the Special

Joint Senate, House of Commons Committee on Child Custody and Access, Toronto, Canada: Easton Alliance

Easton, Steven A., *Who Are Male Victims of Spousal Abuse?*, web document (2001)

English, Diana J., "The Extent and Consequences of Child Maltreatment," *The Future of Children*, vol. 8, no. 1 (Spring 1998)

Ensminger-Vanfossen, B., "Intersexual violence in Monroe County, New York," *Victimology* 4(2): 299-305 (1979)

Ernst, Amy A., et. al., "Domestic violence in an inner-city ED," *Annals of Emergency Medicine*: 30, 190-197 (August, 1997)

Fagan, Jeffrey, *The Criminalization of Domestic Violence: Promises and Limits*. Washington, D.C.: National Institute of Justice (1996)

Farrell, Warren, *The Myth of Male Power: Why Men Are the Disposable Sex*. New York: Simon & Schuster (1993)

Farrell, Warren, *Women Can't Hear What Men Don't Say*. New York: Tarcher/Putnam (1999)

Feather, N. T., "Domestic violence, gender and perceptions of justice," *Sex Roles*, 35, 507-519 (1996)

Fiebert, M. S., "College students' perception of men as victims of women's assaultive behavior," *Perceptual & Motor Skills*, 82, 49-50 (1996)

Fiebert, M. S., and D.M. Gonzalez, "Women who initiate assaults: The reasons offered for such behavior," *Psychological Reports*, 80, 583-590 (1997)

Finkelhor, David, "The Victimization of Children: A Developmental Perspective," *American Journal of Orthopsychiatry* 63(2): 177-193 (April, 1995)

Finkelhor, David, et. al., eds., *Coping with Family Violence: Research and Policy Perspectives*. Newbury Park, Calif.: Sage Publications (1988)

Finkelhor, David, et. al., eds., *The Dark Side of Families*, Beverly Hills, Calif.: Sage (1983)

Finn, Peter and Sarah Colson, *Civil Protection Orders: Legislation, Current Court Practice, and Enforcement*, NCJ 123263. Washington, D.C.: U.S. Department of Justice (1990)

Flood, Michael, "Claims About Husband Battering," *DVIRC Newsletter* (Summer, 1999), pp. 3-8

Flournoy, P. S. and G.L. Wilson, "Assessment of MMPI profiles of male batterers," *Violence and Victims*, 6(4), 309-320 (1991)

Flynn, C. P., "Relationship violence by women: issues and implications," *Family Relations*, 36, 295-299 (1990)

Follingstad, D. R., S. Wright, and J.A. Sebastian, "Sex differences in motivations and effects in dating violence," *Family Relations*, 40, 51-57 (1991)

Foshee, V. A., "Gender differences in adolescent dating abuse prevalence, types and injuries," *Health Education Research*, 11, (3) 275-286 (1996)

Fremouw, W. J., D. Westrup and J. Pennypacker, "Stalking on campus: The prevalence and strategies for coping with stalking," *Journal of Forensic Science*, 42, 666-669 (1997)

Frodi, A., J. Macaulay, J. and P.R. Thome, "Are women always less aggressive than men? A review of the experimental literature," *Psychological Bulletin*, 84(4), 634-660 (1977)

Ganz, Richard L., ed., *Thou Shalt Not Kill*. New Rochelle, New York: Arlington House (1978)

Garbarino, James, et. al., *Special Children--Special Risks: The Maltreatment of Children with Disabilities*. New York: Aldine de Gruyter (1987)

Garbarino, James, Edna Guttmann and Janis Wilson Seeley, *The Psychologically Battered Child*. San Francisco: Jossey-Bass (1986)

Garcia, Jane, "The Cost of Escaping Domestic Violence," *Los Angeles Times*, May 6, 1991

Gardner, Richard A., *The Parental Alienation Syndrome and the Differentiation Between Fabricated and Genuine Child Sex Abuse*. New York: Creative Therapeutics (1987)

Gardner, Richard A., *True and False Accusations of Child Sex Abuse*. Cresskill, N.J.: Creative Therapeutics (1992)

Garnefski, N. and E. Arends, "Sexual Abuse and Adolescent Maladjustment: Differences Between Male and Female Victims," *Journal of Adolescence*, 21(1): 99-107 (February, 1998)

Gelles, Richard J., "Research and advocacy: Can one wear two hats?" *Family Process*, 33, 93-95 (1994)

Gelles, Richard J., "Violence toward children in the United States," *American Journal of Orthopsychiatry*, 48(4), 580-592 (1978)

Gelles, Richard J. *The Violent Home: A Study of Physical Aggression Between Husbands and Wives*, Beverly Hills, Calif.: Sage (1974)

Gelles, Richard J. and C.P. Cornell, *Intimate Violence in Families*, 2d ed., Beverly Hills, Calif.: Sage (1990)

Gelles, Richard J. and Donileen R. Loseke, eds., *Current Controversies On Family Violence*. Newbury Park, Calif.: Sage (1993)

Gelles, Richard J. and Murray A. Straus, *Intimate Violence: The Causes and Consequences of Abuse in the American Family*, New York: Simon & Schuster (1988)

Gelles, Richard J. and Murray A. Straus, "Violence in the American family," *Journal of Social Issues*, 35(2), 15-39 (1978)

George, M. J., "Riding the donkey backwards: Men as the unacceptable victims of marital violence," *Journal of Men's Studies*, 3, 137-159 (1994)

George, M. J., "A victimization survey of female perpetrated assaults in the United Kingdom," *Aggressive Behavior*, 25, 67-79 (1999)

Giles-Sims, Jean, "The Psychological and Social Impact of Partner Violence," *Domestic Violence Literature Review, Synthesis, and Implications for Practice*, United States Air Force and the National Network for Family Resiliency (1997)

Gilligan, James, *Violence: Our Deadly Epidemic and Its Causes*. New York: Grosset/Putnam (1996)

Goelman, Deborah and Roberta Valente, *When will they ever learn? Educating to End Domestic Violence: A Law School Report*, Chicago, IL: American Bar Association (1997)

Gold, Allan R., "Sex Bias Is Found Pervading Courts," *New York Times*, July 2, 1989

Goldberg, Carey, "Spouse Abuse Crackdown, Surprisingly, Nets Many Women," *New York Times*, November 23, 1999

Goldberg, W. G., and M.C. Tomlanovich, "Domestic violence victims in the emergency department," *Journal of the American Medical Association*, 251, 3259-3264 (1984)

Gondolf, E. W., "Who are those guys? Toward a behavioral typology of batterers," *Violence and Victims*, 3(3), 187-203 (1988)

Goodyear-Smith, F. A. and T.M. Laidlaw, "Aggressive acts and assaults in intimate relationships: Towards an understanding of the literature," *Behavioral Sciences and the Law*, 17,285-304 (1999)

Green, A. H., "Factors Contributing to the Generational Transmission of Child Maltreatment," *Journal of the American Academy of Child and Adolescent Psychiatry*, 37(12):1334-1336 (1998)

Greenfeld, Lawrence A., et. al., *Violence by Intimates: Analysis of Data on Crimes by Current or Former Spouses, Boyfriends, and Girlfriends*, NCJ 167237, Washington, DC: U.S. Bureau of Justice Statistics (1998)

Greenfeld, Lawrence, et. al., *Violence by Intimates*, Bureau of Justice Statistics Factbook, NCJ 167237. Washington, D.C.: U.S. Department of Justice (1998)

Greenfield, Margaret, "Beaten Husbands," *Women's Post*, July 8, 1992, p. 2

Hamberger, L. K. and J.E. Hastings, "Personality correlates of men who abuse their partners: A cross-validation study," *Journal of Family Violence*, 1(4), 323-341 (1986)

Hamberger, L.K. and C. Renzetti, eds., *Domestic Partner Abuse*, New York: Springer (1996)

Hampton, Robert L., et. al., eds., *Family Violence: Prevention and Treatment*. Thousand Oaks, Calif.: Sage(1999)

Hampton, R. L., R.J. Gelles and J.W. Harrop, "Is violence in families increasing? A comparison of 1975 and 1985 National Survey rates," *Journal of Marriage and the Family*, 51, 969-980 (1989)

Harmon, R. B., R. Rosner and H. Owens, "Sex and violence in a forensic population of obsessional harassers," *Psychology, Public Policy, and Law*, 4, 236-249 (1998)

Harders, R. J., et. al., *Verbal and physical abuse in dating relationships*, paper presented at the meeting of American Psychological Association, San Francisco, Calif. (1998)

Hastings, J. E. and L.K. Hamberger, "Personality characteristics of spouse abusers: A controlled comparison," *Violence and Victims*, 3(1), 31-47 (1988)

Headey, B., D. Scott and D. de Vaus, *Domestic Violence in Australia: Are Women and Men Equally Violent?* (1999)

Healey, Kerry, Christine Smith and Chris O'Sullivan, *Batterer Intervention: Program Approaches and Criminal Justice Strategies*, NCJ 168638. Washington, DC: U.S. Department of Justice (1998)

Hechler, David, *The Battle and the Backlash: The Child Sexual Abuse War*. Lexington, Mass.: Lexington Books (1988)

Helfer, M.E., R. S. Kempe and R.D. Krugman, eds., *The Battered Child*, 5th ed. Chicago: Chicago University Press (1997)

Heineman, Toni Vaughn, *The Abused Child: Psychodynamic Understanding and Treatment*. New York: Guilford Press (1998)

Henderson, Helene, ed., *Domestic Violence and Child Abuse Sourcebook: Basic Consumer Health Information About Spousal/Partner, Child, Sibling, and Elder Abuse*. Detroit, Mich.: Omnigraphics (2000)

Henton, J., et. al., "Romance and violence in dating relationships," *Journal of Family Issues*, 4, 467-482 (1983)

Hofford, M. and A. Harrell, *Family Violence: Interventions for the Justice System*, Program Brief, NCJ 144532. Washington, DC: Bureau of Justice Assistance (1993)

Holtzworth-Munroe, A., "Social skill deficits in maritally violent men: Interpreting the data using a social information processing model," *Clinical Psychology Review*, 12, 605-617 (1992)

Holtzworth-Munroe, A., et. al., "The need for marital violence prevention efforts: A behavioral-cognitive secondary prevention program for engaged and newly married couples," *Applied and Preventative Psychology*, 4(2), 77-88 (1995)

Holtzworth-Munroe, A. and G. L. Stuart, "Typologies of male batterers: Three subtypes and the differences among them," *Psychological Bulletin*, 116(3), 476-497 (1994)

Hornung, C. A., B.C. McCullough and T. Sugimoto, "Status relationships in marriage: Risk factors in spouse abuse," *Journal of Marriage and the Family*, 43, 675-692 (1981)

Hotaling, G.P., et. al., eds., *Family Abuse and its Consequences: New Directions in Research*. Beverly Hills, Calif.: Sage (1988)

Hotaling, G. T. and D.B. Sugarman, "An analysis of risk markers in husband to wife violence: The current state of knowledge," *Violence and Victims*, 1(2), 101-124 (1986)

Hotaling, G. T. and D.B. Sugarman, "A risk marker analysis of assaulted wives," *Journal of Family Violence*, 5(1), 1-13 (1990)

Hudson, W. W. and S.R. McIntosh, "The assessment of abuse: Two quantifiable dimensions," *Journal of Marriage and Family*, 43, 873-885 (1981)

Hunter, Mic, *Abused Boys: The Neglected Victims of Sexual Abuse*. Lexington, Mass.: Lexington Books (1990)

Hunter, Mic, ed., *The Sexually Abused Male*. Lexington, Mass.: Lexington Books (1990)

Hutchinson, J. and K. Langlykke, *Adolescent Maltreatment: Youth as Victims of Abuse and Neglect* (Maternal and Child Health Technical Information Bulletin), Arlington, Va.: National Center for Education in Maternal and Child Health (1997)

Jackson, S. M., F. Cram, F. and F.W. Seymour, "Violence and sexual coercion in high school students' dating relationships," *Journal of Family Violence*, 15, 23-36 (2000)

Jasinski, J. L., *Structural inequalities, family and cultural factors, and spousal violence among Anglo and Hispanic Americans*, doctoral dissertation, University of New Hampshire, Durham (1996)

Jaudes, Paula and Leslie Mitchel, *Physical Child Abuse*, 2nd ed. Chicago, Ill.: National Committee for Prevention of Child Abuse (1992)

Johnson, M. P., "Patriarchal terrorism and common couple violence: Two forms of violence against women," *Journal of Marriage and the Family*, 57, (1995), pp. 283-294.

Jones, Lisa and David Finkelhor, *The Decline in Child Sexual Abuse Cases*, NCJ 184741. Washington, DC: Office of Juvenile Justice and Delinquency Prevention (2001)

Jouriles, E. N., and K.D. O'Leary, "Interpersonal reliability of reports of marital violence," *Journal of Consulting and Clinical Psychology*, 53, 419-421 (1985)

Jurik, N. C. and R. Winn, "Gender and homicide: A comparison of men and women who kill," *Violence and Victims*, 5(4), 227-242 (1990)

Kalmuss, D., "The intergenerational transmission of marital aggression," *Journal of Marriage and the Family*, 46, 11-19 (February, 1984)

Kalmuss, D. and J.A. Seltzer, "Continuity of marital behavior in remarriage: The case of spouse abuse," *Journal of Marriage and the Family*, 48, 113-120 (February, 1986)

Kammer, Jack, *Good Will Toward Men*. New York: St. Martin's Press (1994)

Karr-Morse, R. and M.S. Wiley, *Ghosts from the Nursery: Tracing the Roots of Violence*, New York: Atlantic Monthly Press (1997)

Kaufman Kantor, Glenda, *Ethnicity, alcohol, and family violence: A structural and cultural interpretation*, paper presented at the Forty-second Annual Meeting of the American Society of Criminology, Baltimore, Md (1990)

Kaufman Kantor, Glenda, *Refining the brushstrokes in portraits of alcohol and wife assaults. In Alcohol and Interpersonal Violence: Fostering Multidisciplinary Perspectives*, NIH Research Monograph No. 24, Rockville, Md.: U.S. Department of Health and Human Services (1993)

Kaufman Kantor, Glenda and Jana L. Jasinski, "Dynamics of Partner Violence and Types of Abuse and Abusers," in *Domestic Violence Literature Review, Synthesis, and Implications for Practice*, a collaborative publication of the United States Air Force and the National Network for Family Resiliency (1997)

Kaufman Kantor, Glenda and Jana L. Jasinski, eds., *Out of the Darkness: Contemporary Perspectives on Family Violence*, Thousand Oaks, CA: Sage Publications (1997)

Kaufman Kantor, G., J. Jasinski, J. and E. Aldorondo, "Sociocultural status and incidence of marital violence in Hispanic families," *Violence and Victims*, 9(3), 207-222 (1994)

Kaufman Kantor, G. and M.A. Straus, "The 'drunken bum' theory of wife beating," *Social Problems*, 34(3), 213-230 (1987)

Kaufman Kantor, G. and M.A. Straus, "Substance abuse as a precipitant of wife abuse victimization," *American Journal of Drug and Alcohol Abuse*, 15, 173-189 (1989)

Kellerman, A. L. and J.A. Mercy, "Men, women, and murder: Gender specific differences in rates of fatal violence and victimization," *Journal of Trauma*, 33(1), 1-5 (1992)

Kelley, Barbara Tatem, et. al., *In the Wake of Childhood Maltreatment*, Youth Development Series. Washington, D.C.: U.S. Office of Juvenile Justice and Delinquency Prevention (1997)

Kempe, C. Henry, "The Battered Child Syndrome," *Journal of the American Medical Association* (1962)

Kempe, C. Henry and Ruth S. Kempe, *Child Abuse*. Cambridge, Mass.: Harvard University Press (1978)

Kennedy, L.S. and D. G. Dutton, "The Incidence of Wife Assault in Alberta," University of Alberta, Canada: Population Research Laboratory (1987)

Kirsta, Alix, "6 Ft., Macho, and Beaten by his Wife," *Sunday Times*, December 10, 1989

Kirsta, Alix, "Could You Batter Him?" *New Woman*, January 1991

Knudsen, D.D. and J.L. Miller, eds., *Abused and Battered. Social and Legal Responses to Family Violence*. Hawthorne, NY: Aldine de Gruyter (1991)

Lane, K. and P.A. Gwartney-Gibbs, "Violence in the context of dating and sex," *Journal of Family Issues*, 6, 45-49 (1985)

Laner, M.R., "Courtship abuse and aggression: Contextual aspects," *Sociological Spectrum*, 3, 69-83 (1983)

Laner, M. R. and J. Thompson, "Abuse and aggression in courting couples," *Deviant Behavior*, 3, 229-244 (1982)

Lang, A. R., et. al., "Effects of alcohol on aggression in male social drinkers," *Journal of Abnormal Psychology*, 84, 508-518 (1975)

Langan, Patrick A. and Christopher A. Innes, *Preventing Domestic Violence Against Women*, NCJ 102037, Washington DC: U.S. Bureau of Justice Statistics (1986)

Langhinrichsen-Rohling, J. and D. Vivian, "The correlates of spouses' incongruent reports of marital aggression," *Journal of Family Violence*, 9, 265-283 (1994)

Langley, Roger and Richard C. Levy, *Wife Beating: The Silent Crisis*, New York: Pocket Books (1977)

Lau, J. T. F., et. al., "Prevalence and Correlates of Physical Abuse in Hong Kong Chinese Adolescents: A Population-Based Approach," *Child Abuse and Neglect*, 23(6):549-557 (1999)

Leonard, K. E., "Drinking patterns and intoxication in marital violence: Review, critique, and future directions for research," *Alcohol and interpersonal violence: Fostering multidisciplinary perspectives*, NIH Research Monograph No. 24 (pp. 253-280), Rockville, Md.: U.S. Department of Health and Human Services (1993)

Leonard, K. E. and M. Senchak, "Alcohol and premarital aggression among newlywed couples," *Journal of Studies on Alcohol*, Supp. No. 11, pp. 96-108 (1993)

Letellier, P., "Gay and Bisexual Male Domestic Violence Victimization: Challenges to Feminist Theory and Response to Violence," *Violence and Victims*. 9(2):95-106 (1994)

Levin, A. and M. Sheridan, eds., *Munchausen Syndrome by Proxy*. New York: Lexington Books (1995)

Lindman, R., et. al., "Serum testosterone, cortisol, glucose, and ethanol in males arrested for spouse abuse," *Aggressive Behavior*, 18(6), 393-400 (1992)

Lo, W. A. and M.J. Sporakowski, "The continuation of violent dating relationships among college students," *Journal of College Student Development*, 30, 432-439 (1989)

Lobel, Kerry, ed., *Naming The Violence: Speaking Out About Lesbian Battering*. Seattle, Wash.: Seal Press (1986)

Loftus, Elizabeth F., *The Myth of Repressed Memory: False Memories and Allegations of Sexual Abuse*. New York : St. Martin's (1996)

Macchietto, J. "Aspects of male victimization and female aggression: Implications for counseling men," *Journal of Mental Health Counseling*, 14, 375-392 (1992)

Magdol, L., et. al., "Gender Differences in Partner Violence in a Birth Cohort of 21-Year-Olds: Bridging the Gap Between Clinical and Epidemiological Approaches," *Journal of Consulting and Clinical Psychology*, 65, no. 1 (1997): 68-78

Makepeace, J. M. "Gender differences in courtship violence victimization," *Family Relations*, 35, 383-388 (1986)

Makepeace, J. M., "Life events stress and courtship violence," *Family Relations*, 32, 101-109 (January, 1983)

Malone, J., A. Tyree, and K.D. O'Leary, "Generalization and containment: Different effects of past aggression for wives and husbands," *Journal of Marriage and the Family*, 51, 687-697 (1989)

Mann, Coramae Richey, "Getting Even? Women Who Kill In Domestic Encounters," *Justice Quarterly*, vol. 5, no. 1, (March, 1988)

Mann, Coramae Richey, *When Women Kill*, Albany, N.Y.: State University of New York Press (1996)

Margolin, G., "The multiple forms of aggressiveness between marital partners: how do we identify them?" *Journal of Marital and Family Therapy*, 13 , 77-84 (1987)

Marshall, L. L. and P. Rose, "Family of origin violence and courtship abuse," *Journal of Counseling and Development*, 66, 414-418 (1988)

Marshall, L. L. and P. Rose, "Gender, stress and violence in the adult relationships of a sample of college students," *Journal of Social and Personal Relationships*, 4, 299-316 (1987)

Marshall, L. L. and P. Rose, "Premarital violence: The impact of family of origin violence, stress and reciprocity," *Violence and Victims*, 5, 51-64 (1990)

Martin, Susan E., ed., *Alcohol and Interpersonal Violence: Fostering Multidisciplinary Perspectives*. NIH Research Monograph No. 24, Rockville, Md.: U.S. Department of Health and Human Services (1993)

Mason, A., & V. Blankenship, "Power and affiliation motivation, stress and abuse in intimate relationships," *Journal of Personality and Social Psychology*, 52, 203-210 (1987)

Matthews, W. J., "Violence in college couples," *College Student Journal*, 18, 150-158 (1984)

McDowell, Charles P., Ph.D., M.P.A., M.L.S., "False Allegations," *Forensic Science Digest*, vol. 11, no. 4, December 1985, p. 64

McKenry, P. C., T. W. Julian and S. M. Gavazzi, "Toward a biopsychosocial model of domestic violence," *Journal of Marriage and the Family*, 57, 307-320 (1995)

McKinney, K., "Measures of verbal, physical and sexual dating violence by gender," *Free Inquiry in Creative Sociology*, 14, 55-60 (1986)

McLaughlin, I. G., K.E. Leonard and M. Senchak, "Prevalence and distribution of premarital aggression among couples applying for a marriage license," *Journal of Family Violence*, 7(4), 309-319 (1992)

McLeod, M., "Women Against Men: An examination of domestic violence based on an analysis of official data and national victimization data," *Justice Quarterly*, Fall 1984: 1: 171-193

McNeely, R. L., C.R. Mann, "Domestic violence is a human issue," *Journal of Interpersonal Violence*, 5, 129-132 (1990)

McNeely, R. L., and G. Robinson-Simpson, "The truth about domestic violence: A falsely framed issue," *Social Work*, 32, 485-490 (1987)

Mercy, James A. and Linda E. Saltzman, "Fatal Violence Among Spouses in the United States, 1976-85," *American Journal of Public Health*, 79(5): 595-599 (1989)

Meredith, W. H., D.A. Abbot, and S.L. Adams, "Family violence in relation to marital and parental satisfaction and family strengths," *Journal of Family Violence*, 1, 299-305 (1986)

Mihalic, S. W., and D. Elliot, "A social learning theory model of marital violence," *Journal of Family Violence*, 12, 21-46 (1997)

Milardo, R. M., "Gender asymmetry in common couple violence," *Personal Relationships*, 5, 423-438 (1998)

Miller, S. L., "Expanding the boundaries: Toward a more inclusive and integrated study of intimate violence," *Violence and Victims*, 9(2), 183-194 (1994)

Minnesota Center Against Violence and Abuse, *Incidence Rates of Violence Against Women: A Comparison of the Redesigned National Crime Victimization Survey and the 1985 National Family Violence Survey*, Washington, D.C.: U.S. Violence Against Women Office (1998)

Moffitt, Terrie E. and Avshalom Caspi, *Findings About Partner Violence From the Dunedin Multidisciplinary Health and Development Study*, NCJ 170018, Washington DC: National Institute of Justice (1999)

Morse, Barbara, "Beyond the Conflict Tactics Scale: Assessing Gender Differences in Partner Violence," *Violence and Victims* 10(4) (Winter 1995): 251-272

Mouradian, Vera, *Abuse in Intimate Relationships: Defining the Multiple Dimensions and Terms*, Wellesley College: National Violence Against Women Prevention Research Center (2000)

Muehlenhard, Charlene L. and Stephen W. Cook, "Men's Self Reports of Unwanted Sexual Activity," *Journal of Sex Research*, vol. 24 (1988): 58-72

Murphy, C. M., S.L. Meyer and K.D. O'Leary, "Family of origin violence and MCMI-II psychopathology among partner-assaultive men," *Violence and Victims*, 8(2), 165-176 (1993)

National Center for Prosecution of Child Abuse, *Investigation and Prosecution of Child Abuse*, 3rd ed. Alexandria, VA: American Prosecutors Research Institute (1994)

National Center on Child Abuse and Neglect, *Child Abuse and Neglect: A Shared Community Concern,* Washington DC: U.S. Department of Health and Human Services (1992)

National Center on Child Abuse and Neglect, *National Study of the Incidence and Severity of Child Abuse and Neglect*, Washington DC: U.S. Department of Health and Human Services (1981)

National Center on Child Abuse and Neglect, *A Report on the Maltreatment of Children with Disabilities.* Washington DC: U.S. Department of Health and Human Services

National Center on Child Abuse and Neglect, *The Third National Incidence Study of Child Abuse and Neglect.* Washington, DC: U.S. Department of Health and Human Services (1996)

National Institute of Justice, *The Cycle of Violence Revisited.* Washington, D.C.: U.S. Department of Justice (1996)

National Institute of Justice, *Domestic Violence, Stalking and Anti-Stalking Legislation*: Annual Report to Congress under the Violence Against Women Act. Washington, DC: U.S. Department of Justice (1996)

National Institute of Justice, *Partner Violence Among Young Adults*, NIJ Research Preview, U.S. Department of Justice (1997)

National Institute of Justice, *The Prevalence and Consequences of Child Victimization*, Research in Brief, Washington DC: U.S. Department of Justice (1997)

National Research Council, *Understanding Child Abuse and Neglect.* Washington, D.C.: National Academy Press (1993)

Neidig, P. H. et. al., "The development and evaluation of a spouse abuse treatment program in a military setting," *Evaluation and Program Planning*, 9, 275-280 (1986)

Nelson, Wyman, *About Spouse Abuse,* South Deerfield, Mass.: Channing L. Bete Co. (1986)

Nicholson, E. Bruce and Josephine Bulkley, *Sexual Abuse Allegations in Custody and Visitation Cases.* Chicago, Ill.: American Bar Association (1988)

Nisonoff, L., and I. Bitman, "Spouse abuse: Incidence and relationship to selected demographic variables," *Victimology*, 4, 131-140 (1979)

O'Keeffe, N. K., K. Brockopp, and Chew, E., "Teen dating violence," *Social Work*, 31, 465-468 (1986)

O'Leary, K. D., et. al., "Premarital Physical Aggression," unpublished ms., State University of New York at Stony Brook and Syracuse University (1985)

O'Leary, K. D., et. al., "Prevalence and stability of physical aggression between spouses: A longitudinal analysis," *Journal of Consulting and Clinical Psychology*, 57, 263-268 (1989)

O'Leary, K. D. and A. D. Curley, "Assertion and family violence: Correlates of abuse," *Journal of Marital and Family Therapy*, 12, 281-289 (1986)

O'Morain, Padraig, "Domestic Violence More Likely From Women--Report," *Irish Times*, June 14, 2001

Pagelow, M. D., *Family Violence*, New York: Praeger Scientific (1984)

Parker, R. N., "The effects of context on alcohol and violence," Special Issue: Alcohol, aggression, and injury, *Alcohol Health and Research World*, 17, 117-122 (1993)

Paterno, Susan, "A Legacy of Violence," *Los Angeles Times*, April 14, 1991, pp. E-1 and E-14

Pearson, Patricia, *When She Was Bad: Violent Women and the Myth of Innocence*. New York: Viking (1997)

Pirog-Good, M.A. and J.E. Stets, eds., *Violence in Dating Relationships: Emerging Social Issues*. New York: Praeger. (1989)

Pizzey, Erin, *Prone to Violence*, Feltham, Middlesex, England: Hamlyn (1982)

Pizzey, Erin, *Scream Quietly or the Neighbors Will Hear*, Short Hill, N.J.: Ridley Enslow (1974)

Pizzey, Erin, "Working with Violent Women," *The Backlash!*, December, 1997

Pleck, Elizabeth, *Domestic Tyranny* (New York: Oxford University Press, 1987)

Pleck, Elizabeth, "Wife Beating in Nineteenth-Century America," *Victimology: An International Journal* 4 (1979): 4

Plass, M. S. and J.C. Gessner, "Violence in courtship relations: a southern sample, *Free Inquiry in Creative Sociology*, 11, 198-202 (1983)

Prince, J. E. and I. Arias, "The role of perceived control and the desirability of control among abusive and nonabusive husbands," *American Journal of Family Therapy*, 22(2), 126-134 (1994)

Ray, J.A. and D.J. English, "Comparison of female and male children with sexual behavior problems," *Journal of Youth and Adolescence* 24(4): 439-451 (1995)

Ray, Nancy, "Judge Allows 'Battered Woman' Defense," *Los Angeles Times*, September 21, 1982

Reiss, Albert J., Jr., and Jeffrey A. Roth, eds., *Understanding and Preventing Violence*, vol. 3, Washington DC: National Academy Press (1994)

Rennison, Callie Marie, *Criminal Victimization 2000, Changes 1999-2000 with Trends 1993-2000*, Bureau of Justice Statistics National Crime Victimization Survey, NCJ 187007, Washington, DC: U.S. Department of Justice (2001)

Rennison, Callie Marie and Sarah Welchans, *Intimate Partner Violence*, NCJ 178247, Washington DC: U.S. Bureau of Justice Statistics (2000)

Renzetti, C. M., "Building Its Second Closet: Third Party Responses to Victims of Lesbian Partner Abuse," *Family Relations*, 38:157-163 (1989)

Renzetti, C. M., "On dancing with a bear: Reflections on some of the current debates among domestic violence theorists," *Violence and Victims*, 9(2), 195-200 (1994)

Renzetti, C. M., "Violence in Lesbian Relationships: A Preliminary Analysis of Causal Factors," *Journal of Interpersonal Violence*, 3(4):381-399 (1988)

Riggs, D. S., K.D. O'Leary, and F.C. Breslin, "Multiple correlates of physical aggression in dating couples," *Journal of Interpersonal Violence*, 5, 61-73 (1990)

Rohsenow, D. J. and J.A. Bacharowski, "Effects of alcohol and expectancies on verbal aggression in men and women," *Journal of Abnormal Psychology*, 93, 418-432 (1984)

Rollins, B. C., and Y. Oheneba-Sakyi, "Physical violence in Utah households," *Journal of Family Violence*, 5(4), 301-309 (1990)

Rooke, Margaret, "Violence in the Home," *Radio Times* (March, 1991)

Rosenbaum, A. et. al., "Head injury in partner-abusive men," *Journal of Consulting and Clinical Psychology*, 62(6), 1187-1193 (1994)

Rosenfeld, R., "Changing relationships between men and women. A note on the decline in intimate partner violence," *Homicide Studies*, 1, 72-83 (1997)

Rounsaville, B., "Theories in marital violence: Evidence from a study of battered women," *Victimology*, 3(1/2), 11-31 (1978)

Rouse, L. P., "Abuse in dating relationships: A comparison of Blacks, Whites, and Hispanics," *Journal of College Student Development*, 29, 312-319 (1988)

Rouse, L. P., R. Breen, and M. Howell, "Abuse in intimate relationships. A Comparison of married and dating college students," *Journal of Interpersonal Violence*, 3, 414-429 (1988)

Roy, M., ed., *Battered Women: A psychosociological study of domestic violence*. New York: Van Nostrand, Reinhold (1977)

Russell, R. J. H., and B. Hulson, "Physical and psychological abuse of heterosexual partners," *Personality and Individual Differences*, 13, 457-473 (1992)

Ryan, K. A., "The relationship between courtship violence and sexual aggression in college students," *Journal of Family Violence*, 13, 377-394 (1998)

Sack, A. R., J.F. Keller, and R.D. Howard, "Conflict tactics and violence in dating situations," *International Journal of Sociology of the Family*, 12, 89-100 (1982)

Schafer, J., R. Caetano and C.L. Clark, "Rates of intimate partner violence in the United States," *American Journal of Public Health*, 88, 1702-1704 (1998)

Scott, Lisa, "Gender profiling prevalent in domestic violence," *East Side Journal*, February 13, 2001

Saenger, G., "Male and female relation in the American comic strips," in White, M. and R.H. Abel, eds., *The Funnies: An American Idiom*, Glencoe, Ill.: Free Press (1963), pp. 219-223

Saunders, D.G., "When battered women use violence: Husband abuse or self defense," *Violence and Victims* 1:47-60 (1986)

Shepard, M. F. and J.A. Campbell," The Abusive Behavior Inventory: a measure of psychological and physical abuse," *Journal of Interpersonal Violence*, 7, 291-305 (1992)

Shupe, A., W. A. Stacey and L.R. Hazlewood, *Violent Men, Violent Couples: The dynamics of domestic violence*. Lexington, Mass.: Lexington Books (1987)

Sigelman, C. K., C.J. Berry, and K.A. Wiles, "Violence in college students' dating relationships," *Journal of Applied Social Psychology*, 5(6), 530-548 (1984)

Sleek, Scott, "Sorting out the reasons couples turn violent: Data on violence between men and women tell only part of the story," *APA Monitor* (American Psychological Association), vol. 29, no. 4 (April, 1998)

Smith, M. D., "Sociodemographic risk factors in wife abuse: Results from a survey of Toronto women," *Canadian Journal of Sociology*, 15(1), 39-58 (1990)

Smith, S., et. al., "Adult Domestic Violence," *Health Trends* 24: 97-99 (1992)

Smithey, M., "Infant Homicide: Victim-Offender Relationship and Causes of Death," *Journal of Family Violence*, 13(3):285-297 (1998)

Snow, Misti, "Psychiatrist James Gilligan has studied society's most violent people and concludes the theories underpinning our criminal-justice system are all wrong," *Minneapolis Star-Tribune*, July, 1996

Sommer, R., G.E. Barnes, and R.P. Murray, "Alcohol consumption, alcohol abuse, personality and female perpetrated spouse abuse," *Journal of Personality and Individual Differences*, 13, 1315-1323 (1992)

Sommers, Christina Hoff, *Who Stole Feminism? How Women Have Betrayed Women*. New York: Simon and Schuster (1994)

Sorenson, S. B., and C.A. Telles, "Self reports of spousal violence in a Mexican-American and non-Hispanic white population," *Violence and Victims*, 6, 3-15 (1991)

Spencer, G. A., and S.A. Bryant, "Dating violence: A comparison of rural, suburban and urban teens," *Journal of Adolescent Health*, 25 (5) 302-305 (2000)

Stacey, Sarah and Maria Cantacuzino, "And Then She Hit Me," *Esquire*, p. 84 (1993)

Stacey and Hazlewood, eds., *Violent Men, Violent Couples*, Lexington, Mass.: Lexington (1986)

Statistics Canada, *Family Violence in Canada: A Statistical Profile* (2000)

Steinmetz, Suzanne, "The Battered Husband Syndrome," *Victimology: An International Journal*, 2: 499-509 (1977-1978)

Steinmetz, Suzanne, "A cross cultural comparison of marital abuse," *Journal of Sociology and Social Welfare*, 8, 404-414 (1981)

Steinmetz, Suzanne, *The Cycle of Violence: Assertive, Aggressive and Abusive Family Interaction*, New York; Praeger (1977)

Steinmetz, Suzanne, "The Truth About Domestic Violence: A Falsely Framed Issue," *Social Work, The Journal of the National Association of Social Workers*, November/December, 1987

Steinmetz, Suzanne, "Women and violence: victims and perpetrators," *American Journal of Psychotherapy*, 34, 334-350 (1980)

Steinmetz, Suzanne and Murray Straus, eds., *Violence in the Family*, New York: Harper & Row (1994)

Stets, J. E. and D.A. Henderson, "Contextual factors surrounding conflict resolution while dating: results from a national study," *Family Relations*, 40, 29-40 (1991)

Stets, J. E. and M.A. Pirog-Good, "Patterns of physical and sexual abuse for men and women in dating relationships: A descriptive analysis," *Journal of Family Violence*, 4, 63-76 (1989)

Stets, J. E., and M.A. Pirog-Good, "Violence in dating relationships," *Social Psychology Quarterly*, 50, 237-246 (1987)

Stets, J. E. and M.A. Straus, "The marriage license as a hitting license: A comparison of assaults in dating, cohabiting, and married couples," *Journal of Family Violence*, 4(2), 161-180 (1989)

Stich, S.M. and M. A. Straus, eds., *Understanding Partner Violence: Prevalence, Causes, Consequences, and Solutions*. Minneapolis, Minn.: National Council on Family Relations (1995)

Stith, S. M. and S.C. Farley, "A predictive model of male spousal violence," *Journal of Family Violence*, 8(2), 183-201 (1993)

Straus, Murray A., *Beating the Devil Out of Them: Corporal Punishment in American Families*. New Brunswick, N.J.: Transaction (2001)

Straus, Murray A., *The controversy over domestic violence by women: A methodological, theoretical, and sociology of science analysis*, paper presented at the Claremont Symposium on Applied Social Psychology, Claremont, Calif. (1998)

Straus, Murray A., "A general systems theory approach to a theory of violence between family members," *Social Science Information*, 12, 105 (1973)

Straus, Murray A., "Measuring intrafamily conflict and violence: The Conflict Tactics (CT) scale," *Journal of Marriage and the Family*, 41(1), 75-88 (1979)

Straus, Murray A., "Victims and aggressors in marital violence," *American Behavioral Scientist*, 23, 681-704 (1980)

Straus, Murray A., "Wife-beating: How common and why?" *Victimology*, 2, 443-458 (1977)

Straus, Murray A. and Richard J. Gelles, eds., *Physical Violence in American Families: Risk Factors and Adaptions to Violence in 8,145 Families*. New Brunswick, N.J.: Transaction Publishers (1990)

Straus, Murray A. and Richard J. Gelles, "Societal Change and Change in Family Violence from 1975 to 1985 as Revealed by Two National Surveys," *Journal of Marriage and the Family*, 48: 465-479 (August, 1986)

Straus, Murray A., Richard J. Gelles and Suzanne K. Steinmetz, *Behind Closed Doors: Violence in the American Family*. Garden City, N.J.: Anchor (1980)

Straus, Murray A. and S. L. Hamby, "The Revised Conflict Tactics Scales (CTS2): Development and preliminary psychometric data," *Journal of Family Issues*, 17(3), 283-316 (1996)

Straus, Murray A. and G. Kaufman Kantor, *Change in spouse assault rates from 1975-1992: A comparison of three national surveys in the United States*, paper presented at the Thirteenth World Congress of Sociology, Bielefeld, Germany (July, 1994)

Straus, Murray A., G. Kaufman Kantor and D.W. Moore, *Change in cultural norms approving marital violence from 1968 to 1994*, paper presented at the American Sociological Association, Los Angeles, Calif. (August, 1994)

Straus, Murray A. and G. Kaufman Kantor, "Corporal punishment of adolescents by parents: A risk factor in the epidemiology of depression, suicide, alcohol abuse, child abuse, and wife beating," *Adolescence*, 29(115), 543-562 (1994)

Strauss, Murray A. and V.E. Mouradian, "Impulsive Corporal Punishment by Mothers and Antisocial Behavior and Impulsiveness of Children," *Behavioral Sciences and the Law*, 16(3):353-374 (1998)

Straus, Murray A. and C.L. Yodanis, "Corporal punishment by parents: Implications for primary prevention of assaults on spouses and parents," *The University of Chicago Law School Roundtable*, 2(1), 35-66 (1995)

Straus, Murray A., et. al., "The Revised Conflict Tactics Scales (CTS2). Development and preliminary psychometric data," *Journal of Family Issues*, 17, 283-316 (1996)

Sugarman, D. B., E. Aldarondo and S. Boney-McCoy, "Risk marker analysis of husband-to-wife violence: A continuum of aggression," *Journal of Applied Social Psychology*, 26(4), 313-337 (1996)

Szinovacz, M. E., "Using couple data as a methodological tool: The case of marital violence," *Journal of Marriage and the Family*, 45, 633-644 (1983)

Tang, C. S., "Prevalence of spouse aggression in Hong Kong," *Journal of Family Violence*, 9, 347-356 (1994)

Thomas, David, *Not Guilty: The Case In Defense of Men*, N.Y.: William Morrow (1993)

Thompson Jr., E. H., "Courtship violence and the male role," *Men's Studies Review*, 7, (3) 1, 4-13 (1990)

Thompson Jr., E. H., "The maleness of violence in data relationships: an appraisal of stereotypes," *Sex Roles*, 24, 261-278 (1991)

Tifft, L. L., *Battering of Women: The failure of intervention and the case for prevention*, Boulder, Colo.: Westview Press (1993)

Tjaden, Patricia and Nancy Thoennes, *Prevalence, Incidence and Consequences of Violence Against Women: Findings From the National Violence Against Women Survey*, Washington, DC: National Institute of Justice and Centers for Disease Control (1998)

Tondonato, P. and B. K. Crew, "Dating violence, social learning theory, and gender: A multivariate analysis," *Violence and Victims*, 7(1), 3-14 (1992)

Tong, Dean, *Don't Blame Me, Daddy : False Accusations of Child Sexual Abuse.* Norfolk, Va.: Hampton Roads (1992)

Tyree, A., J. Malone, *How can it be that wives hit husbands as much as husbands hit wives and none of us knew it?*, paper presented at the annual meeting of the American Sociological Association (1991)

Urban Institute, *The Violence Against Women Act of 1994.* Washington, DC: Urban Institute (1996)

U.S. Bureau of Justice Statistics, *Criminal Victimization in the United States, 1994: A National Crime Victimization Survey Report,* NCJ-162126, Washington DC: U.S. Department of Justice (1997)

U.S. Bureau of Justice Statistics, *Domestic Violence: Violence Between Intimates,* Selected Findings, NCJ 149259. Washington, DC: U.S. Department of Justice (1994)

U.S. Bureau of Justice Statistics, *Murder in Families,* NCJ-143498, Washington, D.C.: U.S. Department of Justice (1994)

U.S. Bureau of Justice Statistics, *Report to the Nation on Crime and Justice,* 2nd ed., NCJ 105506, Washington, DC: U.S. Department of Justice (1988)

U.S. Bureau of Justice Statistics, *Sourcebook of Criminal Justice Statistics,* Washington DC: U.S. Department of Justice

U.S. Bureau of Justice Statistics, *Violence by Intimates,* NCJ-167237, Washington, D.C.: U.S. Department of Justice (1998)

U.S. Department of Justice, *Validity and Use of Evidence Concerning Battering and Its Effects in Criminal Trials,* Report Responding to Section 40507 of the Violence Against Women Act, NCJ 160972. Washington, D.C.: U.S. Government Printing Office (1996)

U.S. House of Representatives, Select Committee on Children, *Youth and Families, Abused Children in America: Victims of Official Neglect,* 100th Congress, 1st Sess. Washington, D.C.: U.S. Government Printing Office (1987)

U.S. Senate, "Women and Violence Hearing before the Commission on the Judiciary, U.S. Senate," part I, June 20, 1990 and part II, August 29, 1990 and December 11, 1990 (Order No. J-101-80.)

U.S. Violence Against Women Grants Office, *Domestic Violence and Stalking: The Second Annual Report to Congress under the*

Violence Against Women Act, Washington DC: U.S. Government Printing Office (1997)

Van Hasselt, Vincent B., et al., eds., *Handbook of Family Violence*, New York: Plenum Press (1991)

Viano, E.C., ed., *Intimate Violence: Interdisciplinary Perspectives*. Bristol, Pa.: Taylor & Francis (1992)

Vivian, D. and J. Langhinrichensen-Rohling, "Are bi-directionally violent couples mutually victimized? A gender-sensitive comparison," *Violence and Victims*, 9(2), 107-124 (1994)

Waiping, A. L., and M.J. Sporakowski, "The continuation of violent dating relationships among college students," *Journal of College Student Development*, 30, 432-439 (1989)

Wakefield, H. and R. Underwager, *Accusations of Child Sexual Abuse*. Springfield, Ill.: Charles C. Thomas (1988)

Walker, Lenore E., *The Battered Woman*. New York: Harper and Row (1979)

Walker, Lenore E., *The Battered Woman Syndrome*. New York: Springer (1984)

Walsh, M.R., ed., *Women, Men and Gender: Ongoing Debates*, New Haven: Yale University Press (1997)

Weiner, N. and M. Wolfgang, eds., *Pathways to Criminal Violence*, Thousand Oaks, Calif.: Sage (1989)

Wekerle, C. and D.A. Wolfe, "The Role of Child Maltreatment and Attachment Style in Adolescent Relationship Violence," *Development and Psychopathology*, 10:571-586 (1998)

Whitbeck, L. B., et. Al., "Intergenerational continuity of parental rejection and depressed affect," *Journal of Personality and Social Psychology*, 63(6), 1036-1045 (1992)

White and Humphrey, "Women's aggression in heterosexual conflicts," *Aggressive Behavior*, 20, 195-202 (1994)

White, J. W. and M.P. Koss, "Courtship violence: Incidence in a national sample of higher education students," *Violence and Victims*, 6, 247-256 (1991)

White, J. W., and R. M. Kowalski, "Deconstructing the myth of the nonaggressive woman: A feminist analysis," *Psychology of Women Quarterly*, 18, 487-508 (1994)

Wilson, M. and M. Daly, "Spousal homicide risk and estrangement," *Violence and Victims*, 8(1), 3-16 (1993)

Wilson, M. I. and M. Daley, "Who kills whom in spouse killings? On the exceptional sex ratio of spousal homicides in the United States," *Criminology*, 30, 189-215 (1992)

Woffordt, S., D.E. Mihalic and S. Menard, "Continuities in marital violence," *Journal of Family Violence*, 9(3), 195-225 (1994)

Wolff, Isobell, "Beyond the Rolling Pin: Domestic Violence and the Other Side," *Spectator Magazine*, p. 22, November 28, 1992

Zeichner, A., and R.O. Pihl, "Effects of alcohol and behavior contingencies on human aggression," *Journal of Abnormal Aggression*, 88(2), 153-160 (1979)

Zingraff, Matthew and Randall Thompson, "Differential Sentencing of Women and Men in the USA," *International Journal of the Sociology of Law*, no. 12: 401-13 (1984)

Notes

[1]"[T]he statistics [on female violence] are likely to be misused by misogynists and apologists for male violence."--Murray Straus, "Physical Assaults by Wives: A major social problem," in R. J. Gelles and D. R. Loseke, eds., *Current Controversies on Family Violence*, Newbury Park, Calif.: Sage (1993), pp. 67-87. *See also* Kristiansen, C. M., et. al., "The Sociopolitical Context of the Delayed Memory Debate," in Williams, L.M. and V.L. Banyard, eds., *Trauma and Memory*, Thousand Oaks, Calif.: Sage (1999)(suggesting that people who express skepticism about female victimization claims are misogynists.)

[2]Responding to increasing reports of domestic violence against men, Patricia Ireland, then president of the National Organization for Women, asserted that the domestic abuse issue is being "hijacked by anti-feminist advocates." Associated Press, "In the gender wars, another flashpoint: battered men," *Seattle Times*, June 16, 2001. When *Mother Jones* published the results of the Dunedin study, *infra* (a study showing that women perpetrate as much violence against their intimate partners as men do), it was immediately attacked by the media watchdog group, F.A.I.R., on the grounds that disclosing the truth to the general public might jeopardize funding for battered women's shelters and "serves the ideological agendas of conservative pundits who wear the anti-feminist label with pride." *Extra!*, November/December, 1999. Ironically, F.A.I.R. stands for Fairness and *Accuracy* In Reporting.

[3]Rita Smith, executive director of the National Coalition Against Domestic Violence, has been quoted as saying that the movement

to provide advocacy and services for battered men is coming
from men who are themselves guilty of abuse. *See* Crary,
David, "Domestic Violence Strikes Men," *Amarillo Globe-
News* (Associated Press), June 18, 2001. Battered women's
advocates almost invariably maintain that if a man is assaulted
by a woman, it can only be because he deserved it--he must
have hit her first. Respectable research, however, has debunked
the "self-defense" myth. (See Chapter 3.) Still, psychologists
and other professionals have expressed a fear that if the truth
about domestic abuse is made public, then men may use the
information to avoid responsibility for their own acts of violence.
Cf. Beaupre, Becky, "No place to run for male victims of
domestic abuse," *Detroit News*, April 20, 1997. This, of course,
assumes that it is *not* a problem if women use the false societal
belief that women are never aggressive to avoid responsibility
for their own acts of aggression. In other words, fear of the
truth, in this context, is really little more than a manifestation of
the American cultural belief that a woman's place is on a pedestal
while it is a man's lot in life to be perpetually devalued.

[4]Dunn, Katherine, "Just As Fierce," *Mother Jones*, November/
December, 1994.

[5]Male victims of domestic abuse are actually members of
two minority groups: men (who, according to the latest
Census figures, are significantly outnumbered by women
in the population of the United States); and male victims of
domestic abuse (who, according to the government at least, are
outnumbered by female victims by a ratio of 20-to-1.)

[6]Easton, Steven A., *Abuse of Men in Families and the Interacting
Legacy of Abuse in the Justice System*, testimony before the
Special Joint Senate, House of Commons Committee on Child
Custody and Access, Toronto, Canada: Easton Alliance

[7]Beaupre, Becky, "Spotlight on female abuser: For 13 years, he
never hit back," *Detroit News*, April 20, 1997. Names have been
changed to protect privacy.

[8]Some states have gone so far as to enact the "95%" figure into
law. *See, e.g.,* Wash. Adm. Code 388-60-140(7), which actually
makes it a law that "a victim of domestic violence is female
in ninety-five percent of domestic violence incidents." This

law was enacted at a time when even the U.S. Department of Justice's National Violence Against Women Act Survey could not avoid coming to the conclusion that at least one-third of all victims of domestic violence are men. The Violence Against Women Survey is discussed in more detail *infra.*

[9]An interesting detail about the Super Bowl Sunday hoax is the fact that a representative of an organization calling itself F.A.I.R. ("Fairness and Accuracy In Reporting"), supposedly a media watchdog group, was in attendance at this press conference. Even this media "watchdog" group swallowed the hoax hook, line and sinker. Indeed, FAIR's publicists actively helped spread it--mass-mailing a document telling women: "Don't remain home with him during the game." A F.A.I.R. representative was also in attendance at a *Good Morning America* show during which Lenore Walker repeated the claim about violence against women on Super Bowl Sunday. Again, F.A.I.R. accepted the claim without question. It was F.A.I.R., in fact, that had supplied the Boston *Globe* with the false information it printed in the January 29, 1993 article. After the Washington *Post* ran an exposé of the hoax, F.A.I.R. representative Linda Mitchell, who had been present at the original news conference with Ms. Kuehl, admitted that she knew at the time that Ms. Kuehl was lying about the Old Dominion study. She said she just didn't feel right about challenging her. Why anyone would join a media "watchdog" group dedicated to promoting "fairness and accuracy in reporting" if she felt comfortable with simply standing by and saying nothing when she knows that the media is being used to perpetrate a deliberate fraud upon the American news-reading public is difficult to comprehend. For a full exposition of the Super Bowl Sunday Hoax, *see* Sommers, Christina Hoff, *Who Stole Feminism? How Women Have Betrayed Women*, New York: Simon and Schuster (1994.)

[10]The term "cycle of abuse" is also used to refer to a repetitive pattern of violence perpetrated by the same person against the same victim, a characteristic that has been observed among some batterers. *See* Walker, Lenore E., *The Battered Woman*, New York: Harper and Row (1979.)

[11]*See* Straus, M. A. and C.L. Yodanis, "Corporal punishment by parents: Implications for primary prevention of assaults on spouses and parents," *The University of Chicago Law School Roundtable*, 2(1), 35-66 (1995); *and* Straus, Murray A., Richard J. Gelles and Suzanne K. Steinmetz, *Behind Closed Doors: Violence in the American Family,* Garden City, N.J.: Anchor (1980). The Minnesota Legislative Child Protection Study Commission estimates that 95% of Minnesota prisoners who perpetrated violent crimes were maltreated as children. Snow, Misti, "Psychiatrist James Gilligan has studied society's most violent people and concludes the theories underpinning our criminal-justice system are all wrong," *Minneapolis Star-Tribune*, July, 1996.

[12]*Ibid. See also* Karr-Morse, R. and M.S. Wiley, *Ghosts From the Nursery: Tracing the Roots of Violence*, New York: Atlantic Monthly Press (1997); Langhinrich-Rohling, P. Neidig and G. Thorn, "Violent Marriages: Gender differences in levels of current violence and past abuse," *Journal of Family Violence*, 10, 2, pp. 159-176 (1995); Malone and Tyree, *Cycle of Violence: Explanation of marital aggression and victimization*, paper presented at the 86th Annual Meeting of the American Society of Anthropology, Cincinnati, Ohio (1991); Pearson, P., *When She Was Bad: How and Why Women Get Away With Murder*, New York: Putnam (1997); Bowker, L. H., *Beating Wife Beating*, Lexington, Mass.: Lexington (1983); Fagan, J. A., D.K. Stewart and K.V. Hansen, "Violent men or violent husbands? Background factors and situational correlates," in D. Finkelhor, et. al., eds., *The Dark Side of Families*, Beverly Hills, Calif.: Sage (1983), pp. 49-68; Walker, Lenore E., *The Battered Woman Syndrome*, New York: Springer (1984); Shupe, A., W.A. Stacey and L.R. Hazlewood, Violent Men, Violent Couples: The Dynamics of Domestic Violence, Lexington, Mass.: Lexington Books (1987)

[13]By "empirical data" is meant data about the incidence of abuse, not information about societal responses to abuse. Information about arrest and prosecution rates, or about the utilization of battered women's shelters and medical services, tells about how our society *responds* to abuse victims; it doesn't tell us what the actual *incidence* of abuse is.

Law enforcement reports from 15 years ago do seem to suggest that in 95% of domestic altercations, it was the man who was arrested. As we will see, however, the arrest rate today is closer to 80% than 95%, and in some parts of the country 35% of domestic violence arrests are of females. If arrest rates were determinative of the actual incidence of abuse, then it would be necessary to conclude that in some parts of the country, women have become 7 times more violent than they were just a few years ago. While there is some evidence that women are getting more violent (see Chapter 8), it seems highly unlikely that they have become *7 times* more violent. That is to say, it is more likely that the data is simply telling us that the societal *response* to domestic violence has changed, not that the actual incidence of domestic violence has changed that much.

[14]U.S. Bureau of Justice Statistics, *Report to the Nation on Crime and Justice*, 2nd ed., NCJ 105506, Washington, DC: U.S. Department of Justice (1988), p. 26.

[15]*Ibid; see also* U.S. Bureau of Justice Statistics, *Criminal Victimization in the United States, 1987*, NCJ 115524 (1989), p. 16, and Federal Bureau of Investigation, *Crime in the United States* (1988), p. 11.

[16]U.S. Bureau of Justice Statistics, *Report to the Nation on Crime and Justice, supra*. The homicide victimization rate for American males between 15 and 24 years of age is 8 times higher than the homicide rate in any other country, including Middle Eastern countries like Iraq, Iran and Afghanistan. Fingerhut, L.A. and J.C. Kleinman, "International and Interstate Comparisons of Homicide Among Young Males," *Journal of the American Medical Association*, 263 (1990), 3292-3295.

[17]U.S. Bureau of Justice Statistics, *Report to the Nation on Crime and Justice, supra*, at p. 27.

[18]*Ibid.* at p. 28; *see also* U.S. Bureau of Justice Statistics, *Criminal Victimization in the United States, 1987, supra*, at p. 16; and Federal Bureau of Investigation, *Crime in the United States, supra*, at p. 11. As long ago as 1967, it was known that males are the primary targets of violence in our country. According to the President's Commission on Law Enforcement and Administration of Justice, "The Challenge of Crime in a Free

Society" (1967), which is cited in the *Statistical Abstracts of the United States, 1972,* at p. 145, men at that time were victims of aggravated assault 143% more often than women were; were burglarized 404% more often than women were; were the victims of larceny 150% more often than women; and were the victims of robbery 45% more often than women were. Even back then, 80% of all murder victims were male. *See* Federal Bureau of Investigation, "Crime in the United States," *Uniform Crime Reports,* Washington DC, August 8, 1973, p. 6.

[19]U.S. Bureau of Justice Statistics, *Report to the Nation on Crime and Justice, supra,* at p. 29; and U.S. Bureau of Justice Statistics, *Criminal Victimization in the United States, 1987, supra.*

[20]U.S. Bureau of Justice Statistics, *Criminal Victimization in the United States, 1994: A National Crime Victimization Survey Report,* NCJ-162126, Washington DC: U.S. Department of Justice (1997)

[21]Greenfeld, Lawrence A., et. al., *Violence by Intimates: Analysis of Data on Crimes by Current or Former Spouses, Boyfriends, and Girlfriends,* NCJ 167237, Washington, DC: U.S. Bureau of Justice Statistics (1998), p. 4.

[22]*Ibid.* at p. 6.

[23]Rennison, Callie Marie, *Criminal Victimization 2000, Changes 1999-2000 with Trends 1993-2000,* Bureau of Justice Statistics National Crime Victimization Survey, NCJ 187007, Washington, DC: U.S. Department of Justice (2001.)

[24]*Id.,* at p. 6.

[25]Although law enforcement records generally only tell us about the societal response to crime, not the actual incidence of crime, unfortunately they are the only source of information about the crime of homicide. A homicide victim is, by definition, dead. Consequently, the probability that he will be able to respond to survey questions is not great.

[26]"Men and violence: From being hurt to hurting," *Minneapolis Star Tribune,* October 7, 1992, p. 18A

[27]Attorney General Daniel E. Lungren's Policy Council on Violence Prevention, *Violence Prevention: A Vision of Hope* (1995), p. 42.

[28]Mcleod, M., "Women Against Men: An Examination of Domestic Violence Based on an Analysis of Official Data and National

Victimization Data," *Justice Quarterly*: 1(2)(1984), 171-93, at pp. 185-86.

[29]U.S. Bureau of Justice Statistics, *Criminal Victimization in the United States, 1987, supra*, at p. 16; *see also* Federal Bureau of Investigation, Uniform Crime Reports, *Crime in the United States* (1990), pp. 15 and 51 and U.S. Bureau of Justice Statistics, *Criminal Victimization in the United States*, National Crime Survey Report (1973-1988), p. 15. None of this is intended to mean that men are never the victims of sex crimes. Indeed, according to the Bureau of Justice Statistics, over 14,700 males over the age of 12 were raped or sexually assaulted in the year 2000 alone. Rennison, *Criminal Victimization 2000, Changes 1999-2000 with Trends 1993-2000, supra*, at p. 8

[30]Rennison, *Criminal Victimization 2000, Changes 1999-2000 with Trends 1993-2000, supra*, at p. 8; *compare* Federal Bureau of Investigation, Uniform Crime Reports, *Crime in the United States* (1990.)

[31]As of 1999, there were 251,200 people serving time in state prisons whose most serious crime was a drug offense. As of December 31, 1995, less than a thousand federal prison inmates were serving time for homicide, while 51,737 federal prison inmates were serving time for drug offenses. Beck, Allen J. and Paige M. Harrison, *Prisoners in 2000*, Washington, DC: U.S. Department of Justice (2001), p. 12. In 1999 alone, 22,372 people were sentenced by federal judges to prison for drug crimes. Scalia, John, *Federal Drug Offenders, 1999 with Trends 1984-99*, NCJ 187285, Washington DC: U.S. Bureau of Justice Statistics (2001). 7,128 of the federal prisoners who were sentenced in 1999 were convicted of a crime involving marijuana only; and the average sentence imposed by federal judges on marijuana offenders is about 3 years. *Ibid.*, at p. 9. Prisoners sentenced for drug offenses now constitute 61% of the federal prison population. Beck and Harrison, *supra*, at p. 13.

[32]U.S. Bureau of Justice Statistics, *Correctional Populations in the United States*, NCJ 118762, (1989), p. 105; and U.S. Bureau of the Census, *Statistical Abstracts of the United States: 1991*, 111th ed., p. 195.

[33]Tjaden, Patricia and Nancy Thoennes, *Prevalence, Incidence and Consequences of Violence Against Women: Findings From the National Violence Against Women Survey*, Washington, DC: National Institute of Justice and Centers for Disease Control (1998)

[34]Koss, Mary, Christine A. Gidycz and Nadine Wisniewski, "The Scope of Rape: Incidence and Prevalence of Sexual Aggression and Victimization in a National Sample of Higher Education Students," *Journal of Consulting and Clinical Psychology*, vol. 55, no. 2 (1987), pp. 162-70, reprinted in the *New York Times*, April 21, 1987.

[35]Gilbert, Neil, "Examining the Facts: Advocacy Research Overstates the Incidence of Date and Acquaintance Rape," in Gelles and Loseke, eds., *Current Controversies in Family Violence, supra,* pp.120-132; Schoenberg, Nara and Sam Roe, "The Making of an Epidemic," *Toledo Blade*, October 10, 1993; Warshaw, Robin, *I Never Called It Rape: The Ms. Report, with afterword by Mary Koss*, New York: Harper Perennial (1988); Koss, Mary, et. al., "Stranger and Acquaintance Rape," *Psychology of Women Quarterly*, vol. 12 (1988), pp. 1/24.

[36]U.S. Department of Education, *Campus Crime and Security*, Washington, D.C.: U.S. Government Printing Office (1997).

[37]Muehlenhard, Charlene L. and Stephen W. Cook, "Men's Self Reports of Unwanted Sexual Activity," *Journal of Sex Research*, vol. 24 (1988), pp. 58-72.

[38]Aizenman, M., and G. Kelley, "The incidence of violence and acquaintance rape in dating relationships among college men and women, *Journal of College Student Development*, 29, 305-311(1988).

[39]Straus, M. A., et. al., "The Revised Conflict Tactics Scales (CTS2). Development and preliminary psychometric data," *Journal of Family Issues*, 17, 283-316 (1996)

[40]Similar frauds have been perpetrated on the American public concerning the incidence of sexual harassment. For example, in 1998 the National Organization of Women issued a report declaring that "Our schools are training grounds for sexual harassment" and urging schools to punish severely any boys who were caught doing it. National Organization of Women,

Issue Report: Sexual Harassment (April, 1998.) The organization relied on an American Association of University Women ("AAUW") study--*Hostile Hallways* (1993)--according to which "85%" of girls experienced sexual harassment at school. What NOW (and the media) failed to mention is that the AAUW study *also* found that 76% of *boys* had experienced sexual harassment, as that term was defined by the AAUW. Four scholars at the University of Michigan did a follow-up study of the AAUW data and found that "The majority of both genders (53%) described themselves as having been both victim and perpetrator of harassment--that is most students had been harassed and had harassed others." Moreover, they concluded that "Our results led us to question the simple perpetrator-victim model..." *American Education Research Journal*, Summer, 1996.

[41]The usual response to examples like these is to categorize them as aberrational exceptions to the rule that women are incapable of violence. I have even heard it argued that these women were not really female--that psychologically, they were male. Of course, it is merely the presence of a Y chromosome, not violence, that causes a person to be male. The "psychological male" argument is simply an example of circular reasoning at its worst.

[42]Goldberg, Carey, "Spouse Abuse Crackdown, Surprisingly, Nets Many Women," *New York Times*, November 23, 1999. And these are just the *arrests*. As we will see, the incidence of female abuse is substantially higher than that reflected in data obtained from arrest reports, for a variety of reasons--most notably the strong male reluctance to report victimization by females, and the proliferation of anti-male gender-profiling arrest policies in domestic abuse cases.

[43]Beaupre, Becky, "No place to run for male victims of domestic abuse," *supra*. According to Michigan State Police, police perceive adult men as the victim in about 20% of the domestic abuse cases that are reported to them. *Ibid.*

[44]Greenfeld, et. al., *Violence by Intimates*, *supra*, at pp. 6-7.

[45]All statistics in this paragraph are from Rennison, *Criminal Victimization 2000, Changes 1999-2000 with Trends 1993-2000*, *supra*, p. 8.

[46]*See*, e.g., Mercy, James A. and Linda E. Saltzman, "Fatal Violence Among Spouses in the United States, 1976-85," *American Journal of Public Health*, 1989, 79(5), pp. 595-599 (more black husbands killed by spouses than any other demographic group; but overall, husbands and wives are almost equally likely to kill each other); *see also* Wolfgang, M., *Patterns in Criminal Homicide*, New York: Wiley (1958)(number of wives killed by husbands nearly equal to number of husbands killed by wives); Curtis, L.A., *Criminal Violence: National Patterns and Behavior*, Lexington, Mass.: Lexington Books (1974)(number of murders of women by men about the same as the number of murders of men by women); *and* Wilson, M. I. and M. Daley, "Who kills whom in spouse killings? On the exceptional sex ratio of spousal homicides in the United States," *Criminology*, 30, 189-215 (1992) In some major cities, e.g., Chicago, Detroit and Houston, more wives than husbands were proven to have been perpetrators of spousal murder. *Ibid.*

[47]Greenfeld, et. al., *Violence by Intimates, supra*, at p. 6.

[48]*Ibid.*

[49]U.S. Bureau of Justice Statistics, *Murder in Families*, NCJ-143498, Washington, D.C.: U.S. Department of Justice (1994)

[50]Jurik, N. C. and R. Winn, "Gender and homicide: A comparison of men and women who kill," *Violence and Victims*, 5(4), 227-242 (1990); Kellerman, A. L. and J.A. Mercy, "Men, women, and murder: Gender specific differences in rates of fatal violence and victimization," *Journal of Trauma*, 33(1), 1-5 (1992); Browne, A. and K.R. Williams, "Exploring the effect of resource availability and the likelihood of female-perpetrated homicides," *Law and Society Review*, 23(1), 75-94 (1989); Wilbanks, W., "The female homicide offender in Dade County, Florida," *Criminal Justice Review*, 8, 9-14 (1983)

[51]Attorney General Daniel E. Lungren's Policy Council on Violence Prevention, *supra,* at p. 42.

[52]*Ibid.* at p. 43.

[53]1 in 500 = 0.2%. 1 in 2 = 50%. 50% is 250 times higher than 0.2%. [Note: the figures given here are for illustrative purposes only, and are not intended to express or imply anything whatsoever about racial crime rates.]

[54]The practice isn't just limited to the United States. *See, e.g.,* Gardner, Julie, "Use of Official Statistics and Crime Survey Data in Determining Violence against Women," in Sumner, Chris, et. al., eds., *International Victimology: Selected Papers from the 8th International Symposium,* Canberra: Australian Institute of Criminology (1996). After acknowledging the data showing that twice as many men as women are assaulted in Australia each year (Australian Bureau of Statistics, *Crime and Safety in Australia 1993,* Canberra, Australia (1994)), and that 37.9% of male assault victims are victims of someone they knew, the author declares that these "data found that men were unlikely to be assaulted by someone they knew." *Ibid.,* at p. 53. The data showed nothing of the kind. The 37.9% figure tells us only about the *male risk* for intimate violence; it doesn't tell us anything about the *relative risk* of each gender for victimization by an intimate. To see this, suppose the number of women assaulted is 10. If 3 out of 4 women were assaulted by someone they knew, then 7.5 women would have been assaulted by someone they knew. Since twice as many men were assaulted, the number of male assault victims would be 20. 37.9% of 20 is 7.58. Thus, although men are more likely to be assaulted by strangers than women are, this does not necessarily mean that women are more likely to be assaulted by someone they know than men are. To the contrary, in our example we see that, in terms of actual numbers, men are slightly more likely to be assaulted by someone they know than women are (7.58 men, as compared to 7.5 women.)

[55]Greenfeld, et. al., *Violence by Intimates, supra,* at p. 14.

[56]Straus, Murray A. and Richard J. Gelles, "Societal Change and Change in Family Violence from 1975 to 1985 as Revealed by Two National Surveys," *Journal of Marriage and the Family,* vol. 48, August 1986, pp. 465-79. Actually, this was consistent with a 3-1/2-year survey of 60,000 households conducted by the U.S. Census Bureau which shows that as early as 1977 the government knew that even women acknowledged that they hit men more frequently than men hit them. U.S. Bureau of the Census, *National Crime Survey,* Washington, D.C.: U.S. Government Printing Office (1977)

[57]Tjaden and Thoennes (1998), *supra.* According to the study, male victims average 3.5 victimizations per year and female victims average 3.4 victimizations per year.

[58]The poll was conducted between June 24 and July 3, 1994 with 1,002 adult Minnesotans. It should be noted that for results based on samples of 1,002, there is a 95% certainty that sampling and other random error will be no more than 3.1 percentage points, plus or minus. Minneapolis *Star Tribune,* 1994.

[59]*See generally* Fiebert, M., *References examining assaults by women on their spouses/partners: An annotated bibliography,* paper presented to the American Psychological Society Convention, Washington, D.C., May 24, 1997. There seems to be an inverse correlation between the soundness of the research methodology used and the extent to which the results are publicized in the media.

Many of the studies cited in this chapter utilized a research instrument known as the Conflict Tactics Scale (CTS.) For an explanation of the CTS, and an examination of the criticisms to which it has been subjected, *see* Appendix.

[60]National Institute of Justice, *Partner Violence Among Young Adults,* NIJ Research Preview, U.S. Department of Justice (1997); and Magdol, L., et. al., "Gender Differences in Partner Violence in a Birth Cohort of 21-Year-Olds," *Journal of Consulting and Clinical Psychology,* 65, no. 1 (1997): 68-78

[61]Moffitt, Terrie E. and Avshalom Caspi, *Findings About Partner Violence From the Dunedin Multidisciplinary Health and Development Study,* NCJ 170018, Washington DC: National Institute of Justice (1999), p. 4. Similar findings have been made by other researchers. See, e.g., Morse, Barbara, "Beyond the Conflict Tactics Scale: Assessing Gender Differences in Partner Violence," *Violence and Victims* 10 (Winter 1995): 251-272.

[62]British Home Office findings, based on the British Crime Survey, as reported in *The London Times,* January 22, 1999; and Travis, Alan, "Both sexes equally likely to suffer domestic violence," *Manchester Guardian,* January 22, 1999. The study was conducted by British Home Office researchers Catriona Mirrlees-Black and Carole Byron. When I tried to obtain copies of these reports directly from the British government, I could

not. Instead, I received the following message: "Please note that the British Home Office does not allow the use of...[the British Crime Survey's] domestic violence or stalking data for teaching purposes." As a result, I have had to rely on contemporaneous newspaper accounts of the findings.

[63]Although this information was available to it at the time, the United Nations selectively omitted this particular finding from its report on the international incidence of domestic abuse, "The Greatest Abuse--Violence Against Women," in *The State Of The World's Children* (1995). *Cf.* Coochey, John, "All Men are Bastards." *The Independent Monthly* (November, 1995)

[64]"First Large-Scale Study Reveals Elder Abuse is Primarily by Wives Against Husbands," *Marriage and Divorce Today*, December 15, 1986

[65]Greenfeld, et. al., *Violence by Intimates, supra.*

[66]Mann, Coramae, *When Women Kill*, Albany, N.Y.: State University of New York Press (1996), p. 83.

[67]*See* Note 59.

[68]Archer, John, "Sex differences in aggression between heterosexual partners: A meta-analytic review," *Psychological Bulletin*, 126(5), 651-680 (September, 2000)

[69]Archer, J., and Ray, N, "Dating violence in the United Kingdom: a preliminary study, *Aggressive Behavior*, 15, 337-343 (1989)

[70]Arias, I., Samios, M., and K.D. O'Leary, "Prevalence and correlates of physical aggression during courtship," *Journal of Interpersonal Violence*: 2, 82-90 (1987)

[71]Arias, I., and P. Johnson, "Evaluations of physical aggression among intimate dyads," *Journal of Interpersonal Violence*, 4, 298-307 (1989)

[72]Bernard, M. L., and J.L. Bernard, "Violent intimacy: The family as a model for love relationships," *Family Relations*, 32, 283-286 (1983)

[73]Billingham, R. E. and A. R. Sack, "Courtship violence and the interactive status of the relationship," *Journal of Adolescent Research*, 1, 315-325 (1986)

[74]Bland, R., and H. Orne, "Family violence and psychiatric disorder," *Canadian Journal of Psychiatry*, 31, 129-137 (1986)

[75]Bohannon, J. R., D.A. Dosser Jr. and S.E. Lindley, S. E., "Using couple data to determine domestic violence rates: An attempt to replicate previous work," *Violence and Victims*, 10, 133-41 (1995)

[76]Bookwala, J., et. al., "Predictors of dating violence: A multi variate analysis," *Violence and Victims*, 7, 297-311 (1992)

[77]Breen, R.N., "Premarital Violence: A Study of Abuse within Dating Relationships of College Students," University of Texas at Arlington (1985)

[78]Brinkerhoff, M., and E. Lupri, "Interspousal violence," *Canadian Journal of Sociology*, 13, 407-434 (1988). The study also found that, for women, there was a positive correlation between the perpetration of domestic violence and educational attainment: the more educated a woman is, the more likely she is to behave violently toward a man. The opposite correlation was found among men: the more educated a man is, the less likely it is that he will behave violently toward a woman. Professor Lupri has also noted that the overall violence index rate for women is 23.3, as compared to 17.8 for men. Lupri, Eugene, "Why Does Family Violence Occur?" cited in Easton, *Abuse of Men in Families and the Interacting Legacy of Abuse in the Justice System, supra.*

[79]Brush, L. D., "Violent Acts and Injurious Outcomes in Married Couples: Methodological issues in the National Survey of Families and Households, *Gender & Society*, 4, 56-67 (1990)

[80]Brutz, J., and B.B. Ingoldsby, "Conflict resolution in Quaker families," *Journal of Marriage and the Family*, 46, 21-26 (1984)

[81]Burke, P. J., J.E. Stets, J. E., and M.A. Pirog-Good, "Gender identity, self-esteem, and physical and sexual abuse in dating relationships," *Social Psychology Quarterly*, 51, 272-285 (1988)

[82]Carlson, B. E., "Dating violence: a research review and comparison with spouse abuse," *Social Casework*, 68, 16-23 (1987)

[83]Carrado, M., et. al., "Aggression in British heterosexual relationships: a descriptive analysis, *Aggressive Behavior*, 22, 401-415 (1996)

[84]Cascardi, M., J. Langhinrichsen, and D. Vivian, "Marital aggression: Impact, injury, and health correlates for husbands and wives," *Archives of Internal Medicine*, 152, 1178-1184 (1992)

[85]Barling, et al., "Factor similarity of the conflict tactics scales across samples, spouses, and sites: Issues and implications," *Journal of Family Violence*: 2, 37-54 (1987).

[86]Caulfield, M. B., and D.S. Riggs, "The assessment of dating aggression: Empirical evaluation of the Conflict Tactics Scale," *Journal of Interpersonal Violence*, 4, 549-558 (1992)

[87]Claxton-Oldfield, S. & Arsenault, J., *The initiation of physically aggressive behaviour by female university students toward their male partners: Prevalence and the reasons offered for such behaviors*, unpublished manuscript (1999)

[88]Coney, N. S., & Mackey, W. C., "The feminization of domestic violence in America: The woozle effect goes beyond rhetoric," *Journal of Men's Studies*, 8, (1) 45-58 (1999)

[89]Deal, J. E., and K.S. Wampler, "Dating violence: The primacy of previous experience," *Journal of Social and Personal Relationships*, 3, 457-471 (1986)

[90]Ensminger-Vanfossen, B., "Intersexual violence in Monroe County, New York," *Victimology* 4(2): 299-305 (1979)

[91]Ernst, Amy A., et. al., "Domestic violence in an inner-city ED," *Annals of Emergency Medicine*, 30, 190-197 (1997)

[92]Fekete, John, *Moral Panic: Biopolitics Rising*. Quebec, Canada: Robert Davies (1994)

[93]Fiebert, M. S., and D.M. Gonzalez, "Women who initiate assaults: The reasons offered for such behavior," *Psychological Reports*, 80, 583-590 (1997); the researchers also found that younger women (those in their twenties) are more likely to physically assault a male partner than older women (those in their thirties) are.

[94]Flynn, C. P., "Relationship violence by women: issues and implications," *Family Relations*, 36, 295-299 (1990)

[95]Follingstad, D. R., S. Wright, and J.A. Sebastian, "Sex differences in motivations and effects in dating violence," *Family Relations*, 40, 51-57 (1991)

[96]Foshee, V. A., "Gender differences in adolescent dating abuse prevalence, types and injuries," *Health Education Research*, 11, (3) 275-286 (1996)

[97]Sleek, Scott, "Sorting out the reasons couples turn violent: Data on violence between men and women tell only part of the story,"

APA Monitor (American Psychological Association), vol. 29, no. 4 (April, 1998)

[98]Gelles, Richard J. *The Violent Home: A Study of Physical Aggression Between Husbands and Wives*, Beverly Hills, Calif.: Sage (1974)

[99]Gelles, Richard J., "Domestic Criminal Violence," in Wolfgang, Marvin E., *Criminal Violence*, Beverly Hills, Calif.: Sage (1982), pg. 201-235.

[100]Gelles, Richard J. and Murray A. Straus, *Intimate Violence: The Causes and Consequences of Abuse in the American Family*, New York: Simon & Schuster (1988)

[101]George, M. J., "A victimization survey of female perpetrated assaults in the United Kingdom," *Aggressive Behavior*, 25, 67-79 (1999); *see also* George, M. J., "Riding the donkey backwards: Men as the unacceptable victims of marital violence," *Journal of Men's Studies*, 3, 137-159 (1994)(women as abusive of men as men are of women)

[102]Goodyear-Smith, F. A. and T.M. Laidlaw, "Aggressive acts and assaults in intimate relationships: Towards an understanding of the literature," *Behavioral Sciences and the Law*, 17,285-304 (1999)

[103]Harders, R. J., et. al., *Verbal and physical abuse in dating relationships*, paper presented at the meeting of American Psychological Association, San Francisco, Calif. (1998)

[104]Headey, B., D. Scott and D. de Vaus, *Domestic Violence in Australia: Are Women and Men Equally Violent?* (1999)

[105]Henton, J., et. al., "Romance and violence in dating relationships," *Journal of Family Issues*, 4, 467-482 (1983)

[106]Jackson, S. M., F. Cram, F. and F.W. Seymour, "Violence and sexual coercion in high school students' dating relationships," *Journal of Family Violence*, 15, 23-36 (2000)

[107]Jouriles, E. N., and K.D. O'Leary, "Interpersonal reliability of reports of marital violence," *Journal of Consulting and Clinical Psychology*, 53, 419-421 (1985)

[108]Kalmuss, D., "The intergenerational transmission of marital aggression," *Journal of Marriage and the Family*, 46, 11-19 (1984)

[109]Lane, K. and P.A. Gwartney-Gibbs, "Violence in the context of dating and sex," *Journal of Family Issues*, 6, 45-49 (1985)

[110]Laner, M. R. and J. Thompson, "Abuse and aggression in courting couples," *Deviant Behavior*, 3, 229-244 (1982)

[111]Langhinrichsen-Rohling, J. and D. Vivian, "The correlates of spouses' incongruent reports of marital aggression," *Journal of Family Violence*, 9, 265-283 (1994)

[112]Lo, W. A. and M.J. Sporakowski, "The continuation of violent dating relationships among college students," *Journal of College Student Development*, 30, 432-439 (1989)

[113]Lottes, I. L. and M.S. Weinberg, "Sexual coercion among university students: a comparison of the United States and Sweden" *Journal of Sex Research*, 34, 67-76 (1996)

[114]Magdol, et. al., *supra.*

[115]Makepeace, J. M. "Gender differences in courtship violence victimization," *Family Relations*, 35, 383-388 (1986)

[116]Malone, J., A. Tyree, and K.D. O'Leary, "Generalization and containment: Different effects of past aggression for wives and husbands," *Journal of Marriage and the Family*, 51, 687-697 (1989)

[117]Margolin, G., "The multiple forms of aggressiveness between marital partners: how do we identify them?" *Journal of Marital and Family Therapy*, 13 , 77-84 (1987)

[118]Marshall, L. L., and P. Rose, "Gender, stress and violence in the adult relationships of a sample of college students," *Journal of Social and Personal Relationships*, 4, 299-316 (1987); Marshall, L. L. and P. Rose, "Premarital violence: The impact of family of origin violence, stress and reciprocity," *Violence and Victims*, 5, 51-64 (1990)

[119]Mason, A., & V. Blankenship, "Power and affiliation motivation, stress and abuse in intimate relationships," *Journal of Personality and Social Psychology*, 52, 203-210 (1987)

[120]McCarthy, A., *Gender differences in the incidences of, motives for, and consequences of, dating violence among college students*, unpublished Master's thesis, California State University, Long Beach (2001)

[121]McKinney, K., "Measures of verbal, physical and sexual dating violence by gender," *Free Inquiry in Creative Sociology*, 14, 55-60 (1986)

[122]McLeod, *supra*.

[123]McNeely, R. L., and G. Robinson-Simpson, "The truth about domestic violence: A falsely framed issue," *Social Work*, 32, 485-490 (1987)

[124]Mercy, James A. and Linda E. Saltzman, "Fatal Violence Among Spouses in the United States, 1976-85," *American Journal of Public Health*, 79(5): 595-599 (1989)

[125]Meredith, W. H., D.A. Abbot, and S.L. Adams, "Family violence in relation to marital and parental satisfaction and family strengths," *Journal of Family Violence*, 1, 299-305 (1986)

[126]Milardo, R. M., "Gender asymmetry in common couple violence," *Personal Relationships*, 5, 423-438 (1998)

[127]Morse, Barbara, "Beyond the Conflict Tactics Scale: Assessing Gender Differences in Partner Violence," *Violence and Victims* 10(4) (Winter 1995): 251-272. In 1983 the rate of male-to-female violence (of any kind) was 36.7, while the rate of female-to-male violence (of any kind) was 48; in 1992, the rate of male-to-female violence was 20.2, while the rate female-to-male violence was 27.9. Decreasing rates of violence were attributed to the fact that the participants were getting older as the study progressed, and the perpetration of physical violence tends to decrease with age. Overall, Morse found that more than twice as many women as men assaulted a partner who had not assaulted them.

[128]Murphy, J.E., "Date abuse and forced intercourse among college students," in G. P. Hotaling, D. Finkelhor, J. T. Kirkpatrick, & M. A. Straus, eds., *Family Abuse and Its Consequences: New Directions in Research*, Beverly Hills, Calif.: Sage (1988), pp. 285-296.

[129]Mwamwenda, T. S., *Husband Battery among the Xhosa speaking people of Transkei, South Africa*, unpublished manuscript, University of Transkei, S. A. (1997)

[130]Nisonoff, L., and I. Bitman, "Spouse abuse: Incidence and relationship to selected demographic variables," *Victimology*, 4, 131-140 (1979.) Nisonoff and Bitman also found that men and women reported very similar instances of violence both by themselves and their partners.

[131]O'Keeffe, N. K., K. Brockopp, and Chew, E., "Teen dating violence," *Social Work*, 31, 465-468 (1986)

[132]O'Leary, K. D., et. al., "Prevalence and stability of physical aggression between spouses: A longitudinal analysis," *Journal of Consulting and Clinical Psychology*, 57, 263-268 (1989)

[133]O'Leary, et. al., "Premarital Physical Aggression," State University of New York at Stony Brook and Syracuse University (1985)

[134]Plass, M. S. and J.C. Gessner, "Violence in courtship relations: a southern sample, *Free Inquiry in Creative Sociology*, 11, 198-202 (1983)

[135]Riggs, D. S., K.D. O'Leary, and F.C. Breslin, "Multiple correlates of physical aggression in dating couples," *Journal of Interpersonal Violence*, 5, 61-73 (1990)

[136]Rollins, B. C., and Y. Oheneba-Sakyi, "Physical violence in Utah households," *Journal of Family Violence*, 5, 301-309 (1990)

[137]Rosenfeld, R., "Changing relationships between men and women. A note on the decline in intimate partner violence," *Homicide Studies*, 1, 72-83 (1997)

[138]Rouse, L. P., R. Breen, and M. Howell, "Abuse in intimate relationships. A Comparison of married and dating college students," *Journal of Interpersonal Violence*, 3, 414-429 (1988)

[139]Russell, R. J. H., and B. Hulson, "Physical and psychological abuse of heterosexual partners," *Personality and Individual Differences*, 13, 457-473 (1992)

[140]Ryan, K. A., "The relationship between courtship violence and sexual aggression in college students," *Journal of Family Violence*, 13, 377-394 (1998)

[141]Sack, A. R., J.F. Keller, and R.D. Howard, "Conflict tactics and violence in dating situations," *International Journal of Sociology of the Family*, 12, 89-100 (1982)

[142]Schafer, J., R. Caetano and C.L. Clark, "Rates of intimate partner violence in the United States," *American Journal of Public Health*, 88, 1702-1704 (1998)

[143]Shook, N. J., et. al., *Journal of Family Violence*, 15, 1-22 (2000)

[144]Sigelman, C. K., C.J. Berry, and K.A. Wiles, "Violence in college students' dating relationships," *Journal of Applied Social Psychology*, 5, 530-548 (1984)

[145]Sommer, R., *Male and female partner abuse: Testing a diathesis-stress model*, unpublished doctoral dissertation, University of Manitoba, Winnipeg, Canada (1994)

[146]Smith, S., et. al., "Adult Domestic Violence," *Health Trends* 24: 97-99 (1992)

[147]Sommer, R., G.E. Barnes, and R.P. Murray, "Alcohol consumption, alcohol abuse, personality and female perpetrated spouse abuse," *Journal of Personality and Individual Differences*, 13, 1315-1323 (1992)

[148]Sorenson, S. B., and C.A. Telles, "Self reports of spousal violence in a Mexican-American and non-Hispanic white population," *Violence and Victims*, 6, 3-15 (1991)

[149]Spencer, G. A., and S.A. Bryant, "Dating violence: A comparison of rural, suburban and urban teens," *Journal of Adolescent Health*, 25 (5) 302-305 (2000)

[150]Steinmetz, Suzanne, "The Battered Husband Syndrome," *Victimology: An International Journal*, 2: 499-509 (1977-1978)

[151]Steinmetz, Suzanne, "A cross cultural comparison of marital abuse," *Journal of Sociology and Social Welfare*, 8, 404-414 (1981)

[152]Steinmetz, Suzanne, "Women and Violence: Victims and Perpetrators," *American Journal of Psychotherapy*, 34(3): 334-350 (1980)

[153]Stets, J. E. and D.A. Henderson, "Contextual factors surrounding conflict resolution while dating: results from a national study," *Family Relations*, 40, 29-40 (1991)

[154]Stets, J. E., and M.A. Pirog-Good, "Violence in dating relationships," *Social Psychology Quarterly*, 50, 237-246 (1987)

[155]Stets, J. E. and M.A. Pirog-Good, "Patterns of physical and sexual abuse for men and women in dating relationships: A descriptive analysis," *Journal of Family Violence*, 4, 63-76 (1989)

[156]Stets, J. E. and M.A. Straus, "Gender differences in reporting of marital violence and its medical and psychological consequences," in M. A. Straus and R. J. Gelles, eds., *Physical Violence in American Families: Risk Factors and Adaptations to Violence in 8,145 Families*, New Brunswick, N.J.: Transaction (1990), pp. 151-165.

[157]Stets, J. E. and M.A. Straus, "The marriage license as a hitting license: A comparison of assaults in dating, cohabiting, and married couples," *Journal of Family Violence*, 4(2), 161-180 (1989)

[158]Straus, Murray, "Victims and aggressors in marital violence," *American Behavioral Scientist*, 23, 681-704 (1980)

[159]Straus, Murray A., "Physical assaults by wives: A major social problem," in Gelles and Loseke, eds., *Current Controversies, supra*, at pp. 67-87.

[160]Straus, Murray, *The controversy over domestic violence by women: A methodological, theoretical, and sociology of science analysis*, paper presented at Claremont Symposium on Applied Social Psychology, Claremont, Calif. (1998)

[161]Straus and Gelles (1986), *supra*. The results were the same even when only the women's version of events were believed--that is, even when the men's versions of events were completely disregarded.

[162]Straus and Gelles (1990), *supra*.

[163]Straus, Gelles and Steinmetz (1980), *supra*, pp.21, 22, 128-133.

[164]Straus, Murray A., et. al., "The Revised Conflict Tactics Scales (CTS2). Development and preliminary psychometric data," *Journal of Family Issues*, 17, 283-316 (1996)

[165]Straus, Murray A. and G. Kaufman Kantor, *Change in spouse assault rates from 1975-1992: A comparison of three national surveys in the United States*, paper presented at the Thirteenth World Congress of Sociology, Bielefeld, Germany, July, 1994.

[166]Straus, Murray A. and Vera Mouradian, *Study of college students report of injuries suffered in dating situations*, unpublished data (1999)

[167]Sugarman, D. B., and G.T. Hotaling, "Dating Violence: Prevalence, Context, and Risk Markers," in M. A. Pirog-Good & J. E. Stets, eds., *Violence in Dating relationships: Emerging Social Issues*, New York: Praeger (1989), pp.3-32.

[168]Szinovacz, M. E., "Using couple data as a methodological tool: The case of marital violence," *Journal of Marriage and the Family*, 45, 633-644 (1983)

[169]Tang, C. S., "Prevalence of spouse aggression in Hong Kong," *Journal of Family Violence*, 9, 347-356 (1994)

[170]Thompson Jr., E. H., "Courtship violence and the male role," *Men's Studies Review*, 7, (3) 1, 4-13 (1990); *see also* Thompson Jr., E. H., "The maleness of violence in data relationships: an appraisal of stereotypes," *Sex Roles*, 24, 261-278 (1991)

[171]Vivian, D., and J. Langhinrichsen-Rohling, "Are bi-directionally violent couples mutually victimized?" in L. K. Hamberger and C. Renzetti, eds., *Domestic Partner Abuse*, New York: Springer (1996), pp. 23-52.

[172]National Association of Social Workers, *Social Work* (Nov./Dec. 1986)

[173]White and Humphrey, "Women's aggression in heterosexual conflicts," *Aggressive Behavior*, 20, 195-202 (1994)

[174]White, J. W., & R. M. Kowalski, "Deconstructing the myth of the nonaggressive woman: A feminist analysis," *Psychology of Women Quarterly*, 18, 487-508 (1994)

[175]White, J. W. and M.P. Koss, "Courtship violence: Incidence in a national sample of higher education students," *Violence and Victims*, 6, 247-256 (1991)

[176]McNeely, R. L. and G. Robinson-Simpson, "The Truth about Domestic Violence: A Falsely Framed Issue," in *Gender Sanity*, University Press of America (1988)

[177]Statistics Canada, *Family Violence in Canada: A Statistical Profile* (2000)

[178]Shervin, Judith, Ph.D. and Jim Sniechowski, Ph.D., "Women Are Responsible Too, "*Los Angeles Times*, June 21, 1994. The statistic was derived from the Straus studies that showed, among other things, that women abuse men at least as often and at least as severely as men abuse women.

[179]Fiebert, M. S., "College students' perception of men as victims of women's assaultive behavior," *Perceptual and Motor Skills*, 82, 49-50 (1996) Two-thirds of the female college students, however, said they could believe that women commit more violence against men than vice versa.

[180]"The public has received a dramatically different picture of domestic violence. Other, more widely publicized studies do suggest that women assault their spouses...less frequently than men....But these studies are based on small, self-selected 'treatment group' samples or police records and are statistically less likely to measure accurately the overall rate and form of domestic violence." Dunn, *supra*. Again, the "studies" that supposedly support the 95% figure are about the *societal response* to abuse, not the *incidence* of it. *See* note 13.

[181]Kipnis, Aaron, *Knights Without Armor: A Practical Guide for Men in Quest of Masculine Soul*, New York: Tarcher (1991), p. 3.

[182]In psychotherapeutic parlance, the process of attempting to avoid responsibility for injurious conduct by claiming that the resulting injury was not significant is known as *minimizing*.

[183]Vivian, D. and Langhinrichensen-Rohling, J., "Are bi-directionally violent couples mutually victimized? A gender-sensitive comparison," *Violence and Victims*, 9(2), 107-124 (1994) The 1985 National Family Violence Resurvey found that both male and female victims of violence experienced considerable distress, psychologically as well as physically, even with respect to what was characterized as "mild" domestic abuse. Straus and Gelles (1990), *supra*.

[184]*See, e.g.*, Garnefski, N. and E. Arends, "Sexual Abuse and Adolescent Maladjustment: Differences Between Male and Female Victims," *Journal of Adolescence*, 21(1): 99-107 (February, 1998.) This study analyzed data from a sample of 1,490 teenagers and found that the experience of sexual abuse carries far more consequences for boys in terms of emotional problems, behavioral problems and suicidal ideation than it does for girls. This is not to say that girls do not also experience these things; the study shows that frequently they do. They just do not experience as many negative consequences as boys do, in most cases.

[185]The distinction between the actual incidence of pain and the societal response to it is not always an easy one to grasp, even for social scientists. For example, social scientists have made many broad generalizations about men's experience of pain on the basis of men's uncorroborated self-reported responses to survey questions. *See, e.g.*, Stets and Straus, 1990, *supra*. Yet, asking a man to admit that he felt pain is about as unlikely to produce reliable information as asking a man to admit that he felt afraid of a woman. Even if a man does feel afraid of a woman, our society has trained him to believe that he will become unreal if he admits it: "Real men are not afraid of women." They don't eat quiche, either.

[186]These are just examples. The actual Conflict Tactics Scale classifies a broader range of acts than the ones mentioned here.

For more information about the Conflict Tactics Scale, *see* Straus, M.A., "Measuring intrafamily conflict and violence: The Conflict Tactics (CT) scale," *Journal of Marriage and the Family*, 41(1), 75-88 (1979); Straus and Gelles (1990), *supra*; *and* Straus, M. A. and S. L. Hamby, "The Revised Conflict Tactics Scales (CTS2): Development and preliminary psychometric data," *Journal of Family Issues*, 17(3), 283-316 (1996); *see also* Appendix.

[187] *See* Appendix.

[188] *See, e.g.*, Straus and Gelles (1986), *supra*, a study which found that women are 77% more likely than men to use an object rather than simply their fists when attacking a spouse, and are 54% more likely to throw things.

[189] ABC News, *20/20*, September 19, 1997.

[190] U.S. Bureau of Justice Statistics, *Criminal Victimization in the United States, 1994, supra.*

[191] Straus and Gelles (1986), *supra*, and Straus and Gelles (1990), *supra.*

[192] Straus and Gelles (1986), *supra.*

[193] Arias, Samios and O'Leary, *supra.*

[194] Brinkerhoff and Lupri, *supra.*

[195] George (1999), *supra.*

[196] Headey, Scott and de Vaus, *supra.*

[197] Kalmuss, *supra.*

[198] Langhinrichsen-Rohling and Vivian (1994), *supra.*

[199] Magdol, et. al., *supra.*

[200] Russell and Hulson, *supra*

[201] Rollins and Oheneba-Sakyi, *supra.*

[202] Stets and Henderson, *supra.*

[203] Steinmetz (1981), *supra.*

[204] McNeely and Mann, *supra.*

[205] Vivian and Langhinrichsen-Rohling, J., "Are bi-directionally violent couples mutually victimized?" in L. K. Hamberger and C. Renzetti, eds., *Domestic Partner Abuse, supra*, at pp. 23-52.

[206] Straus, Murray A., "Wife-beating: How common and why?" *Victimology*, 2 (1977), pp. 443-458.

[207] Straus, Murray A., "Yes, physical assaults by women partners: A social problem, in M. R. Walsh, ed., *Women, Men and Gender:*

Ongoing Debates, New Haven: Yale University Press (1997), pp. 210-221, at 215.

[208]*Ibid.*

[209]Straus, Murray A., "Trends in cultural norms and rates of partner violence: An update to 1992," in S. M. Stich and M. A. Straus, eds., *Understanding Partner Violence: Prevalence, Causes, Consequences, and Solutions*, Minneapolis, Minn.: National Council on Family Relations (1996), pp. 30-33.

[210]These trends are discussed in chapters 5 through 8.

[211]The two forms of severe violence that the 1975 survey found were more likely to be committed by a husband than a wife were: using or threatening to use a gun; and beating up one's spouse with one's fists. The survey found that 1.1% of husbands beat up their wives, while 0.6% of wives beat up their husbands; 0.3% of husbands used or threatened to use a gun, as compared to 0.2% of wives. Thus, even in 1975, it was known that at least 282,000 men had been severely (not "mildly") beaten by their wives. These victims have remained invisible all these years entirely because of their gender. Straus (1977), *supra.*

It should be pointed out that although men surpassed women in these two areas in 1975, women were more likely than men to use other kinds of dangerous weapons (knives, physical objects, etc.) It should also be kept in mind that by 1985, women were either equaling or exceeding men in respect to the propensity to use severe violence. For example, by 1985, wives and husbands were equally likely to use a gun (0.2% of men and 0.2% of women), and women and men were about equally as likely to beat up their spouses. Straus and Gelles (1986), *supra.* Moreover, as will be seen in chapters 5 through 8, men have been getting even less violent and women have been getting even more violent since 1985.

[212]Rouse, L. P., "Abuse in dating relationships: A comparison of Blacks, Whites, and Hispanics," *Journal of College Student Development*, 29, 312-319 (1988)

[213]Tjaden and Thoennes (1998), *supra.*

[214]Greenfeld, et. al., *Violence by Intimates, supra*, at p. 29. The disparity is even greater in certain parts of the country. For example, a study of 6,200 spousal abuse cases in the Detroit area

revealed that about one in four men used a weapon, while 86% of the women who perpetrated spousal abuse used a weapon. McLeod, *supra*. The figures on female violence may actually be higher than even these data suggest. As Erin Pizzey, the founder of the first battered women's shelter in England, has pointed out, many men who are treated in hospitals for eye injuries received their injury from glass thrown by a wife or a girlfriend. Cook, Philip W., *Abused Men: The Hidden Side of Domestic Violence*. Westport, Conn.: Praeger (1997), p. 19.

[215]Mcleod, *supra.*

[216]*Ibid.*

[217]*Ibid, at 185, 186.*

[218]National Center for Health Statistics, *National Hospital Ambulatory Medical Care Survey: 1992 Emergency Department Summary* , Hyattsville, Md. (March, 1997)

[219]Straus, et. al. (1996), *supra.*

[220]Stets and Straus (1990), *supra.* These figures demonstrate the importance of distinguishing between the likelihood to *report* needing medical treatment and the likelihood of *actually* needing medical treatment.

[221]Rennison, Callie Marie and Sarah Welchans, *Intimate Partner Violence*, NCJ 178247, Washington DC: U.S. Bureau of Justice Statistics (2000), p. 6.

[222]Tjaden and Thoennes (1998), *supra;* and Rennison and Welchans, *supra.*

[223]Rennison and Welchans, *supra*, at p. 6.

[224]Tjaden and Thoennes (1998), supra, at p. 11.

[225]*Ibid.*, at p. 10.

[226]*Compare* Tjaden and Thoennes (1998), *supra*, at p. 9.

[227]The authors of the MRCS study, after reporting their finding that the "prevalence of domestic violence among men and women, both as victims and as perpetrators, is broadly similar for all types of violence, both psychological and physical, minor and severe," quickly add this intriguing statement: "However, it needs to be emphasised [*sic*] that the outcomes of domestic violence in terms of physical and psychological injuries tend to be considerably more negative for female victims than for male." Marriage and Relationship Counselling Services interim

finding, as reported in *The Irish Times*, June 14, 2001. If, as the researchers themselves report, severe psychological and physical injury is inflicted on males at about the same rate as it is on females (actually, their own study shows that it is inflicted on males *much more often* than on females), then how can it be that there are more "negative outcomes in terms of physical and psychological injuries" for women? The researchers do not really explain why a severe physical and/or psychological injury is a negative outcome if it happens to a woman, but is not a negative outcome if it happens to a man, although they do have the audacity, later on in the report, to *blame the victims* for "causing" the women to be violent. Apparently these researchers believe that when men are abused by women, it is the men's fault because they failed to change their personalities in the manner prescribed for them by their wives.

It bears noting that this is the same kind of rationalization that white slave-owners believed gave them the right to beat their slaves. Supposedly, slaves "deserved" their beatings because they failed to obey their masters' commands to change their personalities from "lazy and uppity" to "hard-working and jovial." In fairness, it should be pointed out that the MCRS study was conducted in Ireland, not the United States. Slavery and its incidents are not condoned in the United States. *See* U.S. Const. Amend. 13.

[228]*See, e.g.*, Dobash, R. E. and R.P. Dobash, *Violence Against Wives: A Case Against the Patriarchy*, Free Press, New York (1979); Pagelow, M. D., *Family Violence*, New York: Praeger Scientific (1984); Saunders, D. G., "When battered women use violence: Husband abuse or self defense," *Violence and Victims* 1:47-60 (1986); Campbell, J., "Prevention of Wife Battering: Insights from Cultural Analysis," *Response*, 80, 14 (3),18 - 24 (1992); *see generally* Browne, A., *When Battered Women Kill*, New York: Macmillan Free Press (1987).

[229]Moffitt and Caspi, *supra*, at p. 9

[230]Billingham, R. E., and A.R. Sack, "Courtship violence and the interactive status of the relationship," *Journal of Adolescent Research*, 1, 315-325 (1986)

[231]Bookwala, et. al., *supra.*

[232]DeMaris, A., "Male versus female initiation of aggression: The case of courtship violence," in E. C. Viano, ed., *Intimate Violence: Interdisciplinary Perspectives*, Bristol, Pa.: Taylor & Francis (1992), pp. 111-120.

[233]Gonzalez, D. M., *Why females initiate violence: A study examining the reasons behind assaults on men*, unpublished master's thesis, California State University, Long Beach (1997.) A more conservative estimate, based on collaborative research, nevertheless places the figure at the undeniably high rate of 29%. *See* Fiebert and Gonzales, *supra.*

[234]Morse, *supra*, at p. 163.

[235]O'Keefe, Brockopp and Chew, *supra.*

[236]Bland and Orne, *supra.*

[237]Sommer (1994), *supra.*

[238]Marriage and Relationship Counselling Services interim finding, *supra.*

[239]*Ibid.*

[240]Sorenson and Telles, *supra.*

[241]Stets and Straus (1990), *supra.* The 1975 National Family Violence Survey had also found that among married couples, most violence that could not be characterized as "mutual" is initiated by the wife. (27.7% female; 22.7% male; 49.5% mutual.) Straus, *supra.*

[242]Stets and Straus, *supra.*

[243]Sleek, *supra.*

[244]Straus, Murray A., "Physical assaults by wives: A major social problem," in Gelles and Loseke, eds., *Current Controversies, supra*, at pp. 67-87.

[245]*See* Tyree, A. and J. Malone, *How can it be that wives hit husbands as much as husbands hit wives and none of us knew it?* paper presented at the annual meeting of the American Sociological Association (1991) and the sources cited therein.

[246]For the proposition that violence is a learned behavior, *see* Karr-Morse and Wiley, *supra*; Langhinrich-Rohling, Neidig and Thorn, *supra;* Malone and Tyree, *supra*; Pearson, *supra*; Straus and Yodanis, *supra*; Kalmuss, D., "The intergenerational transmission of marital aggression," *Journal of Marriage*

and the Family, 46, 11-19 (February, 1984); O'Leary, K. D., "Physical aggression between spouses: A social learning theory perspective," in Van Hasselt, V. B., et. al., eds., *Handbook of Family Violence*, New York: Plenum Press (1988), pp. 31-56; Straus, Gelles and Steinmetz (1980).

[247]Tyree and Malone, *supra.*

[248]*Compare* Fiebert and Gonzalez, *supra*, finding that many women who assault their male partners do so in an attempt to force the man to pay more attention to their desires and needs; *and* Gonzales (1997), *supra* (most common reason for female aggression is frustration, that is, inability to control a person or situation.) *See generally* McKeowan, *supra.*

[249]*See* McCarthy, *supra* (no differences in reported motives for aggression between men and women); *cf.* Mason and Blankenship, *supra.*

[250]Stets and Pirog-Good, *supra.*

[251]Straus, Murray, "Trends in cultural norms and rates of partner violence: An update to 1992," in S. M. Stich and M. A. Straus, eds., *Understanding Partner Violence: Prevalence, Causes, Consequences, and Solutions, supra*, at pp. 30-33. The recent Marriage and Relationship Counselling Services study, *supra*, reported that real or suspected unfaithfulness was a significant factor in about a third of the cases involving female violence, but found that the female desire to control and coerce changes in men's personality styles (and male resistance to such coercion and control) was a more significant factor.

[252]Mason and Blankenship, *supra.*

[253]*Ibid.*

[254]Fiebert and Gonzalez, *supra*. About 1 in 5 of women who abuse their male partners said they are abusive because "I have found that most men have been trained not to hit a woman, and therefore I am not fearful of retaliation from my partner." *Ibid.* A meta-analysis of the research in this area concluded that women's beliefs about the consequences of their aggression was the major factor accounting for differences in the rates at which men and women aggress against each other. Eagly, A. H. and V.J. Steffen, "Gender and aggressive behavior: A meta-analytic review of the social psychological literature," *Psychological Bulletin*, 100(3), 309-330 (1986)

[255]Straus, Murray, "Trends in cultural norms and rates of partner violence: An update to 1992," in S. M. Stich and M. A. Straus, eds., *Understanding Partner Violence: Prevalence, Causes, Consequences, and Solutions, supra,* at pp. 30-33.

[256]Greenblat, C. S., "A hit is a hit is a hit ... or is it? Approval and tolerance of the use of physical force by spouses," in Finkelhor, et. al., eds., *The Dark Side of Families,* Beverly Hills, Calif.: Sage (1983), p. 254.

[257]Fiebert and Gonzalez, *supra.*

[258]13.1% of *all* the women surveyed (including both abusive and non-abusive women) assaulted their male partners for allegedly not being sensitive to the woman's needs and desires, and 12.6% had assaulted their partners for allegedly not paying enough attention to them. This suggests that at least 1 out of every 10 women believe it is acceptable for women to use violence simply to control and dominate their men. *Ibid.*

[259]Some of the other reasons for abusing men that women cited included such things as: feminism (13%); makes her feel powerful (12%); sexual exhilaration (8%); belief that it is normal and healthy for a woman to be physically violent toward male partner (6%); and "women are in charge...and have the right to strike their partners if they break the rules" (6%.) Participants were permitted to select more than one reason. *Ibid.*

[260]Sleek, *supra.*

[261]*Ibid.*

[262]Technically, "battered women's syndrome" is not really a separate legal defense. It's really just a fuzzy conglomeration of the self-defense and duress defenses. It sometimes *appears* to be a separate legal defense because of the fact that women have been able to invoke it successfully to win acquittal, or a more lenient sentence, even though all the elements of a valid self-defense or duress defense are not actually present. For example, it has been successfully invoked in defense of women who carry out premeditated plans to kill men in their sleep, a circumstance in which self-defense normally cannot be claimed.

[263]Mann, Coramae Richey, "Getting Even? Women Who Kill In Domestic Encounters," *Justice Quarterly,* vol. 5, no. 1, (March, 1988); *see also* Ms. Mann's article in *Behavior Today* (July 25, 1988.)

[264]Mann, Coramae Richey, "Getting Even? Women Who Kill in Domestic Encounters," *supra*, at p. 49.

[265]U.S. Department of Justice, "Trend Analysis: Expert Testimony on Battering and Its Effects in Criminal Cases," in *Validity and Use of Evidence Concerning Battering and Its Effects in Criminal Trials*, Report Responding to Section 40507 of the Violence Against Women Act, NCJ 160972, Washington, DC (1996); *see also* Paterno, Susan, "A Legacy of Violence," *Los Angeles Times*, April 14, 1991, pp. E-1 and E-14; Wilkerson, Isabel, "Clemency Granted to 25 Women Convicted for Assault or Murder," *New York Times*, December 22, 1990, p. A-1; Ray, Nancy, "Judge Allows 'Battered Woman' Defense," *Los Angeles Times*, September 21, 1982.

[266]Parrish, Janet, National Clearinghouse for the Defense of Battered Women, "Family Violence and the Courts: Exploring Expert Testimony on Battered Women," in U.S. Department of Justice, *Validity and Use of Evidence Concerning Battering and Its Effects in Criminal Trials*, Report Responding to Section 40507 of the Violence Against Women Act, NCJ 160972, Washington, DC (1996.)

[267]National Institute of Justice, *The Prevalence and Consequences of Child Victimization*, Research in Brief, Washington DC: U.S. Department of Justice (1997.) Children represent at least one-quarter of all American crime victims. U.S. Office for Victims of Crime, *Breaking the Cycle of Violence: Recommendations to Improve the Criminal Justice Response to Child Victims and Witnesses*, NCJ-176983, Washington, DC: U.S. Government Printing Office (1999), p. 1.

[268]National Institute of Justice, *The Prevalence and Consequences of Child Victimization, supra.*

[269]U.S. Office of Juvenile Justice and Delinquency Prevention, *Children as Victims, supra,* at p. 19.

[270]Federal Bureau of Investigation, *National Incident-Based Reporting System* master files for the years 1991-1996 (machine-readable data files.)

[271]Federal Bureau of Investigation, *Supplementary Homicide Reports for the Years 1980-1997* (machine-readable data files). California Attorney General Daniel E. Lungren also reported

that 83% of California's juvenile homicide victims are male. *See* Attorney General Daniel E. Lungren's Policy Council on Violence Prevention, *supra,* at p. 43. The U.S. Office of Juvenile Justice and Delinquency Prevention reports that 71% of all juvenile victims of homicide are male, and 81% of homicide victims between the ages of 12 and 17 are male. U.S. Office of Juvenile Justice and Delinquency Prevention, *Children as Victims,* 1999 National Report Series, Washington DC: U.S. Department of Justice (2000), p. 3

[272]*Children as Victims, supra,* at p. 5.

[273]Hutchinson, Janice and Kristin Langlykke, *Adolescent Maltreatment: Youth as Victims of Abuse and Neglect,* Arlington , VA: National Center for Education in Maternal and Child Health (1997), p. 14. The bulletin focused on children in the 15-19 age category.

[274]U.S. Department of Health and Human Services, Children's Bureau, *Child Maltreatment 1996: Reports from the States to the National Child Abuse and Neglect Data System,* Washington DC: U.S. Government Printing Office (1998); *see also* U.S. Office of Juvenile Justice and Delinquency Prevention, *Children as Victims, supra,* at p. 20.

[275]U.S. Bureau of Justice Statistics, *Murder in Families,* NCJ-143498, Washington, D.C.: U.S. Department of Justice

[276]National Center on Child Abuse and Neglect, *National Child Abuse and Neglect Data System: Working Paper 2, 1991 summary data component,* Washington DC: U.S. Department of Health and Human Services (1993); *cf.* Kelley, Barbara Tatem, et. al., *In the Wake of Childhood Maltreatment,* Youth Development Series, Washington DC: U.S. Office of Juvenile Justice and Delinquency Prevention (1997.)

[277]National Center on Child Abuse and Neglect, *Child Maltreatment 1992: Reports From the States to the National Center on Child Abuse and Neglect,* Washington, D.C.: U.S. Government Printing Office (1994), pp. 26-28. Males are about equally as likely to be victims of a parental kidnapping as females are. Finkelhor, David and Richard Ormrod, *Kidnapping of Juveniles: Patterns From NIBRS,* NCJ 181161, Washington DC: U.S. Office of Juvenile Justice and Delinquency Prevention (2000), pp. 2-4.

278Minnesota Department of Human Services, *Child Maltreatment: A 1994 Minnesota Report* (1996), pp. 8-9. According to the National Center on Child Abuse and Neglect, the incidence of *neglect*, on the other hand, is about the same for both boys and girls, although male children are somewhat more likely than female children to be victims of emotional neglect. National Center on Child Abuse and Neglect, *Child Abuse and Neglect: A Shared Community Concern,* Washington DC: U.S. Department of Health and Human Services (1992), citing Sedlak, A., *National Incidence and Prevalence of Child Abuse and Neglect 1988: Revised Report* (1991).

279ChildHelp USA, *The National Child Abuse Hotline Information Guide*, pp. 4-5.

280U.S. Office of Juvenile Justice and Delinquency Prevention, *Children as Victims, supra,* at p. 10.

281Snyder, Howard N., *Sexual Assault of Young Children as Reported to Law Enforcement: Victim, Incident and Offender Characteristics*, NCJ 182990, Washington DC: U.S. Department of Justice (2000), pp. 4 and 12.

282National Center on Child Abuse and Neglect, *A Report on the Maltreatment of Children with Disabilities*, Washington DC: U.S. Department of Health and Human Services, pp. 3-3 and 3-5.

283Gilligan, James, *Violence: Our Deadly Epidemic and Its Causes*, New York: Grosset/Putnam (1996.)

284case histories from prison psychiatrist James Gilligan, reported in Snow, *supra.*

285National Center on Child Abuse and Neglect, *The Third National Incidence Study of Child Abuse and Neglect*, Washington, DC: U.S. Department of Health and Human Services (1996); *accord*: U.S. Office of Juvenile Justice and Delinquency Prevention, *Children as Victims, supra,* at p. 14.

286Greenfeld, et. al., *Violence by Intimates, supra,* at p. 3.

287Rennison and Welchans, *supra,* at p. 3.

288Straus and Gelles (1986), *supra*; *see also* Hampton, R. L., R. J. Gelles and J. W. Harrop, "Is violence in families increasing? A comparison of 1975 and 1985 National Survey rates," *Journal of Marriage and the Family*, 51, 969-980 (1989)(rate of overall violence by wives against husbands increased 33% from 1975 to

1985, and the rate of severe violence by wives against husbands increased 42% from 1975 to 1985.)

[289]Federal Bureau of Investigation, Uniform Crime Reports, *Crime in the United States* (1990), pp. 15 and 51; and U.S. Bureau of Justice Statistics, *Criminal Victimization in the United States*, National Crime Survey Report (1973-1988), p. 15.

[290]Greenfeld, et. al., *Violence by Intimates, supra.*

[291]*Ibid.* There was a slight increase in the rate of murder of white girlfriends (committed by either a male or a female intimate) between 1976 and 1996 (up from 0.0017% to 0.002%), but for all other categories and combinations of categories (white spouses, black ex-husbands, etc.) the rates of murder between 1976 and 1996 have been steadily decreasing. *Ibid.*, at pp. 8-9.

[292]*Ibid.*

[293]Straus and Gelles (1986), *supra.*

[294]Greenfeld, et. al., *Violence by Intimates, supra*, at p. 3.

[295]Rennison and Welchans, *supra*, at p. 3.

[296]Jones, Lisa and David Finkelhor, *The Decline in Child Sexual Abuse Cases*, NCJ 184741, Washington DC: Office of Juvenile Justice and Delinquency Prevention (2001.)

[297]Rennison, *Criminal Victimization 2000, Changes 1999-2000 with Trends 1993-2000, supra.*

[298]*Id.*, at p. 3.

[299]*Id.*, Table 1.

[300]*Id.*

[301]U.S. Bureau of Justice Statistics, *Sourcebook of Criminal Justice Statistics*, Washington DC: U.S. Department of Justice; and Federal Bureau of Investigation, *Uniform Crime Reports*, Washington DC: U.S. Department of Justice (1999).

[302]Federal Bureau of Investigation, *Crime in the United States*, Washington DC: U.S. Government Printing Office (1996, 1997, 1998); and Snyder, Howard N. and Melissa Sickmund, *Juvenile Offenders and Victims: 1999 National Report*, Washington, DC: Office of Juvenile Justice and Delinquency Prevention (1999.)

[303]Federal Bureau of Investigation, *Crime in the United States*, Washington DC: U.S. Government Printing Office (1996, 1997, 1998); and Snyder and Sickmund, *supra.*

[304]Federal Bureau of Investigation, *Crime in the United States*, Washington DC: U.S. Government Printing Office (1996, 1997, 1998) and Snyder and Sickmund, *supra*.

[305]Greenfeld, et. al., *Violence by Intimates, supra.*

[306]Straus and Gelles (1986), *supra*.

[307]Hampton, R. L., R. J. Gelles, R. J. and J.W. Harrop, "Is violence in families increasing? A comparison of 1975 and 1985 National Survey rates," *Journal of Marriage and the Family*, 51, 969-980 (1987)

[308]Morse, *supra*.

[309]Brown, Mareva, "Arrests of Women Soar in Domestic Abuse Cases," *Sacramento Bee,* December 7, 1997.

[310]Of course, the data cited in the *Sacramento Bee* article was archival (police reports.) In this case, though, the archival data has been corroborated by survey data, as the other sources cited in this chapter demonstrate.

[311]Rennison, *Criminal Victimization 2000, Changes 1999-2000 with Trends 1993-2000, supra*, at p. 8; *compare* Greenfeld, et. al., *Violence by Intimates, supra*, at p. 4.

[312]Jones and Finkelhor, *supra*.

[313]quoted in Goldberg, *supra*.

[314]U.S. Bureau of Justice Statistics, *Report to the Nation on Crime and Justice, supra,* at p. 46

[315]Steinmetz, Suzanne K. and Joseph S. Lucca, "Husband Battering," in Van Hasselt, Vincent B., et. al., eds., *Handbook of Family Violence*, New York: Plenum Press (1988), pp. 233-246 ("the greatest increase in female criminal activity parallels the increasing number of women who hold positions of [responsibility] in the business world.")

[316]Federal Bureau of Investigation, *Uniform Crime Reports.*

[317]Federal Bureau of Investigation, *Uniform Crime Reports 1995,* Washington, D.C.: U.S. Department of Justice (1996)

[318]Conly, Catherine, *The Women's Prison Association: Supporting Women Offenders and Their Families*, National Institute of Justice Program Focus, NCJ 172858, Washington DC: U..S. Department of Justice (1998), p. 2.

[319]*Ibid.*, at p. 4.

[320]Greenfeld, et. al., *Violence by Intimates, supra*, at p. 28.

[321]U.S. Bureau of Justice Statistics, *Sourcebook of Criminal Justice Statistics* (1991), p. 442; and Kirkpatrick, John T. and John A. Humphrey, "Stress in the Lives of Female Criminal Homicide Offenders in North Carolina," *Human Stress: Current Selected Research*, vol. 3, ed. by James H. Humphrey, New York: AMS Press (1989.)

[322]Johnston, Janet R., et. al., *Early Identification of Risk Factors for Parental Abduction*, NCJ 185026, Washington, DC: U.S. Office of Juvenile Justice and Delinquency Prevention (2001), p. 4; Johnston, Janet R. and Linda K. Girdner, *Family Abductors: Descriptive Profiles and Preventive Interventions*, NCJ 182788, Washington DC: U.S. Office of Juvenile Justice and Delinquency Prevention (2001); Finkelhor and Ormrod, *Kidnapping of Juveniles, supra*, at pp. 2-4.

[323]National Center for Juvenile Justice, *National Juvenile Court Data Archive: Juvenile court case records 1987-1996* (machine-readable data files), Pittsburgh, PA: NCJJ (1998), cited in Snyder and Sickmund, *supra*.

[324]Federal Bureau of Investigation, *Crime in the United States*, Washington DC: U.S. Government Printing Office (1996, 1997, 1998) and Snyder and Sickmund, *supra*.

[325]Straus and Gelles (1986), *supra*.

[326]Steinmetz, Suzanne, "The Truth About Domestic Violence: A Falsely Framed Issue," *Social Work, The Journal of the National Association of Social Workers*, November/December, 1987.

[327]Steinmetz, "The Battered Husband Syndrome," *supra*, at p. 501.

[328]*Ibid.*

[329]Straus, M.A., "Physical Assault by Wives: A Major Social Problem," in Gelles and Loseke, eds., *Current Controversies, supra*, pp. 67-87. Even the more conservative U.S. Bureau of Labor Statistics estimates the male-to-female ratio of domestic assaults to be about 1.5 to 1, at least among Hispanics. U.S. Bureau of Labor Statistics, *The National Longitudinal Survey of Youth* (machine-readable data file), Washington, DC: U.S. Department of Labor (1997.)

[330]Straus and Gelles (1986), *supra*, at pp. 465-79.

[331]*Ibid.*; see also Straus and Gelles (1990)

[332]Straus, M. A. and G. Kantor Kaufman, *Change in spouse assault rates from 1975-1992: A comparison of three national surveys in the United States*, paper presented at the Thirteenth World Congress of Sociology, Bielefeld, Germany, July, 1994.

[333]Bennett, R., "A new side to domestic violence," *The Family Bulletin*, Coalition of Parent Support, p. 4-5, January, 1997

[334]Brown (1997), *supra*. According to Kate Killeen, Sacramento's lead prosecutor, "few women are arrested in error," and the rate of mutual arrests (cases where both the man and the woman involved in a domestic dispute are arrested) had been declining during the same period. *Ibid.* Thus, it is not likely that the increased arrest rate was a result of either faulty police work or failure to give adequate consideration to which party is "the primary aggressor."

[335]California Department of Justice, Criminal Justice Statistics Center, Special run on April 21, 1997.

[336]Federal Bureau of Investigation, *Uniform Crime Reports* (1996), supra. Of course, the data cited in this paragraph is archival in nature. In this case, though, the trend documented in the archival data has been corroborated by survey data, as the other sources cited in this chapter demonstrate

[337]National Institute of Justice, *Partner Violence Among Young Adults*, *supra*; and Magdol, *supra*, at pp. 68-78

[338]Moffitt and Caspi, *supra*, at p. 4.

[339]Marriage and Relationship Counselling Services study, reported in O'Morain, Padraig, "Domestic violence more likely from women--Report," *Irish Times*, June 14,2001. The research was conducted by a team of social researchers led by Dr. Kieran McKeown, who specifically concluded that the "prevalence of domestic violence among men and women, both as victims and as perpetrators, is broadly similar...." It is interesting that the researchers chose to characterize a ratio of 1.6 to 1 as "broadly similar." Can you guess how the results would have been characterized if the study had found a 1.6 to 1 ratio of male to female violence instead of a 1.6 to 1 ratio of female to male violence?

[340]U.S. Department of Health and Human Services, *Child Maltreatment 1992, supra*, at pp. 26-28; *see also* U.S. Office

of Juvenile Justice and Delinquency Prevention, *Children as Victims*, *supra*, at p. 22; Martin, Susan E. and Douglas J. Besharov, *Police and Child Abuse: New Policies for Expanded Responsibilities*, Washington DC: National Institute of Justice (1991); Minnesota Department of Human Services, *Child Maltreatment, supra*, at pp. 17-19; and Nagi, Saad, *Child Maltreatment in the United States*, New York: Columbia University Press (1977)

[341]Contrary to the popular belief that child molestation is entirely "a guy thing," a lot of child molesters are female. In fact, according to estimates from the American Medical Association, one-third of all male children who are victims of sexual abuse are victimized by women. *Journal of the American Medical Association*, December 2, 1998

[342]U.S. Department of Health and Human Services, as reported in Snyder and Sickmund, *supra*.

[343]National Center on Child Abuse and Neglect, *A Report on the Maltreatment of Children with Disabilities*, *supra*, at pp. 3-15 and 3-19.

[344]U.S. Bureau of Justice Statistics, "Murder in Families," NCJ-143498, Washington, D.C.: U.S. Department of Justice.

[345]U.S. Office of Juvenile Justice and Delinquency Prevention, *Children as Victims*, *supra*, at p. 21

[346]U.S. General Accounting Office, *Child Abuse: Prevention Programs Need Greater Emphasis*, GAO/HRD-92-99 (1992)

[347]U.S. Department of Health and Human Services, *Child Fatalities Fact Sheet*, Washington, D.C.: U.S. Government Printing Office (2001)

[348]U.S. Department of Health and Human Services, *Study Findings: Study of National Incidence and Prevalence of Child Abuse and Neglect* (1988) and Sedlak, *supra*.

[349]U.S. Office of Juvenile Justice and Delinquency Prevention, *Children as Victims*, *supra*, at p. 14.

[350]*Ibid.*

[351]Jones and Finkelhor, *supra*.

[352]U.S. Office of Juvenile Justice and Delinquency Prevention, *Children as Victims*, *supra*, at p. 1; rates of crime against children are also about 2 to 3 times higher than crimes against adults.

Turman, Kathryn M. and Kimberly L. Poyer, *Child Victims and Witnesses: A Handbook for Criminal Justice Professionals*, Washington DC: U.S. Attorney's Office (1998), p. 3.The rate of child maltreatment fatalities has steadily increased throughout the 1990's. The National Child Abuse and Neglect Data System reported that in 1997 about 1.7 children per 100,000 in the general population were confirmed by state child protective services agencies to have died as a result of child abuse or neglect. U.S. Department of Health and Human Services, *Child Maltreatment 1997: Reports From the States to the National Child Abuse and Neglect Data System*, Washington, D.C.: U.S. Government Printing Office (1999.) The U.S. Advisory Board on Child Abuse and Neglect estimates that there are about 2,000 child deaths per year that result from abuse or neglect. U.S. Advisory Board on Child Abuse and Neglect, *A Nation's Shame: Fatal Child Abuse and Neglect in the United States*, Washington, D.C.: U.S. Department of Health and Human Services (1995.) By the year 2001, the number of child deaths resulting from maltreatment had grown to an estimated 5,000 per year. U.S. Department of Health and Human Services, *Child Fatalities Fact Sheet, supra*. Most of the children who are abused to death are under 5 years old. *Ibid.*

[353]Greenfeld, Lawrence A., *Child Victimizers: Violent Offenders and Their Victims*, NCJ- 153238, Washington DC: U.S. Department of Justice (1996).

[354]White and Humphrey, "Women's aggression in heterosexual conflicts," *Aggressive Behavior*, 20, 195-202 (1994)

[355]*See* Chapter 11.

[356]Of course, it's not all the fault of feminists. Some men are just as guilty of unrealistically idealizing women as feminists are.

[357]Pizzey, Erin, "Working with Violent Women," *The Backlash!*, December, 1997

[358]*Ibid.*

[359]*Ibid.*

[360]Steinem, Gloria, *Revolution From Within*, Boston: Little, Brown (1992), pp. 259-61.

[361]Pizzey, *Working with Violent Women, supra.*

[362]*Ibid.*

[363]U.S. Bureau of Justice Statistics, *Report to the Nation on Crime and Justice, supra,* at p. 62.

[364]Greenfeld, et. al., *Violence by Intimates, supra,* at p. 19.

[365]*See, e.g.,* Rennison and Welchans, *supra,* at p. 7.In the year 2000, the overall rate at which men were willing to report that they had been a victim of any crime (property, etc.) was 42.9%, as compared to 54.5% of women. Rennison, *Criminal Victimization 2000, Changes 1999-2000 with Trends 1993-2000, supra,* at p. 10. White males are the least likely of all demographic categories to report to police the crimes that have been committed against them. *Ibid.* The fact that the numbers are much further apart than this when the crime involved is domestic abuse suggests that there must be additional reasons why male victims are reluctant to report when they have been victims of domestic violence, over and beyond the general white male inhibition against reporting that they have been victims.

[366]*Ibid.,* at p. 6; U.S. Bureau of Justice Statistics, *Report to the Nation on Crime and Justice, supra,* at p. 34 (majority of women who are victims of violence report the incident to police, but the majority of men who are victims do not); U.S. Bureau of Justice Statistics, *Criminal Victimization in the United States, 1994, supra* (female victims 142% more likely to report assault committed by someone they know than male victims are); Ernst, et. al., *supra* (19% of female victims seeking emergency medical treatment were willing to acknowledge that they had been victims of past abuse, while only 6% of male victims were willing to voluntarily report that); *see also* Langhinrichsen-Rohling and Vivian (1994), *supra* (even among couples in marriage counseling, husbands are substantially more likely to under-report their partner's aggression than wives are; at the same time, substantially more wives than husbands over-reported aggression on their partner's part); *and* Nelson, Wyman, *About Spouse Abuse,* South Deerfield, Mass.: Channing L. Bete Co. (1986)

[367]Rennison and Welchans, supra, at p. 7.

[368]*Ibid.*

[369]Greenfeld, et. al., *Violence by Intimates, supra.*

[370]Stets and Straus (1990), *supra*. Women are also 5 times more likely than men to tell their friends about it. *Ibid.*

[371]*Compare* Tjaden and Thoennes (1998), *supra*; *and* Rennison and Welchans, *supra*, at p. 6.

[372]Phillip Cook notes that he observed the fear of this kind of reaction (being called or thought of as a wimp) to be present in nearly every male victim of domestic abuse that he interviewed. Cook, *supra*, at p. 52.

[373]*See* Warren Farrell's *The Myth of Male Power: Why Men Are the Disposable Sex*, New York: Simon & Schuster (1993).

[374]Gregorash, Lesley, "Family Violence: An Exploratory Study of Men Who Have Been Abused By Their Wives" (unpublished study, University of Calgary, 1993), p. 92.

[375]Recent studies case serious doubt on the validity of this assumption. For example, it has been found that low-income women are actually *more* likely than affluent women to leave an abusive relationship. McNeely and Robinson-Simpson, *supra*, p. 487

[376]Another fraud perpetrated on the American public in recent times is the "pay inequity" statistic according to which women supposedly are paid only 75% of what men earn. The figure is misleading because it is based on a simplistic analysis that fails to control for non-gender-discriminatory factors. Specifically, it does not take into account the things that really do determine wage levels--length of employment; education; occupation; and number of hours worked. Because men are more prone to be held responsible--both legally and socially--for the support of their families (women are only rarely expected or ordered to support men; women are only rarely expected or ordered to pay alimony and child support to men; and although many states are adopting "male responsibility" laws, no states are adopting "female responsibility" laws), men tend to work longer hours and to have longer work histories than women. This isn't true of every member of the work force--some women work longer hours and have longer work histories than some men--but given our legal and societal expectations, it would be reasonable to expect it to be true in most cases. When non-discriminatory variables such as length of employment and number of hours

worked are correctly factored in, the supposed "pay equity gap" virtually disappears. Furchtgott-Roth, Diana and Christine Stolba, *Women's Figures: An Illustrated Guide to the Economic Progress of Women in America*, Washington, D.C.: Independent Women's Forum and the American Enterprise Institute (2000)

[377]Economic concerns and religious beliefs are often cited by abused men as their reasons for not leaving a relationship. Hammond-Saslow, C., *Domestic violence and levels of depression, self-esteem and assertiveness in battered men*, unpublished doctoral dissertation, San Diego, Calif.: United States International University (1997); see also Steinmetz, Suzanne, "The Battered Husband Syndrome," *Victimology* 2 (1977): 499.

[378]Television star Phil Hartman believed that all he had to do was leave the house until his wife cooled down. That belief cost him his life.

[379]A study of college men and women revealed that the same proportion of men as women were inclined to interpret an act of domestic violence as a sign of "love," at least when the violent act in question is committed by a woman against a man. Matthews, W. J., "Violence in college couples," *College Student Journal*, 18, 150-158 (1984)

[380]Abused men often cited religious beliefs as one of their principal reasons for not leaving an abusive relationship. Hammond-Saslow, *supra*.

[381]Some battered women's shelters claim that they provide shelter services to men, but there is no evidence that many of them really do. Why would they call themselves shelters for battered women if their services are intended for battered men, too? Regardless of what shelters claim in their statements to the media, the truth is that nearly all male victims who call battered women's shelters are turned away, and a large number are treated with hostility and contempt, to boot. Beaupre, "No place to run for male victims of domestic abuse," *supra*.

[382]For some real-life examples of this phenomenon in operation, *see* Cook, *supra*, at pp. 79-81.

[383]For some examples of cases in which abused men have been arrested and/or told to leave the house as a result of calling the police for help, see Cook, *supra*, at pp. 79-81.

[384]quoted in Beaupre, "No place to run for male victims of domestic abuse," *supra*.

[385]Righthand, Sue and Carlann Welch, *Juveniles Who Have Sexually Offended: A Review of the Professional Literature*, Office of Juvenile Justice and Delinquency Prevention (2001); *see also* Charles, G. and M. McDonald, "Adolescent sexual offenders," *Journal of Child and Youth Care* 11(1): 15-25 (1997); and Travin, S., K. Cullen and B. Protter, "Female sex offenders: Severe victims and victimizers," *Journal of Forensic Sciences* 35(1): 140-150 (1990.)

[386]The conception of children as their parents' "chattel" is why the first organized movement to raise consciousness about child abuse came from the Society for the Prevention of Cruelty to Animals, rather than a human rights organization.

[387]Hutchinson and Langlykke, *supra*, at p. 10.

[388]*Ibid*, at p. 8, citing American Medical Association Council on Scientific Affairs, "Adolescents as Victims of Family Violence," *Journal of the American Medical Association* 270(15): 1850-1856 (1993).

[389]Hutchinson and Langlykke, *supra*, at p. 11; *see also* Finkelhor, D., "The Victimization of Children: A Developmental Perspective," *American Journal of Orthopsychiatry* 63(2): 177-193 (April, 1995).

[390]Men who abuse female children are substantially more likely to be reported than are women who abuse female children, women who abuse male children, and men who abuse male children. Even so, confirmed reports of child maltreatment perpetrated by women against male children still outnumber every other form of child maltreatment. This is remarkable, in light of the fact that nearly every publication I've seen on the subject of child abuse reporting treats it as if it were "a male phenomenon." This is especially true of publications directed at children; these kinds of publications invariably devote considerable time and attention to the task of encouraging children to report unwanted sexual contact from a father, stepfather or male relative (which, of course, is a good thing to encourage children to do), but they fail to let children know that mothers, stepmothers and female relatives can also be guilty of abuse. None of these publications

lets children know that it is just as "okay" to report mothers as it
is to report fathers and stepfathers. A few publications I've seen
do mention, parenthetically or in a footnote, that it is possible for
women to commit child abuse, but they always attempt to make
it seem as if it is highly unlikely that this would ever actually
happen in real life.

[391]Easton, *Abuse of Men in Families and the Interacting Legacy of
Abuse in the Justice System, supra.*

[392]Unfortunately, many people, including law enforcement officers,
subscribe to the notion that a "real man" should be able to keep
a woman under control. Often, the same people who declare that
"A man is *never* justified in using or threatening to use physical
force of any kind against a woman, under any circumstances"
also say that "real men" can't be victims because they should
be able to control their women, inasmuch as men are physically
bigger and stronger than women are. If it is wrong for men to
use their superior physical size and strength against women,
then telling men that they should be able to control women
by using their superior physical size and strength would seem
to be sending men a conflicting--and dangerous--message.
Unfortunately, this issue never really gets addressed. Since the
net result is to make every woman--even those who are abusing
men--"victims" while denying men the equal protection of the
law, women's advocates have no reason to object to it. Men don't
object because domestic violence has been defined by our society
as a "women's issue," inasmuch as violence is supposedly "a
male phenomenon." Since men so far have been denied a voice,
and since women have no motivation to object on their behalf,
the dual directive to men--use force and don't use force--goes
unchallenged and unabated. To many people in our society, it
goes unnoticed, too.

[393]This is a kind of stigma that is unique to men, originating, as
it does, from the societal assumption that men are physically
stronger than women, and are therefore more capable of
overcoming their partner's will by force than women are. From
this frame of mind, the notion that a woman "let" a man beat her
isn't even a possibility. As a result, it is considered "unmanly"
for a man to "let" a woman beat him up, but it is not considered

"unwomanly" for a woman to acknowledge that she has been beaten up by a man.

[394]"Men also are often kept in their relationships, which can only be likened to 'personal concentration camps,' by the fact that they feel a genuine feeling of 'chivalry' towards their partner." Pizzey (1997), *supra.*

[395]See, e.g., any of the various "Male Responsibility" laws that recently have been enacted by state and federal governments, and the corresponding legislative history for them. Patricia Overberg, executive director of the Valley Oasis Emergency Shelter Programs in Lancaster, California, maintains that it is more difficult for a man to seek help and/or leave an abusive relationship because men are socialized to be the providers and protectors of the family. Most men perceive being beaten up by a woman as something that is inconsistent with having sufficient strength to provide and protect, and as a result a man can be expected to be extremely reluctant to let anyone know about it if it does happen. As she puts it:

[I]t takes a lot to convince [men] they should...do the same things for themselves that the female victim does. It is much more difficult to get a man to make that change. They have been brought up to see their role as being defined as protector of the home. When you get married it's your responsibility to provide, to make sure there is food on the table, clothes. Regardless of the fact that women are going out and working these days, men are still taught that it is their responsibility to provide. So, if you leave, you are abdicating your responsibility, and you are less than a man." Overberg, Patricia, quoted in Cook, pp. 60-61.

[396]Pizzey (1997), *supra.*

[397]Steinmetz, Suzanne K. and Joseph S. Lucca, "Husband Battering" in Van Hasselt, Vincent B., et al., eds., *Handbook of Family Violence*, New York: Plenum Press (1988), pp. 233-246.

[398]In 1963, it was observed that three-fourths of the depictions of domestic violence in American comic strips involved a male being battered by a female. Saenger, G., "Male and female relation in the American comic strips," in White, M. and R.H. Abel, eds., *The Funnies: An American Idiom*, Glencoe, Ill.:

Free Press (1963), pp. 219-223. This was before the successful campaign to educate Americans to take violence against women seriously. Today, it is a cultural taboo in America to depict violence against women in anything but a dead serious manner and context. As a result, approximately 100% of the humorous depictions of domestic violence in America today now involve male victims.

Steven Easton, who founded a support group for battered men in Canada and has counseled thousands of battered men, reports that "Many men who have come to our agency looking for support, have endured laughter and scorn from their families, the police and family violence prevention agencies which are ostensibly set up to deal with victims of abuse." Easton, *Abuse of Men in Families and the Interacting Legacy of Abuse in the Justice System, supra.* Patricia Overberg has observed that "[o]ne of the things that men have to deal with, that women don't have to, is...ridicule. I can tell you that from experience, both from working with these men, and from making speaking engagements. When I mention that we are a shelter that provides shelter to battered men, they all laugh, the men and the women. They think it's funny that a man would be battered. They laugh when I tell them that a man can be raped. Of course,...I know that there are a lot of battered men out there, but part of the reason they don't seek help is this fear of ridicule...[which] is indeed a big factor." Overberg, P., quoted in Cook, p. 54. Sylvia Ashton, an inspector for the domestic violence police unit in England, says that when she tells people about a man who was stabbed by his wife for bleeding on the carpet as a result of a stab wound she had inflicted on him earlier, the universal reaction is laughter. Ashton, S., quoted in Cook, p. 54.

[399]"If there is one defining characteristic of most abused men it is that they are extremely embarrassed by their predicament. Most abused men have attempted to reach out for help and have been laughed at or scorned.....Many men that have been abused know how they are portrayed by society so they minimize their situations out of fear of being ridiculed further or blamed for their victimization." Easton, Steven, *Who Are Male Victims of Spousal Abuse?*, web document (2001.)

[400]Intuitively, it strikes me as highly likely that this double bind, because it guarantees stigmatization for *all* male victims regardless of how they respond to it, is probably at or near the top of the list of male victims' reasons for not reporting.

[401]Cook, *supra*, at p. 85.

[402]Hutchinson and Langlykke, *supra*, at p. 10.

[403]Gregorash, *supra*, p. 89. Patricia Overberg ranks fear of loss of relationship with children as one of the top three reasons that men choose not to leave abusive relationships. (The other two top reasons she cites are: fear of ridicule; and the sense of responsibility to provide and protect.) Cook, *supra*, p. 78.

[404]Straus, Gelles and Steinmetz, *supra; cf.* Langley, Roger and Richard C. Levy, Wife Beating: The Silent Crisis, New York: Pocket Books (1977)

[405]U.S. Office of Juvenile Justice and Delinquency Prevention, *Children as Victims, supra*, pp. 7 and 14; *and* U.S. Office for Victims of Crime, *Responding to Child Victims and Witnesses: Innovative Practices for Prosecutors*, Washington DC.: U.S. Department of Justice

[406]Noble, Kenneth B., "Key Abortion Plaintiff Now Denies She Was Raped," *New York Times*, September 9, 1987, p. A-23.

[407]Webb, Cathleen and Mary Chapian, *Forgive Me*, Old Tappan, NJ: Fleming H. Revell Co. (1985.)

[408]For example, in California and many other states, jurors in rape cases are specifically instructed that a rape conviction can be based on the accuser's testimony alone; that corroborating evidence is not necessary. Associated Press, "Ruling Favors Victim's Word in Rape Cases," *San Diego Union-Tribune*, May 8, 1992.

[409]For example, in many states evidence of the woman's sexual character and habits is generally not admissible in a rape proceeding, notwithstanding it may be relevant to the issue of whether force was used to procure her consent. Evidence of the accused man's sexual character and habits, on the other hand, *is* admissible and can be used against him to obtain a conviction, at least if he takes the stand to testify in his own defense.

[410]"To my considerable chagrin, we found that at least 60 percent of all the rape allegations were false." McDowell, Charles P., Ph.D.,

M.P.A., M.L.S., "False Allegations," *Forensic Science Digest*, vol. 11, no. 4, December 1985, p. 64

[411]Buckley, Stephen, "Unfounded Rape Reports Baffle Investigators," *The Washington Post*, June 7, 1992, pp. B-1 and B-7.

[412]Bedau, Hugo Adam and Michael L. Radelet, "Miscarriages of Justice in Potentially Capital Cases," *Stanford Law Review*, vol. 40, no. 1, November 1987, pp. 21-179.

[413]*compare* Lee, Harper, *To Kill a Mockingbird*, New York: J.B. Lippincott (1960)

[414]*See generally* Schooler, J.W., "Seeking the Core: The Issues and Evidence Surrounding Recovered Accounts of Sexual Trauma," in Williams and Banyard, eds., *Trauma and Memory, supra.*

[415]For an excellent theoretical exposition of how false memories are constructed in psychotherapeutic settings, *see* Hyman, I.E. and E.E. Kleinknecht, "False Childhood Memories: Research, Theory, and Applications," in Williams and Banyard, eds., *Trauma and Memory, supra.*

[416]About one out of five allegations of child sexual abuse are proven to be false even before an arrest is made. Martin and Besharov, *supra*, at p. 17. According to the U.S. Bureau of Justice Statistics, only about one-half of the females who allege that they are victims of domestic abuse have actually been injured, and only about 10% required or sought medical treatment. Greenfeld, et. al., *Violence by Intimates, supra*, at p. 21. Of the 10% that sought or required medical treatment, about half were treated for a bruise and half were treated for something more serious than a bruise. *Ibid.* at p. 22.

None of this is meant to imply that it is only women who make false accusations of abuse. I have no doubt that men sometimes do make false accusations, too. When a man accuses a woman of abuse, however, he already bears the burden of proof. My only reason for focusing on women is to make the point that women should also bear the burden of proof when they accuse a man of abuse.

[417]A bigot is a person who holds blindly and intolerantly to a particular creed, opinion or point of view even when presented with irrefutable evidence that he or she is wrong. *Webster's New*

World Dictionary of the American Language (New York: Prentice Hall Press, 1984.) The term is usually used in the context of race relations, but it is broad enough to encompass gender relations as well. In modern Western cultures, such as the United States, it is politically and socially correct to accuse only white males of it. Nevertheless, as the examples cited in this chapter will demonstrate, there is ample evidence that many women are just as capable of it as some men are.

[418]Kirby, Sandra, "What do Feminist Methods Have to do with Ethics?" in *Women Changing Academe* (Winnipeg, 1991) p.168.

[419]Fagan, Jeffrey, *The Criminalization of Domestic Violence: Promises and Limits*. Washington DC: National Institute of Justice (1996)

[420]quoted in Thomas, David, *Not Guilty: The Case In Defense of Men*, N.Y.: Wm. Morrow (1993)

[421]Sacks, Glenn, "Domestic violence is harsh reality for men also," *UCLA Daily Bruin*, May 12, 2000.

[422]Koss, Gidycz and Wisniewski, *supra*, at pp. 162-70, reprinted in the *New York Times*, April 21, 1987. *See* Chapter 1.

[423]"Every gender bias commission in the United States echoed the finding...that there was 'a reluctance to acknowledge the criminality of domestic violence at every stage of the law enforcement and judicial process' due to a willingness to accept 'still prevalent beliefs that violence against women can be acceptable.'" --Judge C. S. Lederman, "Report on Dade County," *Family Law Commentator* XIX (3) February 1994, citing the *Report of the Florida Supreme Court Gender Bias Commission* (1990), p. 14. "Echo" is the right word. If you take a look at these reports, you'll see that these supposed "findings" are usually based on the supposed "findings" that some other gender bias commission supposedly has made, which, in turn, is simply the "findings" that some other gender biased commission supposedly has made, and so on and so on. If you follow these citations through to the end, in some cases they will lead you around in a circle, right back to the original citation! This may be a fine procedure for the proliferation of urban legends, but it can hardly be considered a worthwhile use of taxpayer-funded

governmental resources on a subject of as vital importance as gender discrimination in the judicial branch of government.

[424]Wikler, Norma Juliet, "Water on Stone: A Perspective of the Movement to Eliminate Gender Bias in the Courts," keynote address, National Conference on Gender Bias in the Courts, Williamsburg, Virginia, May 18, 1989. Usually well over 75% of the people appointed to these commissions are female, and at least half are women's advocates. Hight, Bruce, "Male Group Says Too Many Women on Panel," *Austin American-Statesman*, January 31, 1992.

[425]Farrell, *supra*, at p. 247.

[426]Morgan, Robin, *The Demon Lover*, New York: Norton & Co. (1989)

[427]Edleson, Jeffrey L. and Andrea L. Bible, "Forced Bonding or Community Collaboration? Partnerships Between Science and Practice in Research on Woman Battering," in Kennedy, David, et. al., *Viewing Crime and Justice From a Collaborative Perspective: Plenary Papers of the 1998 Conference on Criminal Justice Research and Evaluation*, NCJ 176979, U.S. Government Printing Office (1998), p. 30. According to the Minnesota Center Against Violence and Abuse, woman-centered advocacy "greatly enhances a research project." *Ibid.*

[428]Not all do. In fact, some women, seeking to distance themselves from these kinds of researchers and advocates, have started to refer to these "other" feminists as "gender feminists," "difference feminists" or "radical feminists," not "real" feminists. Meanwhile, some men, reacting to the anti-male propaganda and legislative policies engendered by these "other" feminists, have invented a new term for themselves, too: "masculists." It really shouldn't be necessary to invent any of these terms. The English language already contains terms that are quite adequate to the task. A person who believes in the superiority of one class of persons over another is a *supremacist*. A person who believes women are superior to men, and/or that women should have rights and privileges not enjoyed by men, should therefore be called what he or she is: a *female supremacist*, just as a person who believes that men are naturally superior to women should be called a *male supremacist*. A person who believes in equal rights

for men and women, not special rights and privileges for either gender at the expense of the other, is an *egalitarian*. Terms like *feminist* and *masculist* connote gender-specific interests. As such, they are inherently gender-polarizing terms. Anyone whose real concern is with equal rights should scrap both of them, and simply call himself or herself what he or she is: an *egalitarian*.

[429]See, e.g., Meis, M., "Liberating Women, Liberating Knowledge: Reflections on Two Decades of Feminist Action Research," *Atlantis* 21(1)(1996): 10-24; Kondrat, M.E. and Julia, M., "Participatory Action Research: Self-reliant Research Strategies for Human Social Development," *Social Development Issues* 19(1)(1997): 32-49; Uehara, et. al., "Toward a Values-Based Approach to Multicultural Social Work Research," Social Work 41(6)(1996): 613-621; Gondolf, E.W., et. al., "Collaboration Between Researchers and Advocates," in G. Kaufman Kantor and J.L. Jasinski, eds., *Out of the Darkness: Contemporary Perspectives on Family Violence*, Thousand Oaks, CA: Sage Publications (1997), pp. 255-267, and Small, "Action-Oriented Research: Models and Methods," *Journal of Marriage and the Family* 57(4)(1995): 941-55. "Advocacy research is intended to support the development of programs and public policies [for] women...." Edleson and Bible, *supra*, at p. 30.

[430]Edleson and Bible, *supra*, at p. 31. Edleson and Bible go on to encourage researchers to share the bounty for their research with women's advocates. *Ibid.*

[431]*Edleson and Bible, supra*, at p. 33

[432]*Ibid.*, at p. 34.

[433]*Ibid.* at p. 34.

[434]*Ibid.* at p. 35.

[435]"[B]attered men and abusive women have received 'selective inattention' by both the media and researchers," despite the fact that "researchers consistently have found that men and women in relationships, both marital and premarital engage in comparable amounts of violence." Flynn, *supra*.

[436]It also tends to confirm the theory that a man is much less willing to report to law enforcement authorities that he has been a victim of a crime perpetrated by a member of the opposite sex than a woman is. Wilt, G.M. and J.D. Bannon, *Violence and the Police:*

Homicides, Assaults and Disturbances, Washington, D.C.: The
Police Foundation (1976)("nonfatal violence committed by
women against men is less likely to be reported to the police than
is violence by men against women; thus, women assaulters who
come to the attention of the police are likely to be those who
have produced a fatal result.")

[437]*See, e.g.,* Greenfeld, et. al., *Violence by Intimates, supra.*

[438]Some examples of studies that exclude young victims are
Bachman, Ronet, *Violence against Women: A National Crime
Victimization Survey Report*, NCJ 145325, Washington DC: U.S.
Bureau of Justice Statistics (1994); Tjaden and Thoennes (1998),
supra, at p. 13; and Greenfeld, et. al., *Violence by Intimates,
supra*; but these are not, by any means, the only ones.

[439]Federal Bureau of Investigation, *Crime in the United States*,
Washington DC: U.S. Government Printing Office (1990), p. 11.

[440]Fagan, *supra.*

[441]U.S. Violence Against Women Grants Office, *Domestic Violence
and Stalking: The Second Annual Report to Congress under the
Violence Against Women Act*, Washington DC: U.S. Government
Printing Office (1997), p. 56, n. 23

[442]This example is for illustrative purposes only, and is not meant
to imply that men really are 100 times more likely to be abused
than women are. Men probably are more likely to be abused
than women are, but they are probably not *100 times* more likely
to be abused than women are.

[443]*Domestic Violence and Stalking, supra*, at p. ix.

[444]Langan, Patrick A. and Christopher A. Innes, *Preventing Domestic
Violence Against Women*, NCJ 102037, Washington DC: U.S.
Bureau of Justice Statistics (1986); Greenfeld, et. al., *Violence by
Intimates, supra.*

[445]The U.S. Department of Health and Human Services has
acknowledged that "the actual number of child fatalities may
be underreported...because some deaths labeled as accidents,
child homicides, and/or Sudden Infant Death Syndrome (SIDS)
might be attributed to child maltreatment if more comprehensive
investigations were conducted," noting that "It is difficult to
distinguish a child who has been suffocated from a child who has
died as a result of SIDS, or a child who was dropped, pushed,

or thrown from a child who dies from a legitimate fall." U.S. Department of Health and Human Services, *Child Fatalities Fact Sheet, supra.* The U.S. Department of Health and Human Services ascribes inadequate forensic investigations of child fatalities to the absence of any national standards for child death investigations, lack of medical training for coroners, and the role of child protection service agencies. *Ibid.*

[446]Dworkin, Andrea, *Ice And Fire,* N.Y.: Weidenfeld & Nicolson (1987)

[447]*see* Tjaden and Thoennes (1998), *supra.*

[448]Steinem, *supra.*

[449]Steven Easton, the man who founded a support group for battered men in Canada, says that denial of access to children and vilification of fathers by children's mothers are two of the most frequently complained about forms of emotional abuse that he receives from men. Easton, *Abuse of Men in Families and the Interacting Legacy of Abuse in the Justice System, supra.* In my review of the research literature, I have come across exactly zero studies that include this kind of behavior within their definitions of emotional abuse, although many include the withholding of money from an economically dependent woman by an income-earning man as a form of emotional abuse. Responding to those who adamantly refuse to consider the idea that denial of access to children may be a form of emotional abuse, Easton has this to say: "As men have not been included in any major discussions about abuse, it would be unwise to discount the feelings of the majority of male abuse victims in defining their own issue." *Ibid.*

[450]*Rat,* February 6, 1970.

[451]Koss, Gidycz and Wisniewski, *supra,* at pp. 162-70, reprinted in the *New York Times,* April 21, 1987. See Chapter 1.

[452]Morgan, Robin, "Theory and Practice: Pornography and Rape" in *Going too Far: The Personal Chronicle of a Feminist,* N.Y.: Random House (1977)

[453]Moffitt and Caspi, *supra.*

[454]What the research actually shows is that the experience of abuse perpetrated by one's *mother* is more predictive of abusive behavior as an adult than having an abusive father is. Langhinrich-Rohling, et. al. (1995), *supra*; Malone and

Tyree, *supra;* Straus, M.A. and V.E. Mouradian, "Impulsive Corporal Punishment by Mothers and Antisocial Behavior and Impulsiveness of Children," *Behavioral Sciences and the Law,* 16(3):353-374 (1998)

[455]*Ibid.,* at p. 7

[456]White, A. C., "Family Law and Domestic Violence," *Florida Bar Journal,* October, 1994.

[457]Giles-Sims, Jean, "The Psychological and Social Impact of Partner Violence," *Domestic Violence Literature Review, Synthesis, and Implications for Practice,* United States Air Force and the National Network for Family Resiliency (1997)

[458]Fagan, *supra.*

[459]*Ibid.,* citing Fagan, Jeffrey and Angela Browne, "Violence Against Spouses and Intimates," in *Understanding and Preventing Violence,* vol. 3, ed. by Albert J. Reiss, Jr. and Jeffrey A. Roth, Washington DC: National Academy Press (1994)

[460]Walker, *The Battered Woman, supra.*

[461]Kaufman Kantor, Glenda and Jana L. Jasinski, "Dynamics of Partner Violence and Types of Abuse and Abusers," in *Domestic Violence Literature Review, Synthesis, and Implications for Practice,* United States Air Force and the National Network for Family Resiliency (1997) Johnson concludes that this pattern may only be applicable to one small sub- category of domestic abuse (what he calls the "terroristic" variety of spouse abuse) and may not be a characteristic of the majority of abusers. Johnson, M. P., "Patriarchal terrorism and common couple violence: Two forms of violence against women," *Journal of Marriage and the Family,* 57, (1995), pp. 283-294.

[462]Holtzworth-Munroe, A. and G.L. Stuart, "Typologies of male batterers: Three subtypes and the differences among them," *Psychological Bulletin,* 116(3), 476-497 (1994) *Compare* Dutton, D. G., "The origin and structure of the abusive personality," *Journal of Personality Disorders,* 8(3), 181-191 (1994); Gondolf, E. W., "Who are those guys? Toward a behavioral typology of batterers, Violence and Victims, 3(3), 187-203 (1988); Kaufman Kantor and Jasinski, *supra* ("there is not a singular profile that defines all abusive men"); *accord:* Hamberger, L. K. and J.E. Hastings, "Personality correlates of men who abuse their

partners: A cross-validation study," *Journal of Family Violence*, 1(4), 323-341 (1986)

[463]Kaufman Kantor and Jasinski, *supra.*

[464]This statement appears to have originated with Congressman Joseph Biden, Jr. as part of his effort to ensure the passage of the Violence Against Women Act. Senate Judiciary Hearings, *Violence Against Women Act* (1990). It has been repeated many times by many different politicians, women's lobbyists, law enforcement agencies, journalists, advocates and advocate-researchers. *See, e.g.*, Los Angeles Police Department web site; Diggs, Agnes, "Plan to escape domestic abuse," *North County Times* (San Diego/Riverside, Calif.), October 29, 2001; Edwards, Claudia, "What does domestic violence really mean?" *Hendersonville* (Tennessee) *Star News*, October 10, 2001; Perls, Ester, "Domestic violence tops list of crimes in U.S. against women," *Vocal Point*, October, 1994; Barnstable Police Department, *The Barnstable Police Domestic Violence Unit*, Barnstable, Mass. (2001); Battered Women Fighting Back, *Domestic Violence: The Facts, a handbook to STOP violence*, Boston, Mass. Sen. Paul Wellstone used it during his campaign for the passage of more special legislation exclusively for battered women. Budig, T. W., "Wellstone's legislation would better link battered women's shelters across country," *East Central Minnesota Post Review*, September, 2000.

[465]Crowell, Nancy A. and Ann W. Burgess, *Understanding Violence Against Women*, Washington, D.C.: National Academy of Sciences (1996), citing Plichta, S.B., *Domestic Violence: Building Paths for Women to Travel to Freedom and Safety*, College of Health Sciences, Old Dominion University (1995)

[466]Burt, Martha R., et. al., *Homelessness: Programs and the People They Serve, Findings of the National Survey of Homeless Assistance Providers and Clients*, Washington, D.C.: Interagency Council on the Homeless (1999)

[467]U.S. Bureau of the Census, *Statistical Abstract of the United States, 2000.*

[468]"National shelter census results revealed," *Journal of the American Veterinary Medical Association*, January 15, 1997

[469]A related assertion that one sometimes hears is that domestic violence causes more injuries to women than car accidents, muggings and rapes combined. See, e.g., Former Surgeon General C. Everett Koop's *Comments to the American College of Obstetricians and Gynecologists*, January 3, 1989. Although the Centers for Disease Control is often cited as authority for this statement, the Centers for Disease Control say this is neither their fact nor a reputable fact. The "statistic" appears to be based on a single survey, of the kind I have described in the text, that was conducted in one small emergency room by a pair of "researchers" named Stark and Flitcraft. *See* Stark, E. and A. Flitcraft, "Spouse abuse," in *Surgeon General's Workshop on Violence and Public Health: Source Book*, Leesburg, Va.: October 27-29, 1985. As is discussed elsewhere in this book, what emergency room records really show is that domestic violence only accounts for less than 1% of the injuries treated in emergency rooms--a figure that is substantially lower than the number of women who are treated for injuries resulting from accidents, let alone "car accidents, muggings and rapes combined."

[470]National Center for Health Statistics, *National Hospital Ambulatory Medical Care Survey: 1992 Emergency Department Summary* , Hyattsville, Md. (March, 1997); *see also* U.S. Bureau of Justice Statistics, *Violence-Related Injuries Treated in Hospital Emergency Departments*, Washington, D.C.: U.S. Government Printing Office (1997)

[471]Straus, Gelles and Steinmetz (1980), *supra*.

[472]Shervin and Sniechowski, *supra*.

[473]See Chapter 1.

[474]quoted in Sommers, *Who Stole Feminism?*, *supra*.

[475]*See, e.g., Boston Globe*, September 2, 1991 *and Dallas Morning News*, February 7, 1993.

[476]*Time*, Jan. 18, 1993

[477]Sommers, *Who Stole Feminism?*, *supra*.

[478]Congressional Caucus for Women's Issues, *Violence Against Women*, Washington, D.C. (October, 1992)

[479]See, e.g., Council on Domestic Violence and Sexual Assault, *Annual Report to Governor Hickel and the Alaska Legislature* (March, 1992), at p. 2

[480]See, e.g., *Growing*, 3, November, 1994; *and* Hollyday, Joyce, "Crimes and Obsessions," *Sojourners*, September-October, 1994.

[481]*See, e.g.*, Irons, Richard R., "Comorbidity Between Domestic Violence and Addictive Disease," *Sexual Addiction and Compulsivity*, Vol. 3, No. 2, pp. 85–96 (1996); Irons, Richard R. and Jennifer P. Schneider, "When Is Domestic Violence a Hidden Face of Addiction?" *Journal of Psychoactive Drugs*, Vol. 29, No. 4, pp. 337-344; *and* Eichelman, B.S., "Profiles in violence: Domestic violence," *Audio-Digest Family Practice*, Vol. 42(32), 1 (1994)

[482]See, e.g., the California Youth Authority's *Family Violence Prevention*, a technical bulletin issued by CYA's Office of Prevention and Victim Services; and the City of Chattanooga's *Family Violence Investigations* brochure. The Abington, Massachusetts police department describes the statistic as a "fact" on its web site.

[483]*See State of Alaska v. Huletz*, Alaska Court of Appeals No. 1248, September 18, 1992

[484]Interim House, *Domestic Violence Training Manual*, Detroit, Mich.: YWCA of Metropolitan Detroit

[485]The Federal Bureau of Investigation's *Supplementary Homicide Reports 1976-98* show that 1,217 women were killed in 1997 by an "intimate," where "intimate" is broadly defined to include spouses, ex-spouses, boyfriends and girlfriends, including homosexual as well as heterosexual relationships. Rennison and Welchans, *supra*, pp. 8 and 10. That is to say, not all of the 1,217 female victims were necessarily killed by men; some may have been killed by their lesbian lovers.

[486]U.S. Department of Health and Human Services, *Child Fatalities Fact Sheet, supra.*

[487]Sen. Joseph Biden, U.S. Senate Committee on the Judiciary, *Violence Against Women: Victims of the System*, 1991.

[488]U.S. Conference of Mayors, *Status Report on Hunger and Homelessness in America's Cities* (1997). Sen. Biden infers that because 55% of the mayors of major cities did not cite domestic violence as one of the principal causes of homelessness, "45 percent of homeless women are...fleeing domestic violence." Sen. Joseph Biden, Jr., *Safer Streets, Safer Homes: The Success*

of the Violence Against Women Act and the Challenge for the Future (September, 1999), at p. 48. There is a difference, however, between saying that something is one of several principal causes and saying that it is "the" cause.

[489]National Coalition for the Homeless, *Domestic Violence and Homelessness Fact Sheet* #8 (1999). Why in the world people feel they have to inflate figures like these is beyond me. Even if only 22% of the nation's homeless people are homeless because they are fleeing domestic violence, that still strikes me as pretty solid evidence that way too many victims of domestic violence have no choice but to live on the streets.

[490]The FBI does collate Supplementary Homicide Reports (SHR's) from data it receives from local law enforcement agencies, and these SHR's do provide information about the victim-offender relationship and the circumstances surrounding the crime, but none have ever included the specific kind of data described in the text.

[491]Synder and Sickmund, *supra*, at p. 54.

[492]*Ibid.* at p. 55 (analyzing information from the FBI's Supplementary Homicide Reports.)

[493]*Ibid.*

[494]*Ibid.*

[495]*See*, e.g., *Journal of the American Medical Association*, 276:23, 3132, June 17, 1992; *see also* Note 54.

[496]National Center for Health Statistics (1997), *supra.*

[497]This statement appears to have been made, originally, by Robert McAfee, past president of the American Medical Association, approximately 10 years ago. It continues to be repeated over and over again to this day by politicians, feminists and the media, despite the ease of access to figures that plainly show it is false. For example, it is cited in Pennsylvania Attorney General Mike Fisher's Family Violence Task Force's *Report on How Pennsylvania's Schools & Early Childhood Development Programs Are Addressing Family Violence*; and in a press release issued by Rep. Leonard Boswell ("Boswell calls for action on Violence Against Women Act," *News from Congressman Leonard Boswell* (March 9, 2000.) During a brief search of

the Internet, I found it listed as a "fact" on over 200 web sites, including the official web sites of many governmental entities.

[498]American Medical Association, *Five Issues on American Health* (1992)

[499]*Information Please Almanac* (1991)

[500]U.S. Bureau of the Census, Statistical Abstracts of the United States (1992)(citing data from the National Center for Health Statistics.)

[501]Greenfeld, et. al., *Violence by Intimates, supra*

[502]Only about 30% are. *Ibid.*

[503]McElroy, Wendy, "Redefining Domestic Violence," *Fox News,* September 11, 2001

[504]Pizzey, Erin, *Prone to Violence*, Feltham, Middlesex, England: Hamlyn (1982)

[505]The classic feminist text on rape is Susan Brownmiller's *Against Our Will.* In this book, Ms. Brownmiller takes the position that rape is "a conscious process of intimidation by which all men keep all women in a state of fear." Brownmiller, Susan, *Against Our Will: Men, Women and Rape*, New York: Simon & Schuster (1975), p. 6.

[506]Aggression can manifest itself in less extreme ways than smashing windows and threatening people's lives. Damage or the threat of damage to one's professional reputation can also have a significant chilling effect on academic freedom. For example, it has been reported that after she discovered that college women initiate physical violence against their dating partners more often than men do, Dr. Irene Frieze, Ph.D. of the University of Pittsburgh tried to keep her findings quiet, out of fear of how feminist groups would react. She was able to keep the findings submerged for a few years, but eventually word leaked out. Her fears proved to be well-founded: Almost immediately upon learning of the findings, the National Organization of Women denounced the research as fraudulent. Sleek, *supra.* Of course the research was not fraudulent. NOW simply felt compelled to insist that it must be, because findings like these tend to undercut the "men bad/women good" dichotomy that NOW has a special interest in having people believe.

[507]Pleck, Elizabeth, "Wife Beating in Nineteenth-Century America," *Victimology: An International Journal* 4, p. 4 (1979); *see also* Pleck, Elizabeth, *Domestic Tyranny* (New York: Oxford University Press, 1987)

[508]Kelly, Henry Ansgar, "Rule of Thumb and the Folklaw of the Husband's Stick," *Journal of Legal Education*, September, 1994.

[509]Overall, child maltreatment reports increased 161% between 1980 and 1996. U.S. Office of Juvenile Justice and Delinquency Prevention, *Children as Victims, supra*, at p. 19.

[510]Jones and Finkelhor, *supra*.

[511]Smith, Barbara E., *Prosecuting Child Physical Abuse Cases: A Case Study in San Diego*, Research in Brief, Washington DC: U.S. Department of Justice (1995), p. 3. It is also interesting to note that although a majority of child victims are male, the majority of the cases that child protection agencies choose to investigate and substantiate involve female victims. U.S. Office of Juvenile Justice and Delinquency Prevention, *Children as Victims, supra*, at p. 19

[512]National Center on Child Abuse and Neglect, *A Report on the Maltreatment of Children with Disabilities, supra*, at p. 3-22; *see also* Center for the Future of Children, "Executive Summary," *The Future of Children*, vol. 8, no. 1 (Spring 1998.) The rate of enforcement is slightly higher for disabled children, however.

[513]*See, e.g.*, Minnesota Department of Human Services, *Child Maltreatment, supra*, at pp. 22-23.

[514]Martin and Besharov, *supra*.

[515]National Center on Child Abuse and Neglect, *A Report on the Maltreatment of Children with Disabilities, supra*.

[516]U.S. Department of Justice, *Criminal Investigation of Child Sexual Abuse*, Portable Guides to Investigating Child Abuse, NCJ 162426, Washington DC: U.S. Government Printing Office (1997)

[517]Smithey, M., "Infant Homicide: Victim-Offender Relationship and Causes of Death," *Journal of Family Violence*, 13(3):285-297 (1998)

[518]Langstaff, John and Tish Sleeper, *The National Center on Child Fatality Review*, Washington DC: U.S. Department of Justice (2001.) The "one child every 2 hours" is based on the

estimate that about 5,000 children die as a result of child abuse or neglect every year. *See* U.S. Health and Human Services Department, *Child Fatalities Fact Sheet, supra.* Even using the most conservative estimates, such as those derived from data on substantiated child abuse fatalities reported by child protection agencies, the rate still comes out to be more than one child every five hours. U.S. Department of Health and Human Services, *Child Maltreatment 1997: Reports From the States to the National Child Abuse and Neglect Data System, supra.*

[519]U.S. Office for Victims of Crime, *First Response to Victims of Crime: A Handbook for Law Enforcement Officers on How To Approach and Help Elderly Victims, Victims of Sexual Assault, Child Victims, Victims of Domestic Violence, Survivors of Homicide Victims,* NCJ 176971, Washington, DC: U.S. Department of Justice (2000), p. 14.

[520]Buzawa, Eve S. and Thomas Austin, "Determining Police Response to Domestic Violence Victims," *American Behavioral Scientist,* 36 (5) (May 1993), 610-623. The same study reports that although a majority of female victims were satisfied with police response, *not a single male was,* not even the ones who were still alive enough to answer follow-up questions.

[521]Greenfeld, et. al., *Violence by Intimates, supra,* at p. 20. The report provides no data about the speed with which police respond to reports of domestic violence by males. This may be due to a desire to hide the fact that police response is slow or non-existent in such cases, or it may simply be due to the researchers' belief in the oft-repeated mantra that domestic abuse is "a male phenomenon."

[522]Federal Bureau of Investigation, "Crime in the United States," *Uniform Crime Reports,* August 8, 1973, pp. 8-9.

[523]U.S. Bureau of Justice Statistics, *Report to the Nation on Crime and Justice, supra,* at p. 41.

[524]Ray, J.A. and D.J. English, "Comparison of female and male children with sexual behavior problems," *Journal of Youth and Adolescence* 24(4): 439-451 (1995.)

[525]Snyder and Sickmund, *supra.*

[526]Snyder, *supra,* at p. 12.

[527]*See* Finkelhor, David and Richard Ormrod, *Child Abuse Reported to the Police*, Washington, DC: U.S. Office of Juvenile Justice and Delinquency Prevention (2001), p. 4.

[528]National Center on Child Abuse and Neglect, *National Study of the Incidence and Severity of Child Abuse and Neglect*, Washington DC: U.S. Department of Health and Human Services (1981), p. 34.

[529]Martin and Besharov, *supra*, at p. 17.

[530]*Ibid.*, at p. 19.

[531]Even though the vast majority of child abusers reported to social service agencies are female, 73% of the cases that these agencies choose to report to police for charging criminally are male. That is to say, for all categories of crimes against children, your case is substantially more likely to be reported to the police for criminal charges if you are male than if you are female. Finkelhor and Ormrod, *Child Abuse Reported to the Police, supra.*

[532]Finkelhor and Ormrod observed that over half of all perpetrators of physical child abuse in the child protection system are female, but less than one-third of physical child abusers reported to police are female. They hypothesize that one possible explanation for the discrepancy might be a tendency among child protection workers to view an act as a "crime" if it is committed by a male, but not a "crime" when the very same act is committed by a female. Finkelhor and Ormrod, *Child Abuse Reported to the Police, supra*, at p. 6.

[533]Smith, Barbara E., *supra*, at p. 3

[534]Moreover, the line between "normal" parental affection and sexual contact isn't always clear, either. For example, since sexual abuse is usually broadly defined to include contact by any part of the adult's body with the child's genitals or breasts, even through the child's clothing,--and also can include contact by any part of the child's body with the adult's genitals, even if covered--it could reach situations in which a father is merely giving his daughter a hug. Just as the line between discipline and physical abuse may not always be clear, so the line between normal parental affection and what the law or a child protection worker regards as "sexual contact" may not always be clear, either.

[535]In San Diego, one of the only jurisdictions in which physical abuse is prosecuted almost as vigorously as sexual abuse, conviction rates for both sexual and physical abuse are about equal. *Ibid.*

[536]Consider this excerpt from a recent U.S. Department of Health and Human Services publication:

In 1995, the U.S. Advisory Board on Child Abuse and Neglect recommended a universal approach to...child fatalities that would reach out to all families through the implementation of several key strategies. These efforts would [include] providing services such as home visitation by trained professionals or paraprofessionals, hospital-linked outreach to parents of infants and toddlers, community-based programs designed for the specific needs of neighborhoods, and effective public education campaigns.

U.S. Administration on Children and Families, *Child Fatalities Fact Sheet*, Washington, D.C.: U.S. Department of Health and Human Services (2001). The idea of prosecuting people who physically abuse their children is not even mentioned as a possible method of deterring parents from killing their children.

[537]*Ibid.*, citing Smith, B.E. and S.G. Elstein, *The Prosecution of Child Sexual and Physical Abuse Cases*, American Bar Association, Final Report to the National Center on Child Abuse and Neglect (1993).

[538]American Bar Association, *Legal Interventions in Family Violence: Research Findings and Policy Implications*, Research Report, NCJ 171666, Washington DC: National Institute Justice (1998)

[539]Snyder and Sickmund, *supra*, at pp. 153, 156

[540]Butler, David D., J.D., "Males Get Longer Sentences," *Transitions*, vol. 10, no. 1, January/February 1990, p. 1.

[541]quoted in Kurtz, Howie, "Courts Easier on Women," *The Sunday Record* (Bergen County, N.J.), October 5, 1975.

[542]Greenfeld, et. al., *Violence by Intimates, supra*, at p. 20. The Report states that over 800,000 women visited such agencies between 1992 and 1996. There is no indication as to the number of men who visited these agencies. This suggests either that a larger number of men sought help and protection from domestic

abuse than the researchers are comfortable with reporting, or that abuse of men is simply not considered important enough to even bother mentioning.

[543]California Attorney General Daniel E. Lungren's Policy Council on Violence Prevention, *supra,* at p. 195.

[544]Cothern, Lynn, *Juveniles and the Death Penalty,* U.S. Coordinating Council on Juvenile Justice and Delinquency Prevention, NCJ 184748 (2000), p. 5, citing Lewis, D.O., et. al., "Neuropsychiatric, psychoeducational and family characteristics of 14 juveniles condemned to death in the United States," *American Journal of Psychiatry* 145(5): 585-589.

[545]Actually, if you want to know my personal opinion, it's that this kind of attorney should be made to serve the sentence in place of the child; but that would seem to me to be an even less realistic expectation than that an attorney would be permanently disbarred for providing ineffective assistance in a capital case.

[546]Kurtz, *supra.*

[547]*Ibid.*

[548]Gorman, Tom, "Woman Who Kills Child Remains Free," *Los Angeles Times,* April 26, 1989.

[549]Rosenbaum, Ron, "Too Young to Die?" *The New York Times Magazine,* March 12, 1989.

[550]Webb, *supra.*

[551]Bedau and Radelet, *supra,* at pp. pp. 21-179.

[552]*Time,* June 3, 1991, p. 52.

[553]Gold, Allan R., "Sex Bias Is Found Pervading Courts," *New York Times,* July 2, 1989.

[554]Beck, Allen J., *Prisoners in 2000,* Bureau of Justice Statistics Bulletin, NCJ 188207, Washington, DC: U.S. Department of Justice (2001), pp. 1 and 5.

[555]All statistics in this paragraph are from Brown, Jodi M. and Langan, Patrick A., *State Court Sentencing of Convicted Felons, 1994,* NCJ 164614, Washington DC: U.S. Department of Justice (1998.)

[556]*Ibid.,* at p. 26.

[557]U.S. Bureau of Justice Statistics, *Sentencing Outcomes in 28 Felony Courts: 1985,* NCJ 105743, Washington DC: U.S. Department of Justice (1987.)

[558]Brown and Langan, *supra*, at p. 27.

[559]All statistics in this paragraph are from Brown and Langan, *supra*, at p. 20

[560]*Ibid.*

[561]Zingraff, Matthew and Randall Thompson, "Differential Sentencing of Women and Men in the USA," *International Journal of the Sociology of Law*, no. 12 (1984), pp. 401-13 at 408.

[562]U.S. Bureau of Justice Statistics, *Domestic Violence: Violence Between Intimates*, Washington, D.C.: U.S. Department of Justice (1994). Thus, the oft-repeated myth that "women who kill their batterers receive longer prison sentences than men who kill their partners" is just that--a myth. In fact, it is exactly the opposite.

[563]Washington State Sentencing Guidelines Commission, *Sentencing Practices Under the Sentencing Reform Act: Fiscal Year 1987*, p. 72.

[564]Clark, John, et. al., *'Three Strikes and You're Out': A Review of State Legislation*, National Institute of Justice Research in Brief, U.S. Department of Justice (1997), pp. 5-6.

[565]Greenfeld, *Child Victimizers, supra*, at p. 10.

[566]*Ibid.*, at p. 5.

[567]*Ibid.*, at p. 1.

[568]*Ibid.*

[569]*Ibid.*, at p. 1; and Turman and Poyer, *supra*, at p. 3.

[570]Greenfeld, et. al., *Violence by Intimates, supra*.

[571]*Ibid.*, at p. 29

[572]Cothern, *supra*, at p. 9.

[573]International Covenant on Civil and Political Rights, Article 6(5).

[574]G.A. Res. 44/25, annex, 44 U.N. GAOR, Supp. No. 49, at 167, U.N. Doc. A/44/49 (1989.)

[575]Cothern, *supra*, at pp. 8-9.

[576]Amnesty International, *On the Wrong Side of History: Children and the Death Penalty in the USA*, New York: Amnesty International USA Publications (1998); and Amnesty International, *Betraying the Young: Human Rights Violations Against Children in the U.S. Justice System*, New York: Amnesty International USA Publications (1998)

[577]Cothern, *supra,* at p. 4.

[578]Streib, Victor L., *The Juvenile Death Penalty Today: Death Sentences and Executions for Juvenile Crimes, January 1, 1973--June 30* (2000), Ada, OH: Ohio Northern University Claude W. Pettit College of Law (2000); *see also* Cothern, *supra,* at p. 2

[579]U.S. Bureau of Justice Statistics, *Profile of Felons Convicted in State Courts,* NCJ 120021 (1990), p. 9.

[580]U.S. Bureau of Justice Statistics, *Report to the Nation on Crime and Justice, supra,* at p. 99.

[581]Streib, Victor L., *American Executions of Female Offenders: A Preliminary Inventory of Names, Dates and Other Information,* Cleveland, Ohio: Cleveland-Marshall College of Law (1988)

[582]NAACP Legal Defense and Educational Fund, "Execution Update" (January 18, 1990.)

583

[584]U.S. Bureau of Justice Statistics, *Sourcebook of Criminal Justice Statistics, supra,* at p. 442; and Kirkpatrick and Humphrey, *supra.*

[585]U.S. Bureau of Justice Statistics, *National Corrections Reporting Program, 1992-1996* (machine-readable data file), Washington DC: BJS (1998); and Snyder and Sickmund, *supra,* at p. 210

[586]Austin, James, Kelly Johnson and Maria Gregoriou, *Juveniles in Adult Prisons and Jails: A National Assessment,* NCJ 182503, Washington DC: U.S. Bureau of Justice Assistance (2000) at p. 173.

[587]*Washington v. Furman,* 853 P.2d 1092, 1102 (Wash. 1993)

[588]Vt. Stat. Ann. tit. 13 §2303 (Supp. 1997) and Vt. Stat. Ann. tit. 33 §5506 (1991); *see generally* Cothern, *supra,* at p. 10.

[589]*Workman v. Kentucky,* 429 S.W. 2d 374 (Ky. App. 1968)(later appealed.)

[590]Snyder and Sickmund, *supra,* at pp. 158, 198-199, 202-203 132.

[591]Austin, Johnson and Gregoriou, *supra,* at p. 41

[592]*Ibid.,* at p. 42.

[593]Brown and Langan, *supra.*

[594]*See, e.g.,* U.S. Bureau of Justice Statistics, *Profile of Felons Convicted in State Courts, supra.*

[595]Austin, Johnson and Gregoriou, *supra,* at p. 39

[596]U.S. Bureau of Justice Statistics, *Report to the Nation on Crime and Justice, supra* at p. 109.

[597]*Ibid.*

[598]*Ibid.*

[599]Council on Crime in America, *The State of Violent Crime in America*, Washington DC: The New Citizenship Project (1996), p. 41

[600]Conly, *supra*, at p. 2.

[601]*Ibid.*, at p. 2

[602]Strasser, Fred and Mary C. Hickey, "Running Out of Room for Women in Prison," *Governing* (October, 1989), p. 70.

[603]Snow, *supra*.

[604]*See, e.g.*, Daly, Kathleen, "Neither Conflict Nor Labeling Nor Paternalism Will Suffice: Intersections of Race, Ethnicity, Gender and Family in Criminal Court Decisions," *Crime and Delinquency* 35(1) (January 1989): 136-168

[605]Snyder and Sickmund, *supra*, at p. 132.

[606]National Institute of Justice, *Partner Violence Among Young Adults, supra*; and Magdol, *supra*, at pp. 68-78

[607]Moffitt and Caspi, *supra*, at p. 10.

[608]Straus and Gelles note that "Violence by wives has not been an object of concern. There has been no publicity, and no funds have been invested in ameliorating this problem because it has not been defined as a problem. In fact, our 1975 study was criticized for presenting statistics on violence by wives. Our 1985 finding of little change in the rate of assaults by women on their male partners is consistent with the absence of ameliorative programs." Straus and Gelles (1990), *supra*, at p. 8.

[609]Feather, N. T., "Domestic violence, gender and perceptions of justice, *Sex Roles*, 35, 507-519 (1996)

[610]*See also* Straus, M. A., G. Kaufman Kantor, and D.W. Moore, *Change in cultural norms approving marital violence from 1968 to 1994*, paper presented at the American Sociological Association, Los Angeles, Calif. (1996)(finding that the ratio of the approval rate for wives slapping husbands--which has always been higher than the approval rate for husbands slapping wives--to that for husbands slapping wives has doubled since 1968.) *Accord*: Straus, Murray A., "Trends in cultural norms and rates

of partner violence: An update to 1992," in S. M. Stich and M. A. Straus, eds., *Understanding Partner Violence: Prevalence, Causes, Consequences, and Solutions*, Minneapolis, Minn.: National Council on Family Relations (1996), pp. 30-33.

[611]Gilligan, *supra*.

[612]U.S. Bureau of Justice Statistics, *National Survey of Crime Severity*, NCJ 96017, Washington DC: U.S. Government Printing Office (1985); *see also* Bureau of Justice Statistics, *Report to the Nation on Crime and Justice, supra*, at p. 16.

[613]Tifft, L. L., *Battering of Women: The failure of intervention and the case for prevention*, Boulder, Colo.: Westview Press (1993); *see also* Straus and Yodanis, *supra*.

[614]*See* Wallerstein, Edward, M.D., *Circumcision: An American Health Fallacy*, New York: Springer Publishing Co. (1980)

[615]Special state and federal laws prohibiting the mutilation of female genitals have recently been enacted. Males are excluded from the protection of these laws.

[616]*See, e.g.,* Aaron Kipnis, PhD, "Male Privilege or Privation?" *ReSource* (Summer, 1992), p. 1.; Dr. Frederick Leboyer, *Birth Without Violence* (1975); Dr. Rima Laibow, MD, "Circumcision and its Relationship to Attachment Impairment," *Syllabus of Abstracts, Second International Symposium on Circumcision*, April 30, 1991.

[617]According to the Minnesota Legislative Child Protection Study Commission, 95% of the inmates in Minnesota prisons for perpetrating violent crimes were maltreated as children. Snow, *supra. See also* Strauss, M. A. and V. E. Mouradian, "Impulsive Corporal Punishment by Mothers and Antisocial Behavior and Impulsiveness of Children," *Behavioral Sciences and the Law*, 16(3):353-374 (1998)("the more corporal punishment experienced by the child, the greater the tendency for the child to engage in antisocial behavior and to act impulsively....These relationships hold even after controlling for family socioeconomic status, the age and sex of the child, nurturance by the mother, and the level of noncorporal interventions"); Thompson, K. M. and R. Braaten-Antrim, "Youth Maltreatment and Gang Involvement," *Journal of Interpersonal Violence*, 13(3):328-345 (1998)(abused children 4

times more likely to become members of violent gangs); Green, A. H., "Factors Contributing to the Generational Transmission of Child Maltreatment," *Journal of the American Academy of Child and Adolescent Psychiatry*, 37(12):1334-1336 (1998); Wekerle, C. and D.A. Wolfe, "The Role of Child Maltreatment and Attachment Style in Adolescent Relationship Violence," *Development and Psychopathology*, 10:571-586 (1998); *and* Lau, J. T. F., et. al., "Prevalence and Correlates of Physical Abuse in Hong Kong Chinese Adolescents: A Population-Based Approach," *Child Abuse and Neglect*, 23(6):549-557 (1999); Darby, P. J., et. al., "Analysis of 112 Juveniles Who Committed Homicide: Characteristics and a Closer Look at Family Abuse," *Journal of Family Violence*, 13(4):365-375 (1998); Straus and Yodanis, *supra*; Langhinrich-Rohling, et. al., *supra*; Malone and Tyree, *supra*; and Karr-Morse and Wiley, *supra*. These studies provide clear evidence of a causative correlation between abuse victimization in childhood and subsequent perpetration of domestic violence as an adult.

[618]Cothern, *supra*, at p. 9; *see also* Tifft, *supra*.

[619]"The contribution to later intrafamily aggression of individual biological and neurological factors...as risk markers for relationship aggression are not often incorporated into sociological, feminist or even psychological theories and research on intrafamily aggression." Kaufman Kantor and Jasinski, *supra*.

[620]Kaufman Kantor and Jasinski, *supra*; Holtzworth-Munroe and Stuart, *supra*; *see also* Hamberger, L. K. and J.E. Hastings, "Personality correlates of men who abuse their partners: A cross-validation study," *Journal of Family Violence*, 1(4), 323-341 (1986); Hudson, W. W. and McIntosh, S.R., "The assessment of spouse abuse: Two quantifiable dimensions," *Journal of Marriage and the Family*, 43, 873-885 (1981); Roy, M., ed., *Battered Women: A Psychosociological Study of Domestic Violence*, New York: Van Nostrand, Reinhold (1977); Stith, S. M. and S. C. Farley, S. C., "A predictive model of male spousal violence," *Journal of Family Violence*, 8(2), 183-201 (1993); Gondolf, *supra*; Rounsaville, B., "Theories in marital violence: Evidence from a study of battered women," *Victimology*, 3(1/2), 11-31 (1978); Shields, N. M., G. J. McCall and C. R. Hanneke,

"Patterns of family and nonfamily violence: Violent husbands and violent men," *Violence and Victims*, 3(2), 83-97 (1988)

Neidig, Friedman and Collins used assessments of self-esteem, authoritarianism and attitudes toward women, and found that abusive men differed from non-abusive men only in regard to the lower self-esteem of abusive men and their distrust of others. Neidig, Friedman and Collins, "The development and evaluation of a spouse abuse treatment program in a military setting," *Evaluation and Program Planning*, 9, 275-280 (1986)

[621]Holtzworth-Munroe and Stuart, *supra*; Gilligan, *supra*.

[622]Moffitt and Caspi, *supra; see also* Kaufman Kantor, G., J. Jasinski, and E. Aldorondo, "Sociocultural status and incidence of marital violence in Hispanic families," *Violence and Victims*, 9(3), 207-222 (1994); Dibble, U. and M.A. Straus, "Some social structure determinants of inconsistency between attitudes and behavior: The case of family violence," *Journal of Marriage and the Family*, 42(1), 71-80 (1980); Hotaling, G. T. and D. B. Sugarman, "An analysis of risk markers in husband to wife violence: The current state of knowledge," *Violence and Victims*, 1(2), 101-124 (1986); Straus, M.A. and C. Smith, "Violence in Hispanic families in the United States: Incidence rates and structural interpretations," in Straus, M.A. and R. J. Gelles, eds., *Physical Violence in American Families: Risk factors and adaptations to violence in 8,145 families*, New Brunswick, N.J.: Transaction (1990), pp. 341-368; *see generally* Straus, Murray A., "A general systems theory approach to a theory of violence between family members," *Social Science Information*, 12, 105 (1973); Gelles, R. J. and M.A. Straus, *Intimate Violence*, New York: Simon & Schuster (1988).

The rate of violence among families with incomes under $20,000 has been found to be 500% greater than families with incomes over $20,000. Straus, Gelles and Steinmetz (1980), *supra*.

[623]Gelles, R. J., "Violence toward children in the United States," *American Journal of Orthopsychiatry*, 48(4), 580-592 (1978); Gelles, R. J. and M.A. Straus, "Violence in the American family," *Journal of Social Issues*, 35(2), 15-39 (1978); Hornung, C. A., B.C. McCullough and T. Sugimoto, "Status relationships in marriage: Risk factors in spouse abuse," *Journal of Marriage*

and the Family, 43, 675-692 (1981); Jasinski, J. L., *Structural inequalities, family and cultural factors, and spousal violence among Anglo and Hispanic Americans*, doctoral dissertation, University of New Hampshire, Durham (1996); Kaufman Kantor, G., J. Jasinski and E. Aldorondo, "Sociocultural status and incidence of marital violence in Hispanic families," *Violence and Victims*, 9(3), 207-222 (1994); McLaughlin, I. G., K.E. Leonard and M. Senchak, "Prevalence and distribution of premarital aggression among couples applying for a marriage license," *Journal of Family Violence*, 7(4), 309-319 (1992); Steinmetz, S. K. and M.A. Straus, eds., *Violence in the Family*, New York: Harper & Row (1974). Acknowledging that domestic violence is more about the loss of control over one's own life events than the desire to control another person "is...important because it helps explain the importance of socioeconomic factors such as unemployment to intimate violence." Kaufman Kantor and Jasinski, *supra*. *Compare* Greenfeld, *supra*.

[624]Moffitt and Caspi, *supra*; Brinkerhoff and Lupri, *supra*.

[625]*See, e.g.*, Moffitt and Caspi, *supra;* Hamberger and Hastings, *supra*; Hudson and McIntosh, *supra*; O'Leary (1988), *supra*; *and* Roy, *supra*.

[626]*See, e.g.*, Moffitt and Caspi, *supra;* Hamberger and Hastings, *supra*; Hudson and McIntosh, *supra*; *and* Roy, *supra*.

[627]Moffitt and Caspi, *supra*; Holtzworth-Munroe and Stuart, *supra*. In this connection, it is worth noting that Dutton and Starzomski have uncovered convincing evidence that the intermittent abusive rage and violent behavior of the so-called "patriarchal" or "terroristic" batterer--the kind of abuser with whom shelter employees are probably most familiar--is more likely attributable to a specific, identifiable mental illness than simply "the patriarchy." Dutton, D. G. and A.J. Starzomski, "Borderline personality in perpetrators of psychological and physical abuse," *Violence and Victims*, 8(4), 327-337 (1993)

[628]O'Leary (1988), *supra*; Conger, R.D., et. al., "Linking economic hardship to marital quality and instability," *Journal of Marriage and the Family*, 52(3), 243-656 (1990); Gelles, R.J. and M.A. Straus, "Violence in the American family," *Journal of Social Issues*, 35(2), 15-39 (1978)

[629]*See* Elliott, F. A., "Neurological factors," in Van Hasselt, V. B., et. al., eds., *Handbook of Family Violence*, New York: Plenum Press (1988), pp. 359-382; Warnken, W. J., et. al., "Head injured males: A population at risk for relationship aggression," *Violence and Victims*, 9(2), 153-166 (1994); *and* Kaufman Kantor and Jasinski, *supra*.

[630]Moffit and Caspi, *supra*.

[631]Moffit and Caspi, *supra*.

[632]"A history of violence in the family of origin is probably the most widely accepted risk marker for the occurrence of partner violence." Kaufman Kantor and Jasinski, *supra*; Shupe, et. al., *supra*; *see also* Arias, I., *A social learning theory explication of the intergenerational transmission of physical aggression in intimate heterosexual relationships*, doctoral dissertation, State University of New York (1984); Kalmuss (1984), *supra*; Straus, Gelles and Steinmetz (1980), *supra*. Studies show that there is a strong correlation between the propensity to perpetrate acts of domestic violence as an adult and a history of being maltreated by one's mother during childhood, although there is no such correlation between abusiveness in adulthood and maltreatment by one's father during childhood. Langhinrich-Rohling, et. al. (1995), *supra*; Malone and Tyree, *supra; compare* Straus and Mouradian, *supra*. Ending maternal violence against male children can therefore be expected to go a long way toward reducing the perpetration of domestic violence by adult males.

[633]Moffitt and Caspi, *supra*; Straus and Yodanis, *supra*; Karr-Morse and Wiley, *supra*; Langhinrich-Rohling, Neidig and Thorn, *supra*; Malone and Tyree, *supra*; Pearson, *supra*; Kalmuss (1984), *supra*; O'Leary (1988), *supra*; Straus, Gelles and Steinmetz (1980), *supra*

[634]Tifft, *supra.*

[635]O'Leary (1988), *supra*

[636]It is just as possible that a man might act in self-defense as that a woman might do so, by the way. As a society, however, we permit women much broader leeway to use violence in self-defense than we do men. A woman who kicked her husband in the crotch because he was coming at her with a dangerous weapon would be hailed as a hero, but a man who kicked a

woman in the crotch--even if she were coming at him with a weapon--would be serving time in jail.

[637]Moffitt and Caspi, *supra*, at p. 4. It has been found, for instance, that women in lesbian relationships commit acts of domestic violence against their partners at a rate almost identical to the rate among heterosexual couples. The "male privilege" model also does not account for the disproportionately high rate of physical abuse that is perpetrated by females against children.

[638]Researchers have identified various factors that bear a more positive correlation to domestic violence than gender--e.g., mental illness; substance abuse; lack of education; poverty; weak parent-child attachment, among others. *Ibid.*, at pp. 6, 8. Directing batterers to focus on learning to feel shame about the subjugation of women as a class by men as a class, while denying that any of these other factors might have something to with it, only drives batterers further and further away from discovering within themselves the true source(s) of their problems.

[639]Snow, *supra.*

[640]Easton, *Abuse of Men in Families and the Interacting Legacy of Abuse in the Justice System supra* ("Powerlessness and how it affects peoples' choices will be the key to unlocking the hidden secrets in our abusive families ").

[641]In fact, dependence on one's partner is one of the few things that researchers have found to be consistently present in all three categories of men who abuse their intimate partners. Holtzworth-Munroe and Stuart, *supra. See also* Kaufman Kantor and Jasinski, *supra; and* Shupe, et. al., *supra.*

[642]"Men, particularly those with low self esteem, may defend themselves against feelings of frustration, vulnerability, and personal attack by using violence against a partner." Kaufman Kantor and Jasinski, *supra.* "Men who batter are often emotionally dependent, insecure [and] low in self-esteem." *Ibid. See also* Gondolf, *supra*; Holtzworth-Munroe and Stuart, *supra*; Rounsaville, *supra*; Shields, McCall and Hanneke, *supra; and* Stith and Farley, *supra*; and Neidig, Friedman and Collins, *supra.* Not all violence is a product of low self-esteem, however. Even when self-esteem is high, both men and women can sometimes become violent when they are deprived of control over their

lives. Prince, J. E., and I. Arias, "The role of perceived control and the desirability of control among abusive and nonabusive husbands," *American Journal of Family Therapy*, 22(2), 126-134 (1994.) An anthropologist might attribute the latter variety of violence to the "fight or flight" instinct that appears to be present in nearly all animal species, including humans.

[643]See, e.g., Daniel E. Lungren's Policy Council on Violence Prevention, *supra*, at pp. 194 and 195.

[644]The exclusive focus on improving girls' self-esteem is attributable, in large part, to the myth that girls' self-esteem shrinks radically upon going through adolescence, while boys' self-esteem rises. This myth originated with Carol Gilligan, a feminist professor of gender studies at Harvard University. More responsibly conducted research contradicts Ms. Gilligan's assertions. *See* Offer, Daniel and Kimberly Schonert-Reichl, "Debunking the Myths of Adolescence: Findings from Recent Research," *Journal of the American Academy of Child and Adolescent Psychiatry*, November, 1992. In 1993, *American Psychologist* reported that "It is now known that the majority of adolescents of both genders successfully negotiate this developmental period without any major psychological or emotional disorder [and] develop a positive sense of personal identity...." Petersen, et. al., "Depression in Adolescence," *American Psychologist*, February, 1993. The fact that most Americans insist on believing Ms. Gilligan's mythology despite overwhelming evidence that it isn't true speaks volumes about the relative value our society places on the male and female genders.

[645]The primary responsibility, of course, rests with the violent men themselves. I am not suggesting that violent men should not be held accountable for their violence. To the contrary, I believe that violent men should be held accountable, just as violent women should be. What I am suggesting, though, is that if, in addition to punishing these people, we also desire to *change* them into people who will not be likely to commit violence again in the future, then we have to do that in a responsible way. I am suggesting that those who place themselves in positions of power over other persons (as, for example, educators, courts and domestic violence program coordinators do) thereby undertake a

responsibility to adopt methods and practices that are reasonably designed to effect such changes. A knowing failure, on the part of such a person, to discharge this responsibility does not excuse the perpetrator for any further acts of violence he might commit, but it does give him an accomplice.

[646]Gilligan, *supra.*

[647]Warren Farrell's *Why Men Are The Way They Are*, New York: McGraw-Hill (1986), and *The Myth of Male Power, supra*, do a good job of bringing some of these abuses to light. For those who still need more proof, I might suggest visiting the women's section of a bookstore, taking a few women's studies classes at any major university, or just sitting down and watching a couple of daytime talk shows.

[648]Attorney General Daniel E. Lungren's Policy Council on Violence Prevention, *Violence Prevention: A Vision of Hope* (1995), *supra.*

[649]*Ibid.,* p. 53.

[650]*Ibid.,* at p. 23. If, as the Policy Council contends, countering stereotypes is the way to foster acceptance and respect for people, then the Policy Council's attempt to perpetuate stereotypes about males can only be interpreted as evidence of the Policy Council's desire to *discourage* acceptance and respect for males. As applied to persons who have been held by the Supreme Court to be members of a class that is entitled to the Equal Protection of the Laws, the legal term for this kind of desire would be *"purposeful discrimination."*

[651]*Ibid.,* at p. 20

[652]*Ibid.,* at p. 21.

[653]*Ibid.,* at p. 33

[654]U.S. Bureau of Justice Statistics, *Report to the Nation on Crime and Justice, supra*, at p. 24.

[655]U.S. Senate, "Women and Violence Hearing before the Commission on the Judiciary, U.S. Senate," part I, June 20, 1990 and part II, August 29, 1990 and December 11, 1990 (Order No. J-101-80); see also Young, Cathy, "The Sexist Violence Against Women Act," *Wall Street Journal*, Mar. 23, 1994, at A15.

[656]By the 1980's, most of these protections had been extended to men, too.

[657]Steinmetz, "The battered husband syndrome," *supra*.

[658]Cook, *supra*; Steinmetz, "The battered husband syndrome," *supra*; *see also* Hammond-Saslow, *supra*.

[659]*See* Slovenko, R., *Psychiatry and Law*, Boston, Mass.: Little, Brown & Co. (1973), p. 361.

[660]U.S. Bureau of the Census, *Current Population Reports*, Series P20-537, "America's Families and Living Arrangements: March 2000."

[661]Maccoby, Eleanor and Robert Mnookin, *Dividing the Child: Social and Legal Dilemmas of Custody*, Harvard University Press (1992)

[662]Johnston, et. al. (2001), *supra*; Johnston and Girdner, *supra*; *and* Finkelhor and Ormrod, *Kidnapping of Juveniles, supra*.

[663]Goelman, Deborah and Roberta Valente, *When will they ever learn? Educating to End Domestic Violence: A Law School Report*, Chicago, Ill.: American Bar Association (1997)

[664]Walker, *The Battered Woman, supra*, p. xiii.

[665]See, e.g., Dobash, R.E. and R. Dobash, *Violence Against Wives: A Case Against Patriarchy*, New York: Free Press (1979)

[666]Fiebert and Gonzales, *supra*.

[667]See, e.g., McCarthy, *supra*; Gonzales (1997), *supra*; *and* Stets and Pirog-Good, *supra*.

[668]Contrary to popular belief, statistics reporting that "20%" (or whatever the statistic *du jour* happens to be at the time) of women seen in emergency rooms are victims of domestic abuse are not about the number of women who are at the emergency room to receive treatment for injuries received as a result of domestic violence. Rather, they reflect the number of women who answered "yes" to the survey question, "Do you believe you have experienced domestic abuse *at some time* in your life?" A woman who believes she has been verbally or emotionally abused could answer such a question affirmatively even though the abuse had nothing whatsoever to do with her reason for being in the emergency room on the particular day in question. This is why there is a huge discrepancy between the findings based on archival data concerning women who have actually sought treatment for injuries caused by domestic violence (a comparatively small number), and findings based

on survey questions about domestic violence in general that are asked of women who are in the emergency room for *any* reason. Unfortunately, many unscrupulous politicians, women's organizations and journalists have used data from surveys conducted at emergency rooms as a basis for making statements like, "Emergency room records show that more women are treated in emergency rooms for domestic violence than for all other kinds of injuries combined." The campaign to characterize the male gender as a bunch of vicious misogynists has been so successful that such misrepresentations are rarely, if ever, questioned, even when they are patently absurd.

[669]Straus, et. al. (1996), *supra.* Of course, if a man accused of abuse were to try to defend himself on the ground that it wasn't "severe" or that it only happens "occasionally" rather than "chronically," he would most likely be chastised for trying to minimize the evil he has wrought. Domestic abuse literature almost always asserts that even a single act of domestic abuse, no matter how severe, is sufficient to earn a person the "batterer" label, since a single act of violence, even if mild, creates a perpetual implied threat of additional, potentially more severe, violence in the future. Yet, when research data shows that women commit as many acts of violence as men do, the data is attacked because it might be classifying as "batterers" those women who only "occasionally" batter men or who only do it "mildly." No logical explanation has ever been given for why a single act of violence, no matter how severe, makes a person a "batterer" when the person is male, but does not make a person a "batterer," even if the act is severe, when the person is female.

[670]While attending court in Hennepin County, Minnesota a few years ago, I observed a pro se defendant enter a "guilty" plea to battery for the singular act of attempting to take his wife's car keys away in order to prevent her from driving drunk. A neighbor called police when she heard the drunk woman yelling profanities at the man. When the police arrived, the woman begged them not to take the man to jail, but the police said they had a "mandatory arrest" policy. Under the law, "battery" is defined as any unwanted touching, no matter how slight, so technically the man was guilty. The prosecutor's office pursued the charge because

it had a "no-drop" policy in domestic cases. The end result is that the archival data, which consists simply of a tabulation of arrests and convictions without providing information about the nature or circumstances of the behavior upon which arrests and convictions are based, now reflects that yet another man was arrested and convicted of "battering" his wife in Hennepin County, Minnesota.

[671]Persecution of the male gender has reached a feverish pitch in recent times. For example, male infants and toddlers as young as two years old have been cited, charged, publicly disciplined and sued for such "outrageous" conduct as giving a friendly hug to a female classmate in the day-care center. *See* Sommers, Christina Hoff, *The War Against Boys : How Misguided Feminism Is Harming Our Young Men*, New York: Simon and Schuster (1994)

[672]Straus, et. al. (1996)

[673]See, e.g., Flood, Michael, "Responding to men's rights", *XY: men, sex, politics*, 7(2), Spring 1997; Flood, Michael, "Contemporary Issues For Men," *XY: men, sex, politics*, 5(1), Autumn 1995; Flood, Michael, "Claims About Husband Battering," *DVIRC Newsletter* (Summer, 1999), pp. 3-8; and Orman, Kate, *The Battered Husband Controversy*, web document (2001)

[674]Kennedy, L.S. and D. G. Dutton, "The Incidence of Wife Assault in Alberta," University of Alberta, Canada: Population Research Laboratory (1987).

[675]*Ibid.*

[676]Straus and Gelles (1990), *supra; see also* Straus, et. al., "The Revised Conflict Tactics Scale (CTS2): Development and Preliminary Psychometric Data," *Journal of Family Issues*, vol. 17, no. 3 (May, 1996), pp. 283-316; *and* Minnesota Center Against Violence and Abuse, *Incidence Rates of Violence Against Women: A Comparison of the Redesigned National Crime Victimization Survey and the 1985 National Family Violence Survey*, Washington, D.C.: U.S. Violence Against Women Office (1998)

[677]As a matter of fact, the CTS has also been criticized for *including* "choking" as an item in the "severe" category. *See* Bagshaw, Dale and Donna Chung, *Women, Men and Domestic Violence*, University of South Australia: Pirie (2000)

[678]*Ibid*; *see also* Flood (1995), *supra*; Flood (1999), *supra*; Orman (2001), *supra*; Smith, M. D., "The Incidence and Prevalence of Woman Abuse in Toronto," *Violence and Victims*, 2, p. 173-187 (1987); *and* DeKeseredy, Walter S., *Four Variations of Family Violence: A Review of Sociological Research*, Ottawa, Ont., Canada: National Clearinghouse on Family Violence (1993) The most recent Statistics Profile issued by Statistics Canada includes choking, and finds that men are twice as likely as women to be victims of this kind of violence. Statistics Canada, *supra*.

[679]Mouradian, Vera, *Abuse in Intimate Relationships: Defining the Multiple Dimensions and Terms*, Wellesley College: National Violence Against Women Prevention Research Center(2000.) Mouradian cites Gondolf, E. W., "Who are those guys? Toward a behavioral typology of batterers, *Violence and Victims*, 3, 187-203 (1988); Gray, H. M. and V. Foshee, "Adolescent dating violence: Differences between one-sided and mutually violent profiles," *Journal of Interpersonal Violence*, 12, 126-141 (1997); Hudson, W. W. and S. R. McIntosh, "The assessment of spouse abuse: two quantifiable dimensions," *Journal of Marriage and the Family*, 43, 873-886 (1981); Makepeace, *supra*; Marshall, L.L., "Development of the Severity of Violence Against Women Scales," *Journal of Family Violence*, 7, 103-121 (1992); Marshall, L.L., "The Severity of Violence Against Men Scales," *Journal of Family Violence*, 7, 189-203 (1992); Pan, H. S., P.H. Neidig and K.D. O'Leary, "Male-female and aggressor-victim differences in the factor structure of the modified Conflict Tactics scale," *Journal of Interpersonal Violence*, 9, 366-382 (1994); Sheppard, M. F. and J.A. Campbell, "The Abusive Behavior Inventory: a measure of psychological and physical abuse," *Journal of Interpersonal Violence*, 7, 291-305 (1992); Straus and Gelles (1986), *supra*; Straus, et. al., (1996), *supra*; and Tjaden, P. and N. Thoennes, "Prevalence and consequences of male-to-female and female-to-male intimate partner violence as measured by the National Violence Against Women Survey," *Violence Against Women*, 6, 142-161 (2000). Headey, Scott and de Vaus specifically measured scratching, and found that women perpetrate this kind of violence more frequently than men do. Headey, Scott and de Vaus, *supra*.

[680]Straus, et. al. (1996), *supra.*

[681]*See* Dobash, Russell P., et. al., "The myth of sexual symmetry in marital violence," *Social Problems*, 39 (1992), pp 71-91.

[682]Straus, et. al. (1996), *supra.*

[683]See, e.g., the discussion in Chapter 11 of the Violence Against Women Survey. According to the Violence Against Women Survey, an assault on a vagina or an anus is a "sexual assault," but an assault on a penis or testicle is not.

[684]Straus, et. al. (1996), *supra.*

[685]U.S. Bureau of Justice Statistics, *Sex Offenses and Offenders: An Analysis of Data on Rape and Sexual Assault*, NCJ-163392, U.S. Department of Justice: Washington, D.C. (1997)

[686]Claims about the incidence of domestic violence against women are all over the map. The Violence Against Women Office claims that 1 in 4 (25%) of women are abused. Tjaden and Thoennes (1999), *supra.* UNICEF puts the figure at between 20% and 50%. Kapoor, Sushma, *Domestic Violence Against Women and Girls*, UNICEF: Innocenti Research Centre (June, 2000.) Some sources estimate it's around 5%, while some feminist scholars have maintained that 100% is the correct figure.

[687]The proportion is even lower when the fact that not all rapes and sexual assaults are perpetrated by husbands and boyfriends is taken into consideration. A fair number of rapes and sexual assaults are perpetrated by strangers and acquaintances, not husbands and boyfriends.

[688]See, e.g., Flood (1995), *supra.*

[689]*See, e.g.*, Orman, *supra*; and Flood (1995), *supra.*

[690]Mouradian, *supra.*

[691]Most stalking cases do not involve intimate or romantic partners. Zona, M. A., R.E. Palarea and J.C. Lane Jr., "Psychiatric diagnosis of the offender-victim typology of stalking," in J. R. Meloy, ed., *The Psychology of Stalking: Clinical and Forensic Perspectives*, San Diego, Calif.: Academic Press (1998)

[692]Harmon, R. B., R. Rosner and H. Owens, "Sex and violence in a forensic population of obsessional harassers," *Psychology, Public Policy, and Law*, 4, 236-249 (1998)

[693]Tjaden and Thoennes use a slightly narrower definition, under which some showing of a reasonable possibility of fear on the

part of another person is required. The test is still a subjective one, however, in the sense that it is not necessary to actually *intend* to cause fear, so long as someone else might *experience* fear, as a result of your visual or audible proximity to them. Tjaden and Thoennes (2000), *supra.*

[694]For reasons outlined in Chapter 11, the Violence Against Women Survey funded by the Violence Against Women Grants Office is an example of a study that was conducted in allegiance to this principle.

[695]Statistics Canada (2000), *supra.* Some of the studies that have attempted to measure the incidence of stalking include: Fremouw, W. J., D. Westrup and J. Pennypacker, "Stalking on campus: The prevalence and strategies for coping with stalking," *Journal of Forensic Science*, 42, 666-669 (1997); Harmon, Rosner and Owens, *supra*; Tjaden and Thoennes (2000), *supra*; Walker, L. E. and J. R. Meloy, "Stalking and domestic violence," in J. R. Meloy, ed., *The Psychology of Stalking: Clinical and Forensic Perspectives*, *supra*, pp. 140-161; Meloy, J. R. and S. Gothard, "A demographic and clinical comparison of obsessional followers and offenders with mental disorders," *American Journal of Psychiatry*, 152, 258-263 (1995)

[696]*Cf.* Jouriles and O'Leary, *supra*; *and* Szinovacz, *supra.*

[697]There have been feminist scholars, for example, who have published books and articles detailing how Beethoven's symphonies are "all about rape." Women's magazines are replete with articles such as "The Ten Signs Your Boyfriend Might Be A Batterer," and the like.

[698]Moffitt and Caspi, *supra. See also* Morse, *supra*; National Institute of Justice, *Partner Violence Among Young Adults*, *supra*; *and* Magdol, et. al., *supra.*

[699]*Compare* Moffitt and Caspi, *supra*; Morse, *supra*; National Institute of Justice, *Partner Violence Among Young Adults*, *supra*; Magdol, et. al., *supra;* Burke, Stets and Pirog-Good, *supra;* Minneapolis *Star-Tribune*/WCCO, *supra*; Foshee, *supra*; O'Leary, *supra*; Vivian and Langhinrichsen-Rohling; *and* Straus and Gelles (1986), *supra.*

[700]Straus and Gelles (1986), *supra.*

[701]The Betty Friedan story is instructive in this respect. In one of her feminist tracts, she went into elaborate detail about how she supposedly had been severely abused during her marriage to what she portrayed as a patriarchal monster. Her story had the intended effect: she won immediate favor, sympathy and attention from the media (not to mention increased book sales.) Eventually, however, evidence came out that her ex-husband, far from being a patriarchal monster, had actually been a strong supporter both of Ms. Friedan personally and of the feminist cause in general. Apparently feeling pangs of conscience about smearing an innocent person's reputation for her own personal gain, Ms. Friedan started urging the media to stop talking so much about the nature of her relationship to her ex-husband. Ultimately, she acknowledged that it was she who had been abusive during the relationship.

[702]*See, e.g.,* Giles-Sims, Jean, "The Psychological and Social Impact of Partner Violence," *Domestic Violence Literature Review, Synthesis, and Implications for Practice*, United States Air Force and the National Network for Family Resiliency (1997). In fairness, it should be pointed out that although Ms. Giles-Sims seems to take the position that domestic violence is worse for female victims than for male victims, she does acknowledge that "research on psychological consequences of partner violence has varied in quality of measurement," that "there is a limited amount of information...on males as victims," and that "more research is needed on consequences for male victims. *Ibid.*

[703]*see, e.g.,* Grotevant, H.D. and C.I. Carlson, *Family Assessment: A Guide to Methods and Measures*, New York: *Guilford* (1989); Hertzberger, S.D., "The Conflict Tactics Scales," in D. J. Keyser and R. C. Sweetland, eds., *Test Critiques*, 8, Kansas City Test Corporation of America (1991); Plichta, Stacey B., "Violence and abuse: Implications for women's health," *Women's Health: The Commonwealth Fund* Survey (1996), p. 237-270, at p. 240 ("calling the CTS "a widely used instrument with good reliability and validity.")

[704]Walsh, M.R., ed., *Women, Men and Gender: Ongoing Debates*, New Haven: Yale University Press (1997), p. 218.

[705]Reliance on archival data can also be dangerous when it is used in combination with faulty logic. Consider this passage from Hague and Malos' treatise on domestic violence: "activists [in] the domestic violence field know that it is simply not true that as many men are abused by women as vice versa. There are no refuges for abused men....One phone line exists in the country [for] men...." Hague, G. and E. Malos, *Domestic Violence: Action for Change*, New Clarion Press: Great Britain (1993). Notice how the authors cite evidence of the *societal response* to male victims as if it were evidence of the *incidence* of violence against men. This is like citing the unavailability of colleges for black people in the early twentieth century as if it were evidence of lower levels of intelligence among black people in general.

Index

Printed in the United States
23929LVS00001B/454-459

Hudson, W. W. and S.R. McIntosh, "The assessment of spouse abuse: Two quantifiable dimensions," *Journal of Marriage and the Family*, 43, 873-885 (1981)

Hunter, Mic, *Abused Boys: The Neglected Victims of Sexual Abuse*. Lexington, Mass.: Lexington Books (1990)

Hunter, Mic, ed., *The Sexually Abused Male*. Lexington, Mass.: Lexington Books (1990)

Hutchinson, J. and K. Langlykke, *Adolescent Maltreatment: Youth as Victims of Abuse and Neglect* (Maternal and Child Health Technical Information Bulletin), Arlington, Va.: National Center for Education in Maternal and Child Health (1997)

Jackson, S. M., F. Cram, F. and F.W. Seymour, "Violence and sexual coercion in high school students' dating relationships," *Journal of Family Violence*, 15, 23-36 (2000)

Jasinski, J. L., *Structural inequalities, family and cultural factors, and spousal violence among Anglo and Hispanic Americans*, doctoral dissertation, University of New Hampshire, Durham (1996)

Jaudes, Paula and Leslie Mitchel, *Physical Child Abuse*, 2nd ed. Chicago, Ill.: National Committee for Prevention of Child Abuse (1992)

Johnson, M. P., "Patriarchal terrorism and common couple violence: Two forms of violence against women," *Journal of Marriage and the Family*, 57, (1995), pp. 283-294.

Jones, Lisa and David Finkelhor, *The Decline in Child Sexual Abuse Cases*, NCJ 184741. Washington, DC: Office of Juvenile Justice and Delinquency Prevention (2001)

Jouriles, E. N., and K.D. O'Leary, "Interpersonal reliability of reports of marital violence," *Journal of Consulting and Clinical Psychology*, 53, 419-421 (1985)

Jurik, N. C. and R. Winn, "Gender and homicide: A comparison of men and women who kill," *Violence and Victims*, 5(4), 227-242 (1990)

Kalmuss, D., "The intergenerational transmission of marital aggression," *Journal of Marriage and the Family*, 46, 11-19 (February, 1984)

Kalmuss, D. and J.A. Seltzer, "Continuity of marital behavior in remarriage: The case of spouse abuse," *Journal of Marriage and the Family*, 48, 113-120 (February, 1986)

Kammer, Jack, *Good Will Toward Men.* New York: St. Martin's Press (1994)

Karr-Morse, R. and M.S. Wiley, *Ghosts from the Nursery: Tracing the Roots of Violence,* New York: Atlantic Monthly Press (1997)

Kaufman Kantor, Glenda, *Ethnicity, alcohol, and family violence: A structural and cultural interpretation,* paper presented at the Forty-second Annual Meeting of the American Society of Criminology, Baltimore, Md (1990)

Kaufman Kantor, Glenda, *Refining the brushstrokes in portraits of alcohol and wife assaults. In Alcohol and Interpersonal Violence: Fostering Multidisciplinary Perspectives,* NIH Research Monograph No. 24, Rockville, Md.: U.S. Department of Health and Human Services (1993)

Kaufman Kantor, Glenda and Jana L. Jasinski, "Dynamics of Partner Violence and Types of Abuse and Abusers," in *Domestic Violence Literature Review, Synthesis, and Implications for Practice,* a collaborative publication of the United States Air Force and the National Network for Family Resiliency (1997)

Kaufman Kantor, Glenda and Jana L. Jasinski, eds., *Out of the Darkness: Contemporary Perspectives on Family Violence,* Thousand Oaks, CA: Sage Publications (1997)

Kaufman Kantor, G., J. Jasinski, J. and E. Aldorondo, "Sociocultural status and incidence of marital violence in Hispanic families," *Violence and Victims,* 9(3), 207-222 (1994)

Kaufman Kantor, G. and M.A. Straus, "The 'drunken bum' theory of wife beating," *Social Problems,* 34(3), 213-230 (1987)

Kaufman Kantor, G. and M.A. Straus, "Substance abuse as a precipitant of wife abuse victimization," *American Journal of Drug and Alcohol Abuse,* 15, 173-189 (1989)

Kellerman, A. L. and J.A. Mercy, "Men, women, and murder: Gender specific differences in rates of fatal violence and victimization," *Journal of Trauma,* 33(1), 1-5 (1992)

Kelley, Barbara Tatem, et. al., *In the Wake of Childhood Maltreatment,* Youth Development Series. Washington, D.C.: U.S. Office of Juvenile Justice and Delinquency Prevention (1997)

Kempe, C. Henry, "The Battered Child Syndrome," *Journal of the American Medical Association* (1962)